LOOKING FOR
THE STRANGER

LOOKING FOR
The Stranger

Albert Camus and the
Life of a Literary Classic

ALICE KAPLAN

The University of Chicago Press

Chicago and London

The University of Chicago Press, Chicago 60637
The University of Chicago Press, Ltd., London
© 2016 by Alice Kaplan
All rights reserved. Published 2016.
Printed in the United States of America

25 24 23 22 21 20 19 18 17 16   1 2 3 4 5

ISBN-13: 978-0-226-24167-8 (cloth)
ISBN-13: 978-0-226-24170-8 (e-book)
DOI: 10.7208/chicago/9780226241708.001.0001

Library of Congress Cataloging-in-Publication Data

Names: Kaplan, Alice Yaeger, author.
Title: Looking for The stranger :
Albert Camus and the life of a literary classic / Alice Kaplan.
Description: Chicago ; London : The University of Chicago Press, 2016. |
Includes bibliographical references and index.
Identifiers: LCCN 2016008498| ISBN 9780226241678 (cloth : alk. paper) |
ISBN 9780226241708 (e-book)
Subjects: LCSH: Camus, Albert, 1913–1960. | Authors, French—Biography. |
Philosophers—France—Biography. | Camus, Albert, 1913–1960. L'Étranger. |
Camus, Albert, 1913–1960—Appreciation.
Classification: LCC PQ2605 .A3734 Z6694 2016 | DDC 848/ .91409—dc23
LC record available at http://lccn.loc.gov/2016008498

♾ This paper meets the requirements of ANSI/NISO Z39.48-1992
(Permanence of Paper).

Contents

Prologue

READING *THE STRANGER* is a rite of passage. People all over the world connect the book to their coming of age, to grappling with the toughest questions of existence. The story of Meursault, a man whose name contains a plunge (*saut*) into death (*meur*), is a deceptively simple one: his mother dies in an old people's home and he travels to her funeral.[1] When he gets back, he goes swimming with a girlfriend and takes her to the movies. He writes a letter for a friend who is a pretty rough character. He kills an Arab on a beach in Algiers. He is tried and sentenced to death, and, as the novel ends, he awaits execution. It's not much to go on. Yet *The Stranger* is as gripping and puzzling today as it was in 1942, with its images both ordinary and unforgettable: a view from the balcony on a lazy Sunday, the whimper of a dog being beaten, the light shooting off a steel knife, a view of the sea from a prison window. And those four quick knocks on the door of unhappiness, echoes of a stupid vigilante killing.

My experience teaching *The Stranger*, and giving talks about the novel, is that everyone in the room has read it—usually twice. The debate is always informed and heated. Does Meursault exemplify the human condition? Should we sympathize with him? Why doesn't he cry at his mother's funeral? And why, in the end, does he want people to gather at his execution and greet him with cries of hatred? English-speaking readers of *L'Étranger* want to talk about whether it should be called, in translation, *The Stranger* or *The Outsider*. They want to know why the Algerian setting of the novel matters, what difference it makes that Meursault is an Algerian Frenchman in a colonial setting, and why the Arab he kills is given no name. Every reader of *The Stranger* has a theory, whether they read the book last week or fifty years ago.

The allure of Camus's novel means you can read it again and again and see something different in it each time. The critics have done just that, calling it a colonial allegory, an existential prayer book, an indictment of conventional morality, a study in alienation, or "a Hemingway rewrite of Kafka."[2] That critical commotion is one mark of a masterpiece, but not the only one. Camus was proud of a singular literary innovation, almost a trick: he told his story in the first person, which usually lets the reader inside the narrator's head—but he did it so that there was no getting inside, no way to feel close to Meursault.

How can such a distant and empty narrator capture so much attention, and how can such a disturbing book elicit so much loyalty? The absence of depth in Meursault, his strange indifference, has paradoxically drawn readers to him, since it is natural to hunger for understanding when it's withheld.

Anyone who loves to read knows that books have a life. They come to life as you read them, and they stay alive long after you've turned the last page. Among the intangible factors in *The Stranger*'s long life are certainly the limpid music of the sentences, the rough sensuality of the Algerian setting, the imagistic writing, and the perfect symmetry of the story of a life cut in two by a murder on the beach. All these formal and esthetic elements of the novel have been studied assiduously by scholars and taught to the generations of students who have read *The Stranger* for school since the 1950s—often as their first intense literary experience in an AP English course or a college philosophy seminar, or in the final two years of the French lycée. In fact, you can construct a pretty accurate history of twentieth-century literary criticism by following the successive waves of analysis of *The Stranger*: existentialism, new criticism, deconstruction, feminism, postcolonial studies.

Yet something essential is lacking in our understanding of the author and the book. By concentrating on themes and theories—esthetic, moral, political—critics have taken the very existence of *The Stranger* for granted. Biographies have of course touched on Camus's situation while writing *The Stranger*, but their focus is the man, not his book. The fact that Camus was such a glamorous and admirable person—a political activist, a great humanitarian—has meant that his life story has eclipsed the story of his writing more completely than if he had been mean, or homely. Yes, details about variations in the manuscript are available in small print, in the definitive French edition. But no one has told the story of exactly how Camus created this singular book—I'm tempted to say, how he discovered the novel within himself—and how it came to be published during the Nazi Occupation, in one of the most humiliating and complicated climates for publishing in French history.[3] It's an astonishing success story, with consequences so enormous for the future of the novel, you might consider the appearance of *The Stranger* on the literary landscape as an evolutionary accident that made way for a whole new species.[4]

That is why I thought *The Stranger* deserved a biography, a story of its life, connected to the life of its creator but also separate and distinct from him. I first came upon the idea of a book's biography reading Michael Gorra's excellent *Portrait of a Novel: The Making of an American Masterpiece*, about Henry James's *Portrait of a Lady*. From *Portrait* and from its exquisitely self-conscious creator, writing in his maturity, Gorra drew rich and many-layered reflections on life and work and literary influences.[5] In the case of *The Stranger*, begun by a twenty-six-year-old aspiring writer in the boondocks of Algeria, without reputation or œuvre, the life story of the book is at once more straightforward and more difficult to flesh out.[6] Lloyd Kramer put it another way: "Like an historian looking for the causes of a war, the biographer of a book looks for the causes of that book."[7]

By starting with the first glimmers of the novel in Camus's notebooks and letters, I make my way through the years of its creation, moving from the writer at work to the words on the page. My method resembles what fiction writers call a "close third-person narrative": I follow Camus, month by month, as though I were looking over his shoulder, telling the story of the novel from *his*, rather than my own, point of view. My design is to get as close as I can to his process and his state of mind as he creates *The Stranger*, sends it out for review, and publishes it in wartime France. This is not the "omniscient voice" of standard literary criticism, although my own critical assessments guide the telling, and I use endnotes to complement this history with information about the rich literary criticism on the novel. I've also included maps of Algeria and wartime France, to give the reader a sense of *The Stranger*'s odyssey between North Africa and France as it went from manuscript to book.

The story of *The Stranger* isn't over when the novel is published in 1942: the first responses are dramatic, funny, and strange. Over the years, the book has had friends, enemies, and many offspring, including translations into sixty languages, films, comic books—even a recent recasting of the story in postcolonial Algeria.

No author, no matter how powerful or influential, controls the fate of his or her work. At a certain point, a book leaves the author's purview for points unknown. In the best cases, when the life of a book lasts for many generations, whatever the writer might have thought about what she or he was doing joins a hundred other voices and visions. The life of *The Stranger* has gone well beyond Camus's own life, cut abruptly short by an auto accident in 1960, when he was only forty-six. It shows no signs of dying: seventy-four years after its first publication, and over a century after Camus's birth, over 10.3 million copies of *The Stranger* have sold in France alone.[8] As long as people keep reading novels, the *The Stranger* will live on: that's more of a guarantee of an afterlife than any author, and most books, can hope for.

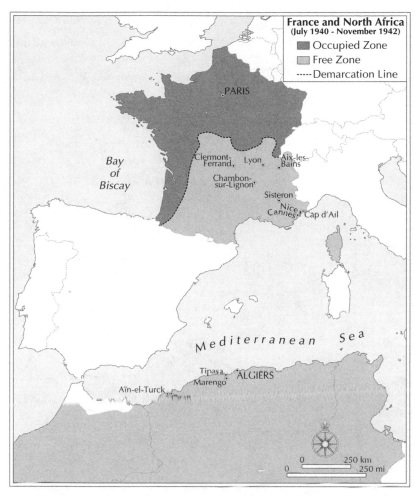

France and North Africa (July 1940–November 1942). Courtesy of Dick Gilbreath, Gyula Pauer Center for Cartography and GIS, University of Kentucky.

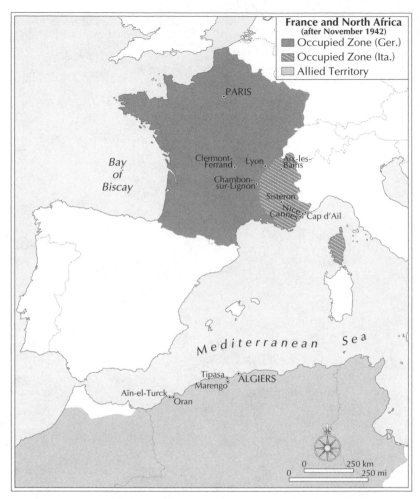

France and North Africa (after November 1942). Courtesy of Dick Gilbreath, Gyula Pauer Center for Cartography and GIS, University of Kentucky. For more detailed maps of the zones of occupation and their evolution, see Julian Jackson, *France: the Dark Years: 1940–1944* (Oxford: Oxford University Press, 2003).

1

A Bonfire

PAGE BY PAGE, the flames transformed paper and ink to ash, and more ash. Into the fire went letters from girlfriends, from teachers, from school chums. It was an unexpected act of destruction for the young man who vowed in his notebook to produce an œuvre, a body of literature, within two years.[1] He underlined the word *œuvre* with a thick stroke of his pen, three times.

He burned the letters in October 1939, a month after France declared war on Germany. Troops were mobilized, waiting on the Maginot Line. Albert Camus, unfit for military service, journalist at a newspaper about to be shut down by the government, was staying with his mother in the apartment where he'd lived for the first seventeen years of his life. A three-room flat on the rue de Lyon in Belcourt, the working-class neighborhood of Algiers. The place was sparsely furnished, with shared toilets on the landing— impoverished, even by the standards of working-class Europeans in Algeria. His brother, three years older, had married and moved downtown; his grandmother was dead. Only his mother remained, and his Uncle Étienne, both of them deaf and nearly mute. The flat was a shabby, silent place.

Albert Camus was twenty-five years old that October 1939. His hooded eyes were grayish green and his brown hair was combed straight back, emphasizing his high forehead. If you had to guess a nationality, you might see something Spanish in his prideful gaze— his mother's people were from Minorca, one of the Balearic Islands.

After work he favored fashionably baggy high-waisted trousers and plaid shirts, but in his job as a reporter he was never without a coat and a tie, and a trenchcoat or tweed overcoat. His face was handsome, but not so handsome as to be uninteresting. Something horsey and asymmetrical about his face, despite his fine features, gave him an expressive force that moved deftly from comic to tragic, from gangster to prince. His scrawny chest, his long legs and arms, his broad hands and physical grace made him seem taller than five feet eight. He was a passionate, deliberate young man whose energy overflowed the small rooms and low ceilings of his childhood.

He dragged out the two trunks of correspondence he had left in the apartment for safekeeping, set himself up in front of the tiny stove in the empty parlor, and fed the pages to the flames in crumpled heaps. "I have five years less weighing on my heart,"[2] he wrote to Francine Faure, his fiancée, after the bonfire did its work. It must have taken him a long time. Five years in the life of an ambitious young writer means a lot of paper.

That apartment was the place where he felt most deeply, where he'd honed his sense of observation, his ear for language, and his sense of what he began to call, from the wisdom of his twenty-five years, the absurd. He had studied the absurd in philosophy class, but his own sense of the concept came from his own body, from an illness contracted at age seventeen that threatened his sensual delight in the world around him. All men were condemned to death, some sooner than others. It was absurd not only that life was finite but also that humans were meaningless before the physical world. He was determined that his first important artistic creations be born out of these simple truths.[3]

·

In the jargon of the colonies, you would say that Albert Camus came of age in a world of *petits blancs* (little white men) or *petits colons* (small-time settlers): "poor white trash" would be too harsh a translation for an expression that meant a working-class European who was neither a colonizer—a big landowner—nor a disenfranchised native. He was part of a settler class, at the bottom of the European hierarchy but with privileges of race and citizenship virtually unknown to the native population. He grew up in Algiers, a city of mixed ethnicities — Spanish, French, Arab, Berber, Jewish — in a country conquered in 1830, which France had not only colonized but annexed, turning the territory into three *départements* (states).

Though technically they were living in France, most Algerians, whatever their ethnicity, had never seen the mainland. That was the case for Camus's father, Lucien, who saw France for the first time as a soldier in the Battle of the Marne, where he promptly lost his life. Albert was less than a year old. His father's death made him a "pupil of the nation" — a scholarship student. His mother worked as a cleaning lady; his uncle made barrels. School gave him his chance. A primary school teacher named Louis Germain recognized his talent and talked his grandmother, the real head of household, into letting him go on to secondary school rather than start an apprenticeship like his brother Lucien. For a boy from this family, from this neighborhood, going on to lycée was an almost unheard-of step, transporting him into a totally unfamiliar environment.

Albert Camus was a child who could barely sit still, whose exuberance in class, on the soccer field, at the beach, was exceptional. He was a force of nature, physically unstoppable until, in 1930, at age seventeen, he began to cough up blood. He'd contracted tuberculosis. He was sent to live with his uncle Gustave Acault, a butcher who had a ground-floor flat on the rue Languedoc with a large library and a courtyard garden. His uncle's comfortable home became a refuge for Camus, the place where he began to read seriously and where he could eat regular portions of red meat, considered essential for a cure. He was told he might die, and if he were lucky, he faced a lifetime of repeated treatments: months of bed rest, x-rays, and injections to collapse the affected lung so that it might heal.

The diagnosis coincided with his most formative intellectual relationship. In 1930, Camus met Jean Grenier, his lycée and then his university teacher, who guided his early reading and encouraged him to take the double path of philosophy and literature. Writing became essential, a conquest of the silence he grew up with and a compensation for the breath that began to elude him. Still only seventeen, he wrote literature and music criticism in a student magazine, *Sud*, with an acumen beyond his years, and he started to draft the barely disguised scenes from his childhood that he would transform, over the next seven years, into a first collection of personal essays, *The Wrong Side and the Right Side*.

He shared his work in progress before it was published with a few loved ones but especially with Jean Grenier, who gave him a steady supply of novels to inspire him. When Camus first discovered Proust's account of his wealthy childhood and Gide's self-conscious intellectual games, he feared that only the rich could become writers. Then Grenier gave him *La Douleur*, published in 1930 by a little-known twenty-three-year-old writer named André de Richaud. *La Douleur*—"grief" in English—is the story of a World War I widow, her loving son, and the German prisoner of war who becomes a deadly wedge between them. The plot, driven by the widow's guilty, sensual longings, ends in betrayal and tragedy. Camus was captivated by the desperate love of mother and son and by an aura of misery that permeates the book—not the economic misery he knew so well, but the moral misery of desperate people. He considered *La Douleur* his license to write, to let the circumstances and feelings of his childhood guide his creative work. Later he went back to Gide and Proust with enthusiasm, but he remained an anxious reader of fiction. When he discovered a writer he loved, he was often struck with a wave of envy, wondering if there was anything more for him to say.[4]

As he dreamed about what it would take to become a real writer, he approached philosophy as a discipline. In the 1930s, French lycées and universities transmitted a brand of continental philosophy that was a close cousin to literature. In courses such as Jean Grenier's survey on esthetic creation, Nietzsche, Schopenhauer, Bergson, and Kierkegaard nourished Camus's thinking about a godless world, and a world of forms. Philosophy also seemed the best path to a stable teaching career. Grenier, who wrote stylish, atmospheric essays for the best literary magazines in Paris, clearly had time to teach and to write, and so would he.

Camus finished his advanced work in philosophy—the equivalent of a master's degree—at the University of Algiers in 1935, with a thesis on two African philosophers, the Greek Plotinus, and the early Christian Saint Augustine. He sympathized with the tubercular Plotinus, and even more with the sensual but disciplined Saint Augustine. Though he refers in the thesis to Augustine's *Confessions*, and to the use Augustine makes of his personal experiences, nowhere in this academic study does Camus mention the detail that links the fourth-century Augustine, in word and deed, to Camus's twentieth-century Meursault, but it must have lodged in a corner of his imagination: miserable over the death of his mother, Augustine refuses to weep at her funeral, and looks for a cure to his sorrow by going to the baths.[5]

Camus's education in philosophy lacked the depth and rigor it might have had in the Paris academy. But the fact that Camus never quite conformed to formal philosophical modes of reasoning was also a feature of his character. Nietzsche was the writer who counted most for Camus in those years, in style and substance; he admired Nietzsche, he wrote, as a poet-philosopher, "susceptible of engaging in contradictions."[6] He might as well have described his own love of paradox, his attraction to images and intuitions above and beyond structured argument. Even when he still hoped that a career as a philosophy professor could buy him freedom for his creative work, he made a note to himself: "If you want to be a philosopher, write novels."[7]

·

The year he finished his philosophy thesis, 1935, Camus's literary ambitions were sparked by a visit. André Malraux, the author of *Man's Fate* and one of Camus's literary and political heroes, flew to Algiers on a hydroplane to address a gathering of antifascist intellectuals. Malraux spoke in a movie theater in Camus's neighborhood to an enthusiastic crowd who greeted the writer with raised fists, signifying their shared commitment to the Popular Front against fascism.[8] When Camus was a child, he used to go to movie houses in Belcourt with his domineering grandmother, who insisted that he shout the subtitles of silent films into her ear, since she couldn't read and couldn't hear very well, what with the piano and the moviegoers' loud reactions.[9] Those were humiliating memories. By 1935, he was just beginning his own career as a writer and a political activist, and his relationship to the places he associated with his childhood was changing. Camus may have had the chance to shake Malraux's hand that day in Belcourt, but that was all. Only in his wildest dreams could he imagine he would ever see Malraux again.

·

By October 1939, when he burned his letters, a hopeful period of political and cultural activism was behind him: he had believed in the Popular Front against fascism, but it failed to stave off Hitler's march through Europe. There was now little left for him in Algiers. With the start of the war in September, between the pressures of censorship and a dwindling paper stock, *Alger-Républicain*, the newspaper that had galvanized his energies since 1938, was reduced to a two-page bulletin called *Le Soir Républicain*, distributed locally and regularly censored for its antiwar positions. Camus, the solitary editor-in-chief, was considered a security risk by the government. He'd applied to compete for a state-sponsored teaching position, the logical next step after his philosophy degree, but he was declared ineligible because of his tuberculosis—one lung infected when he was seventeen and the other lung when he was twenty-one. The government didn't want to invest in a teacher who might not be around for very long, and official policy meant that no one with a contagious disease could join the teaching corps. The academic degree that should have led him to a stable career was worth nothing.[10] The disease also disqualified him from military service while his comrades at the newspaper, and his brother, had all gone off to fight. He canceled a summer trip to Greece because of the war; turned down a temporary teaching position, and used the time instead to finish a first draft of a play about the Roman emperor Caligula, whose story he knew from his studies. He had plenty of time on his hands to ruminate, and to imagine the future.

Over the course of five years, Albert Camus lived in at least six different houses and apartments in Algiers. He even married, but it didn't last. In 1939 he was separated, though still not divorced. After his wife came a new girlfriend, followed by others. Now he had reached a threshold in more ways than one. He had met a brilliant math student and pianist named Francine Faure. She lived in Oran, a smaller city to the west of Algiers, and her intelligent seriousness, the high standards she set for him, made him see himself in a new light. Telling her that he had burned his letters from other women was a way to reassure her, and perhaps himself, that his affairs were a thing of the past.[11]

There were personal reasons to burn letters, and plenty of political reasons as well. In August 1939, following the Hitler-Stalin pact, the French government declared Communist Party membership illegal, and although Camus was expelled from the party in 1937, he feared he was under surveillance. He had begun his work for the Communists going door to door in Belcourt to recruit Muslim members. But Moscow was concerned about the coming war, and activism in favor of indigenous Algerians was not a priority. Camus was purged—a report to the Comintern said he was a "Trotskyist agitator."[12] He found a better outlet for his beliefs as a journalist, and was well known for the positions he defended in *Alger-Républicain*, for his attacks on the colonial government's heartless policies, and for his pacifism. Those positions were reason enough to add political correspondence with his university teachers and his friends to the flames.

The past five years had been mixed, including gratifying work in the theater, where he founded two companies with friends, but also a miserable trip to central Europe, which ended his first marriage. He wrote a story called "Death in the Soul," about lonely days spent in a rundown Prague hotel and concluded, with the sense of paradox already so like him: "Any country where I am not bored is a country that has nothing to teach me."[13] Camus found a home with friends from the theater after his separation, and he spent an idyllic period living with them in a magical house in the heights of Algiers. There on the chemin du Sidi Brahim, in the place he called "The House Above the World," he first tried his hand at writing a novel. *A Happy Death* followed the story of a tubercular young man who commits murder for freedom. Camus wrote, rewrote, and finally abandoned the manuscript. His newspaper work covering trials turned out to be better preparation for *The Stranger* than this first jagged attempt at fiction.

A journalist, a political activist, a writer, a man of the theater, a lover, briefly a husband, a son to his mother, a child of his poor neighborhood, Belcourt—by the time he was twenty-five Camus had played many roles. That was the problem. "I haven't kept the same face for any two people," he wrote Francine, in the tone of melancholy self-deprecation that would be a constant of his character. "I have never made anyone happy who loved me. . . ." And he added: "To really do it right, I'd need to burn your letters as well, since what good are these pieces of evidence? I was about to do it, and I don't know what prevented me."[14] Even as he played on her sentiments, he was trying to stop playing, to strip himself down to the essential elements, to get rid of the pose, the décor. He was ready, he wrote, to destroy even the few precious letters he'd received from well-known writers like Henry de Montherlant and Max Jacob, but he had to think about it. Those belonged to literature, not life, and he wasn't giving up on literature.

In two months, after the demise of *Le Soir Républicain*, he would be without work and without prospects. But he was already the author of two books—*The Wrong Side and the Right Side*, his essays reflecting on childhood and failed love in a discreet, melancholy first person, and *Nuptials*, a joyous ode to the Algerian landscape, including his beloved ruins at Tipasa.[15] Both books were published locally at a small press started by Edmond Charlot, another student in Jean Grenier's circle. Print runs for the books were tiny—350 copies each—and the reviews nearly nonexistent. But Montherlant, the great Henry de Montherlant, wrote from Paris in a dashing stylized hand to praise *Nuptials*: "I feel closer to what you've written than to anything else I've read about Algeria." And if that wasn't praise enough, he added, "you write the way I want to write."[16] Montherlant hoped a future volume would be published in Paris, so that Camus would have a larger audience. In the end, Camus saved the letter.

What Camus saved from the flames that day in October was his literary future: Montherlant's words of praise; the notebooks where he jotted down images and ideas; the manuscript of his failed experiment in fiction, *A Happy Death*. He was at work on three new projects in various states of draft, all of them related in his mind to the concept of the Absurd, the first "negative" phase of his ambitious life plan as a writer. He hoped to create three books in an "absurd cycle," working in three distinct genres. On his desk was the rough draft of his play *Caligula*, still little more than a one-man show, culminating in a scene where the murderous, incestuous young emperor stands before a mirror, contemplating his dreadful freedom. There were notes for a book about other struggles with godless freedom in history and literature, which he was calling *The Myth of Sisyphus*. Most important of all was a new novel, barely begun. He thought he might call it *The Indifferent Man*.[17] Like *Caligula* and *The Myth of Sisyphus*, it explored one man's "negative truth." It was his second try at fiction, on the heels of a frustrating defeat, but the process already felt different. Instead of chasing down the words, they were coming at him.

Between the day he burned his letters and the day he left for Paris five months later, Albert Camus finished a first chapter of the novel that became *The Stranger*. Camus and *The Stranger* were beginning a long and arduous voyage, and the manuscript wouldn't leave his side until it was done. Fiction hadn't come easily to him. Had the bonfire stripped him down to his essence and allowed him to begin writing, or was it an inkling of the universal bonfire to come? What had changed?

2

From Belcourt to Hydra

TO UNDERSTAND THE TALENTED young man who first sat down to write *The Stranger* in the summer of 1939, it helps to return to the five years that Camus wanted to burn out of his existence—years of dizzying change that began with his marriage to Simone Hié. He met her while taking classes for his undergraduate degree at the University of Algiers in 1933. With her mauve and blue eye shadow, her fake lashes and slinky see-through dresses, Simone played the vamp to Albert's man-about-town. When they married a year later, he was twenty-one and she, twenty. Her flamboyant performance covered a starker reality: Simone's mother, a successful ophthalmologist, had given her daughter morphine to ease her terrible menstrual cramps, and she had become addicted to the drug. Camus's friends warned him that the marriage to Simone was nothing but a rescue mission. Louis Bénisti told him he was acting like an angel, or a Saint Bernard puppy.[1] Yves Bourgeois, who traveled with the couple, remembered her bitterly: a "professional seducer . . . vocation, 'femme fatale.'"[2] But seduction is not a one-way street, and the fact that Simone had been engaged to his friend Max-Pol Fouchet and that Camus won her away added an element of triumph that intensified his fervor. Simone was as glamorous as a character in a book—she was Camus's version of Breton's *Nadja*, a seductress-waif.[3] And for a young man determined to become a writer, she appeared to be an ideal writer's wife—a mystery to behold, rather than a partner.

Camus's uncle Gustave Acault, who heartily disapproved of Simone, gave him an ultimatum—either leave her or lose his financial support. Of the two families, only Simone's mother, Martha Sogler, seemed enthusiastic about the match, which she saw as her daughter's salvation. She set the newlyweds up in a little villa with the silly name Villa Frais Cottage on rue no. 12, Parc d'Hydra, a new housing development in Hydra, a suburb in the heights of Algiers. It was a fancy European neighborhood where Camus had often visited his lycée teacher Jean Grenier, who lived in a large villa on rue no. 9.[4] Grenier knew how far a climb Camus had made. At the start of Camus's long illness, the teacher took a taxi to the Belcourt address on file for his best student. He found the boy, speechless and embarrassed, in a flat whose poverty shocked him. The rue de Lyon, a busy artery of working-class Belcourt, was unfamiliar territory to the dapper professor.[5]

·

With his marriage in 1934, Camus found himself transported to his teacher's neighborhood. Hydra represented bourgeois success but also the denial of what Camus loved most in Algiers—the smell of the ocean and a view of the bay on nearly every street corner.[6] In Hydra, when you reached the central commercial roundabout, La Placette, you knew you were high up in the city, but the prospect, beyond the shops, was nothing but walled-off villas in pristine white stretching out in spokes, and thick hedges of laurel and bougainvillea.

·

Camus relied on his mother-in-law for support, and when Simone went to a clinic to detox, he stayed in Martha Sogler's apartment in another neighborhood on a hill, Les Sept Merveilles (the seven marvels), an enticing name. On Dr. Sogler's bookshelves were issues of the surrealist magazine *Le Minotaure* and a copy of the death mask of the legendary "inconnue de la Seine," the anonymous woman fished out of the Seine River around 1900, whose mysterious visage, smiling with eyes closed, became an icon for surrealist artists and writers. Dr. Sogler's apartment was "a nest of luxury and avant-garde culture."[7]

·

During those brief years with Simone and her mother, Camus insinuated to friends that his own mother was off in Oran with relatives, recovering from an illness—which wasn't true—as if he wanted to sweep Belcourt out of his existence.[8] His mother-in-law was an eminent medical specialist, up to date on the latest from Paris: how could Camus not have wondered what it would have been like to have a mother like that? To have grown up in Les Sept Merveilles instead of in Belcourt?

He tried many times to capture in essay form the strange dependence he felt on his mother, and the difficulty of explaining anything about her to his entourage. This fragment, never published, was found inside a folder with the manuscript of *A Happy Death*:

> One day he fell gravely ill. Since that day, age 17, he lived with an uncle. His mother hadn't taken care of him. Indifference? No but a strange personality, almost supernatural. She was from another world . . .
>
> The attitude of this mother towards her son: a mixture of wrongs and rights. Though she had neglected him, and especially had neglected his need for warmth and protection, she hadn't abandoned him.
>
> To the woman he loved, the son told a very different story. A story made of truths but distorted, arranged. A false history that didn't explain the reality. Why? Secret resentment. Pride especially. Pride.[9]

The fragment, for all its frank simplicity, is beautifully complex. The young man from Belcourt who won the hand of Dr. Sogler's daughter is proud, and knows he's lying. He's unable to tell the truth about his mother to the bourgeois woman he loves.

In a later draft about his childhood entitled "Voices from the Poor

Quarter," written during his marriage to Simone and dedicated "to my wife," he backs off from shame and ventures into the safer domain of fiction:

> If the child comes in then, he sees her thin shape and bony shoulders, and stops, afraid. He is beginning to feel a lot of things. He is scarcely aware of his own existence. But this animal silence makes him want to weep in pain. He feels sorry for his mother, is this the same as loving her? She has never hugged or kissed him, for she wouldn't know how. He stands for a long time watching her. Feeling separate from her, he becomes conscious of his suffering. She does not hear him, for she is deaf.[10]

Putting mother and child together in a room, he is able to let the scene express his feelings. Perhaps it was from his mother's silence that he derived his first lesson as a fiction writer: the idea, common currency among novelists today, that there is more power in showing than in telling, more emotion in silence than in speech.

.

Camus's literary efforts were slowed by the pull of political commitment. He joined the Communist Party in 1935, urged on rather cynically by Grenier, who hated the Communists but thought party membership was a rite of passage for any ambitious young man, and by a school friend, Claude de Fréminville.[11] In 1936, Camus spoke at meetings of his cell, the Amsterdam-Pleyel Committee, to enthusiastic applause. He argued that fascism was a generator of violence and of war, and urged support of the Popular Front. A year after Malraux had mesmerized the crowds at the movie house in Belcourt, Camus gave a speech at the movie theater in the neighborhood called the Ruisseau. He warned the audience to beware of the fascist manipulation of language, of "the power of certain words like 'fatherland,' 'glory,' 'honor'—synonyms of the bank vault." Editorializing came more easily to him than fiction. He was a natural whose speeches were limpid, pedagogical without being pedantic. A police informant always filed a report on the Amsterdam-Pleyel Committee meetings, quoting Camus and the other speakers and gauging the audience's response. A typical meeting might have an attendance of around 150 people—140 European men, four or five Arab men, two or three European women.[12]

·

Camus understood his work with the Communist Party as a cultural front against fascism, an appendage supporting the political Popular Front. The various committees and organizations he managed had their equivalents in metropolitan France. But the cultural activism he loved most came from his theater companies, where he thrived as a director and an actor. Following Malraux's dramatic speech in Belcourt, he adapted Malraux's antifascist novel, *Days of Wrath*, for Le Théâtre du Travail. With three friends, he wrote a play about a miner's strike in Spain and its tragic repression. When the performance was canceled by the right-wing mayor of Algiers, Camus presented the play in a public reading to a large crowd, the friends of the theater. Soon he was named general secretary of a cultural center, the Maison de la Culture, where he lectured on how the left might wrest the idea of a Mediterranean culture from Charles Maurras and the far right, who had hijacked it with their notion of a "Latin Genius."[13]

Camus traveled in those years in a left intellectual milieu, whose informal headquarters was Edmond Charlot's bookstore, Les Vraies Richesses. Charlot, who was even younger than Camus, was the friend who published Camus's *The Wrong Side and the Right Side* and *Nuptials* along with books by Jean Grenier and Gabriel Audisio; he shared with them a vision of a vibrant Mediterranean culture. As soon as Camus published with the Éditions Charlot, he began to read manuscripts for Edmond—the beginning of his life-long career as a book editor. If you spotted the young man in those years—meeting with his friends at the Brasserie de la Renaissance across from the University of Algiers, rehearsing with his theater company down by the port—it would have been impossible to see the traces of his impoverished childhood.

In May of 1935, soon after his marriage to Simone Hié, Camus began to jot down his insights in notebooks that would nurture every project to come. In a first entry, he reflected on those origins. Could he stay true to the poverty in which he had been born without giving in to romanticism, and could he ever convey the strangeness of his relationship to his mother? "A certain number of years lived in misery are all it takes to construct a sensibility. In this particular case, the bizarre feeling a son has for his mother constitutes *his entire sensibility*."[14]

That summer, when the university wasn't in session, he tutored adult students in philosophy and got a desk job with the government administration; he even worked for the City of Algiers department of motor vehicle registration—all to make ends meet. He was fed up with his exile to the heights of the city, and after a relapse of his tuberculosis in July kept him bedridden, he wrote to his teacher Jean Grenier, who was vacationing in France, "I'm getting back to work to dissipate this enforced idleness that chills me and also to escape the evening hours you know so well in Hydra Park."[15]

·

In the summer of 1936, during a trip to Eastern Europe with Simone, he intercepted a letter from her doctor in Algiers, who was also her supplier, and who, he now realized, had been her lover for quite some time. For the prideful Camus, it was a deep wound—the worst humiliation of his life. The marriage was already stormy but now any future was out of the question. He wrote to Grenier upon his return to Algiers, "I will no longer be living in Hydra."[16]

Camus separated from Simone in the fall of 1936; it took another year for him to separate from the Communist Party. He published *The Wrong Side and the Right Side* in May 1937, with a dedication to Jean Grenier. The book was an apprenticeship, using the first person while maintaining a curious distance from himself in evocative sketches. These included "Death in the Soul," the piece inspired by his unhappy trip to Eastern Europe with Simone, and "Between Yes and No," which incorporated the passage from "Voices from the Poor Quarter" about the child and his mother. The emotional power of his description, its evocation of estrangement and of a silence by now so far removed from his busy everyday life, continued to inhabit every book he wrote.

3

A First Try

ALONG THE BOULEVARD Telemly in Algiers, where on a clear day you can see the bay and the mountains of Kabylia, is a residential neighborhood that has always attracted artists and intellectuals. Like Hydra, Telemly is considered to be in "the heights" of the city, but beyond the boulevard itself, there is higher still to go. In that place above the world, twenty-three-year-old Albert Camus put his failed marriage behind him, recovered his *joie de vivre*, and dreamed that he could be a novelist.

In 1935 and still today, if you cross the street at the "Algeria" apartment complex, built in 1935, and make your way along the west side of the park,[1] a long sloping greenway set into the hillside, you can follow the Chemin du Sidi Brahim, a remnant of an ancient walkway from the Ottoman era, up a series of terraced steps that hug the length of garden, then leave it far behind. "A steep path, beginning in olive trees and ending in olive trees";[2] indeed, the way up was so steep, Camus wrote in his notebooks, there was no climbing it without feeling as if you had made a conquest.[3] In the fall of 1936, when he first started taking the Chemin du Sidi Brahim, he was in remission from his second bout of tuberculosis. Every time he reached the top of that hill, it was a victory of his growing stamina over the disease. He would climb one set of steps, then another, until he came to a series of looping streets named for nut and fruit trees: the rue des Amandiers, the rue des Oliviers, the rue des Bananiers. There, in what felt like a timeless village, were modest houses whose terraces took advantage of the skyline, and whose tiny gardens had just enough room for two or three trees and a wisteria bush.⁴ Marguerite Dobrenn and Jeanne Sicard, friends from Oran, members of Camus's theater troupe and comrades in the Communist Party, rented the first floor of a house at the corner of the Chemin du Sidi Brahim and the rue des Amandiers: "a kind of balloon-gondola suspended in the brilliant sky over the motley dance of the world."⁵ In the months following his separation from Simone, Camus spent more and more time in the place they baptized "the House Above the World," calling his roommates his "children" and himself "their boy." Marguerite Dobrenn and Jeanne Sicard were a couple, and in their affectionate company Camus experienced for the first time a close platonic friendship with women. A fourth housemate joined the group. Christiane Galindo, a sensual free spirit, became his companion for hiking in the Roman ruins at Tipasa. She worked as a secretary in town and soon began to type Camus's manuscripts. They doted on two housecats Camus dubbed Cali and Gula, mascots for the play he was writing, *Caligula*. This was a period of enormous activity for the young intellectual: adapting plays for his theater troupe, making political speeches at party meetings and at the Maison de la Culture, starting a second theater troupe after his break with the Communist Party. In the fall of 1937 he took a day job as an assistant at an Institute of Meteorology, measuring barometric pressure. When he was in the House Above the World, chaos retreated and the world itself became a character: "there are days when the world lies, days when it tells the truth. It tells the truth tonight—and with what insistent and sad beauty."⁶ It felt like the perfect spot from which to write a novel.

So he tried. In 1937, after the publication of *The Wrong Side and the Right Side*, Camus began working in earnest on the novel he called *A Happy Death*, living sometimes in the house and sometimes in a barren room he rented in the center of town, furnished only with a long trunk—bed by night, desk by day.⁷ The premise of the novel was inspired by his literary hero André Malraux, whose *Man's Fate*, about an uprising in revolutionary Shanghai, was the cult novel of the Popular Front. In the first scene of *Man's Fate*, an insurgent plunges a knife into the heart of a government authority caught unawares in his sleep.[8] Camus began *A Happy Death* with another kind of liberating murder: the morally restless Patrice Mersault befriends a philosophically minded paraplegic, Zagreus (named after the Greek god). He takes Zagreus's gun and shoots him, steals his vast fortune from a safe, and makes it look like a suicide. This successful murder sets the plot in motion, because once Patrice is rich, he is free to seek happiness anywhere.

It is a truism among writers of fiction that to succeed, a novel needs to take flight, to leave the real world for a specific flight of fancy, with its own logic and boundaries. The freedom Camus gave to his protagonist, and his desire to use every landscape and every important person he knew, made it hard for him to set limits for his story. All the characters were based on people in his life: his mother is a partial model for a deformed and diabetic mother who lives and dies in a shabby apartment in Belcourt; a deaf-mute neighbor who works as a barrel maker is based on his Uncle Étienne; Marthe, based on Simone, is a seductress who makes Patrice jealous; and Camus's housemates Marguerite, Jeanne, and Christiane become Rose, Claire, and Catherine.

There are at least four settings: Patrice goes on a long voyage to Europe, stopping in Lyon, Prague, Breslau, Vienna, Genoa. Returning from Italy, he moves into the House Above the World—which keeps its real name—and realizes he has practically forgotten that he murdered a man. He finds happiness temporarily but longs for a more solitary, meditative life. So he moves near the sea, to Chenoua, by the Roman ruins of Tipasa. He acquires a wife, Lucienne, and befriends a doctor. Then in an unprepared and hurried ending, Mersault succumbs to tuberculosis and dies a happy man.

Everything that didn't work in *A Happy Death* was a cautionary tale for the novels to come, a challenge to approach the same themes with authority, to chase away the easy sentiment. *A Happy Death* is full of ruminations on being a man, on the difficulty of sexual love, on the beauty of youth and the beauty of the world. Patrice is vain ("His hair fell in a tangle over his forehead, down to the two deep creases between his eyebrows, which gave him a grave, tender expression, he realized"); romantic (he felt "an enormous silence in himself as he faced the swelling waves and the steep hillsides"); but also sarcastic—he tells Marthe, who wants to know if he loves her, that love is for old people.

Camus wrote about the life he was leading at the time he was writing—the pleasant camaraderie of the house, the day trips to Tipasa, the travel in Eastern Europe and Italy. He wanted to wrestle all of it into fiction, without deciding what was most important or how the pieces fit together. His manuscript was an airplane packed with cargo, too heavy to fly.

Only the ending of the novel, sudden as it is, harbors a deeper fear. Anyone who has struggled with the symptoms of tuberculosis has enough material to write a death scene. Tuberculosis, before the advent of antibiotics, guaranteed an early death in the majority of cases, and the dread and curiosity provoked by the diagnosis were powerful incentives for fiction. Camus wanted the reader to feel the life go out of Mersault, to experience the very instance of his death:

> Slowly, as though it came from his stomach, there rose inside him a stone which approached his throat. He breathed faster and faster, higher and higher. He looked at Lucienne. He smiled without wincing, and this smile, too, came from within himself. He threw himself back on the bed and felt the slow ascent within him. He looked at Lucienne's swollen lips and, behind her, the smile of the earth. He looked at them with the same eyes, the same desire.
>
> "In a minute, in a second," he thought. The ascent stopped. And stone among the stones, he returned in the joy of his heart to the truth of the motionless worlds.[9]

Camus sent the manuscript to Jean Grenier. Camus burned Grenier's response with the rest of his correspondence in October, 1939—burned the harsh words of reproach. We know how harsh the letter must have been because the fussy and often disapproving teacher carefully saved Camus's response:

First of all, thank you. Yours is the only voice today that I can heed with profit. What you say always revolts me for a few hours. But this forces me to reflect and to understand. . . . Today what you are saying is absolutely right. I took great pains over this book. . . . I am still happy that certain parts please you, happy to have made progress. I have to confess that I am not indifferent to this failure. I don't need to tell you that I am not satisfied with the life I'm leading. And so I had given great importance to the novel. Clearly I was wrong.[10]

Then, as he poured out his heart for many pages, Camus asked Grenier a question that gave his teacher enormous power over his future:

Before going back to work, there is one thing I'd like to know from you because you're the only one who can tell me straight: Do you sincerely believe I should continue writing?

After such an abysmal failure, he had to ask. But however much he looked to Grenier to judge his work, Camus realized he could only answer the question for himself:

I'm asking myself with quite some anxiety. You understand that it's not about making this into a profession or extracting gains from it. I don't have many pure things in my life. Writing is one of them. But at the same time, I have enough experience to know that it's better to be a good bourgeois than a bad intellectual or a mediocre writer.

"A bad intellectual, a mediocre writer": he could fail either as a thinker, or as an artist, or both. It would be awful to fail. But he hung on to a basic belief, a knowledge that in writing he found the "pure thing" missing in the rest of his life. He recovered from his disappointment and prepared to revise his novel one more time.

4

The Novel He Didn't Know
He Was Writing

CAMUS WAS A CRAFTSMAN who believed in the benefits of re-writing, in literary sweat equity: "Rewrite. The effort always gets you something, whatever it may be. For those who don't succeed, it's a question of laziness."[1] After the discouraging response to *A Happy Death* from Jean Grenier, followed by his teacher's suggestions as to how he might proceed, the dutiful student went back to his manuscript.[2] He was working from a lot of little slips of paper, from other manuscripts, from images and thoughts jotted down. But no matter how beautiful the sentences, the novel wouldn't take off.

He turned to his notebooks to think about his structure and admonish himself to rewrite. These work-in-progress notebooks tell a frustrating story: there was a first outline, then a second. He told himself to recycle material from "Death in the Soul" that he had published in *The Wrong Side and the Right Side*, inspired by his miserable experience in a Prague hotel.[3] Another year passed. Finally, without saying when it happened, Camus abandoned the manuscript of *A Happy Death*. It might be truer to say that the manuscript abandoned him. To the people around him, his family, his friends in the theater and in the Party, the drama would have been invisible. Many people observed him; they knew him as a charming and seductive man who had separated from his wife and was making a name for himself in politics and theater. He was ambitious and he was busy, rushing from play rehearsals to political and editorial meetings, to odd jobs. For Camus, what was happening in his solitary hours was a gently unfolding mystery he wouldn't have been able to describe. At his writing table, surrounded by piles of books, smoking Bastos, his ever-present Algerian cigarettes, he was more and more surprised. As he tried to figure out the plot, characters, and locale of the novel that wasn't working, elements of a completely different book began to creep into his notebooks. The ambitious writer who wanted to control every aspect of his craft found himself confronted with the unexpected.

The novelist Catherine Lépront once compared the characters in a novel to the neighbors upstairs: you can't see them at first, you don't know exactly what they're doing, but you can hear them stomping around.[4] In Camus's case, there were already plenty of upstairs neighbors making a commotion in *A Happy Death* when suddenly his ear became attuned to different footsteps. On their own, the characters of *The Stranger* entered the apartment of his mind and made themselves heard.

The process began in the summer of 1936, when he returned from his trip to Eastern Europe and ended his marriage to Simone Hié. After one of his attempts at an outline for *A Happy Death*, Camus imagines Patrice, his main character, recounting a story about a man condemned to death. And Patrice says, "I see this man. He is inside me. And every word he says grips my heart. He is living and breathing with me. He is afraid with me."[5]

Camus was learning to use his notebooks as guidebooks to his instincts as a writer. Imagining that Patrice feels this other character, this man condemned to death, entering his body, his breath, was the clue that would lead him to a new character. Camus had no notion that there was a second novel in him, and yet the sentences were a perfect premonition of what would indeed come to pass: a man condemned to death named "Meursault" instead of "Mersault" would grow into the main character of *The Stranger*. The substitution of one name for the other would take a very long time.

In April 1937, Camus wrote in his notebook, "Story: the man who doesn't want to justify himself. He prefers the idea others have of him. He dies, only he retains the consciousness of his truth—vanity

of this consolation."[6] Meursault's principal character trait is born—
the refusal to bend to society's expectations. Two months later, in
June 1937, he imagines a priest visiting a man condemned to death.
"And each time," Camus writes in his notebook, "resistance in the
man who doesn't want this easy way out, who wants to savor his fear.
He dies without a word, his eyes filled with tears."[7] An atheist on
death row, dying in silence: it is the ending for another novel.

July 1937 was a turning point. Camus and his closest friends had
broken with the Communists, and his first collection of essays, *The
Wrong Side and the Right Side*, was in print. The press was silent
about the book, except for a single article in the *Oran Républicain*, by
a young man in Camus's crowd, who said that he sounded too much
like Jean Grenier.[8] Camus decided to leave the heat of Algiers behind
for a vacation in Marseille, then Paris. In the French capital, between
visits to the Exposition Universelle and to the rue Mouffetard, which
reminded him of Belcourt, he grasped the gist of that future novel
and had a first awareness of what would become its title: "A man
who looked for life where people usually find it (marriage, position,
etc.), and who realizes suddenly, reading a fashion catalog, how he
has been a stranger to his life. . . ."[9] Paris, the unfamiliar city, clari-
fied his vision.

There's only one place in the notebooks where Camus reflects
upon the mysterious process by which a new book was coming into
focus. This was after leaving Paris, en route to a mountain resort in
Embrun, in the Alps—not quite a sanitarium but a place where he
could rest and breathe easily. From his train compartment, with
the green pastures and foothills rushing by him, he wrote about the
way words or characters would rise up in him without his knowing why. "Sometimes I need to write things that escape me in part,
but which are proof of precisely what within me is stronger than I
am."[10] Pieces of *The Stranger* were bursting through his consciousness from a source that was becoming more and more accessible—
first the voices, then the characters, then the stories. A lesser writer,
annoyed or frightened, might have pushed those voices aside, because they didn't fit.

There may have come a moment when Camus decided to welcome the incongruous images, and even began to invite them consciously. When he returned to Algiers, he was offered a job teaching grammar in a Foreign Legion outpost, Sidi-bel-Abbès. Turning it down was an act of faith in his future as a writer, and he wrote to his friend Jacques Heurgon: "It finally seems to me that I've made a wager that forces me to create something meaningful, otherwise my life will be totally absurd."[11]

Notebook entries concerning *A Happy Death* continued in August and September 1937. In May 1938, he had an odd experience that turned out to be central to the novel he still didn't know he was writing. His brother's wife moved her grandmother to an old people's home in Marengo, a town on the outskirts of Tipasa. When she died, Camus attended the burial.[12] He wrote in the notebooks, in May and yet again in August, about a little old man, the fiancé of the old woman who had died, following the muddy funeral procession to the church and the cemetery.[13] There was a scene in *A Happy Death* where Patrice Mersault buries his mother, but there was no Marengo, no old people's home.

On a June list of seven things to do that summer, Camus noted as item six "rewrite the novel" and as item seven, "The Absurd." Did "rewrite the novel" mean revising *A Happy Death* one more time or starting another novel?[14] It's possible that Camus didn't know.

In a notebook entry written in the fall of 1938, Camus outlines "the story of R"—a glimpse of two characters who will become, in *The Stranger*, Raymond, Meursault's neighbor, and Raymond's Moorish mistress, who has no name. Camus loved to imitate the familiar *patoùete*, the particular slang and accent of the working-class characters on the streets of Belcourt, and here was an opportunity to put his mimicry to work:

Story of R. I knew a lady. She was for all intents and purposes my mistress. . . . I realized there was cheating going on: story of lottery tickets. . . . He asks for advice. He still thought "she was a good lay." He wants a letter with a "kick in the pants" and "things to make her sorry." Ex: "all you want is to screw around, that's all you care about." "I hit her, but real gentle, you know what I mean? She yelled, I closed the shutters."[15]

Camus adds to this entry, in tiny letters: "C'est une arabe" (she is an Arab).[16] It was an afterthought that would have momentous consequences for his unborn novel.

And so the backbone of *The Stranger* emerged: the bonding of Meursault with his neighbor, Raymond the pimp, who will ask Meursault to write a letter to his Moorish mistress, part of a plan to punish her for her infidelity. Camus had found the larger social reality in which his novel could resonate: the tension between poor and rough-edged Europeans and Arabs in Belcourt and neighboring Bab-el-Oued. He'd found a tone of voice he liked and got a glimpse of his plot, which connects the pimp to his narrator.

Camus started developing a set of principles for his fiction. "The true work of art," he writes, "is the one that says the least."[17] These were truths he had never articulated; his first try at a novel and his essays were lush with description. One of the problems with *A Happy Death* was Patrice's constant ruminations and his tedious explanations of his state of mind, which gave the story a sentimental quality. "To write," Camus now realized, "one must fall slightly short of the expression (rather than beyond it). No chit chat."[18] A single line, set apart in his notebook, became a motto for the work to come: "The dry heart of the creator."[19]

If there was a point of no return, a moment when *A Happy Death* gave way to *The Stranger*, it came in the fall of 1938, in a notebook entry marked "22," with no month. Camus wrote five sentences. It is tempting to say he unearthed them, for they landed on his page exactly as they would appear in print four years later, the first five sentences of *The Stranger*:

Today, Maman died. Or yesterday maybe, I don't know. I got a telegram from the home: "mother deceased. Funeral tomorrow.

Faithfully yours." That doesn't mean anything. Maybe it was yesterday.[20]

Camus added no explanation of the paragraph in his notebook. He'd spent a day with his brother Lucien and Lucien's wife at her grandmother's funeral in Marengo, but that experience couldn't have been more obscure, less connected to his personal dramas. Perhaps a distance from his sources was exactly what was missing from *A Happy Death*, exactly what he needed for his new fiction to take off. The other aspect of those sentences was fundamental: since 1936, Camus had been writing and rewriting a novel narrated in the third person, pouring emotion into his story to make it come alive. Now, two years later, he had come up with a new narrator, who said "I," but coldly. A narrator with no resemblance to Camus.

The day Camus wrote the first paragraph of *The Stranger* in his notebook, pieces of the novel already existed in his imagination. His narrator would have to make sense of all those pieces. A man who didn't know which day his mother died and didn't mind not knowing. Who had a way of talking that was almost mechanical, and strangely empty, given the circumstances. Gone was the pressure he'd felt writing *A Happy Death* to make Patrice Mersault appealing.

The following spring, under the heading "brawl in Tolba," he wrote another notebook entry that would go almost word for word into the mouth of Raymond Sintès, the pimp, and set a rhythm for his prose:

The other guy says: "If you're man enough you'll get off that street-car." I said to him: "Take it easy." He said, "You're not a man." So I got off and I said to him "Enough, you'd better or I'm gonna have to teach you a lesson." And he says "you and who else." So I let him have it.[21]

It was clear by then that *The Stranger* would not be set in the heights of the city, in the lovely house above the world, or in the Roman ruins at Tipasa. It would come from the streets of Belcourt, the place that harbored his earliest memories. *A Happy Death* was a labored effort to create a novel, but by listening to an inner voice, irrepressible, Camus had found another way. In letters, in interviews, and in his many literary essays to come, he rarely referred to *A Happy Death*, his unpublished manuscript.[22]

5

A Reporter on the Beat

AS THE SECOND NOVEL began to emerge, how to make a living
so he could keep writing? Camus's meager 1,000 francs a month at
the Institute of Meteorology weren't enough.[1] Martha Sogler, his
mother-in-law, helped—a kind of alimony—as did Camus's Uncle
Acault, who hadn't stayed angry with his nephew for long. In September 1938, a few weeks after he scribbled, "Today, Maman died,"
in his notebook, a chance meeting and a job offer set his life on a new
course. A man named Pascal Pia arrived in Algiers from Paris to start
a newspaper. He interviewed Camus and hired him on the spot.

If you had to compare Camus's earliest mentors, men whose
opinions were key in the years when he conceived and wrote *The
Stranger*, it would be hard to place Jean Grenier and Pascal Pia in
the same universe. Grenier was an elegant esthete, in his writing
and in his looks. Short and compact, he had wavy black hair, sensual
lips, and a distant gaze that reminded Camus of an oriental sage.[2] He
wore silk ties and matching pocket handkerchiefs. Grenier published
with André Gide's *Nouvelle Revue Française* (known as the *NRF*) in
Paris, and he impressed his students with his insider's knowledge of
the literary scene. Pia, the newspaperman, lanky, with a receding
hairline and a long, forward-leaning neck that made him look like
a tortoise peeking out of its shell, was obviously a man who had
spent too many hours bent over copy. While Grenier went to all the
right schools and had the highest academic degrees, Pia remained

an irregular: a used-book fanatic, a specialist in archaic pornography, a barker, a forger of Baudelaire poems, a magazine writer and art critic. When Pia was seventeen, he and André Malraux worked for the same private library near the Madeleine, rummaging for old books in the stalls along the Seine, and they were still friends. Pia was completely indifferent to literary fame or glamor, and a sudden sense of the futility of all things had caused him to cancel the publication of his own book of poems at Gallimard just as it was going to press. He was a nihilist but was a driven and obsessional worker when it came to other people's writing. He would rather spend hours on footnotes for an obscure encyclopedia than shine as an author. These qualities made him an excellent editor.[3]

In 1938 Pia was hired by an agronomy engineer and urbanist named Jean-Pierre Faure, who was financing a new newspaper. Oran already had a progressive newspaper and Algiers needed one. In the fall of that year, *Alger-Républican* was born—antifascist, anticolonialist, and independent, with scarcely a penny to its name. Pia had no resources to hire professional journalists, so he looked for talented neophytes he could train. He remembered that first encounter with Camus as an instant meeting of minds: "Nothing he said was insignificant, while he was clearly even-handed. Whatever the subject, his comments showed both solid general knowledge and an experience beyond that of the usual man of his age (he was only 25 years old). I didn't have to submit his candidacy to any employer. I invited him immediately to work with me." Camus, he observed, was disillusioned with party politics, but hadn't abandoned his hopes for change.[4]

They didn't talk about literature in that first meeting. Pia was equally at home among artists, writers, and journalists, but the last thing he was looking for was a literary dreamer: he had a newspaper to produce. *The Wrong Side and the Right Side*, *A Happy Death*, Camus's work in the theater—he didn't know anything about them.

Everyday journalism was indeed a completely different form from the lyrical essays that Camus had been learning to write. At *Alger-Républican*, his intense introspection and sensibility were turned outward, and his political and moral judgments put to the test of deadlines and limited space.

Camus wrote Jean Grenier, who had left Algiers for a new teaching position in metropolitan France: "I'm doing journalism (at *Alger-Républicain*): dogs run over by cars and reporting—a few literary articles as well. You know better than I do how disappointing this work can be. Yet I've found something in it—an impression of freedom—I'm not constrained and everything I do seems lively. One finds as well satisfactions of rather base quality, but too bad." In case the literary esthete remained unconvinced, Camus added that a government commission had taken a long time determining whether or not he'd be able to take the state teaching exam, and decided, based on his health, that he wouldn't: "That is why I accepted the job of editor at *Alger-Républicain*."[5] Grenier had been a powerful influence on him since high school, and if Camus had been allowed to take that exam, he would have followed in his teacher's path and become a professor. Tuberculosis threatened his life and and matured him beyond his years. The disease was also going to save him from a conventional academic career.

·

As of October 1938, Camus's theatrical and bohemian habits gave way to the frenetic activities of a journalist on the beat. He would no longer resemble his character Patrice Mersault, "lounging on a couch in the terrace room, a detective story in his hands."[6] Now the detective stories in Camus's hands were real.

The headquarters of *Alger-Républicain* was on the rue Koechlin, in Bab-el-Oued, close to the docks. The paper had a tiny staff and was produced on ancient equipment. What were the "satisfactions of rather base quality" Camus was talking about in his letter to Grenier? Describing low-life criminals and hookers did not have the same descriptive potential as evoking the Roman ruins at Tipasa. At least so it seemed. But right away, Camus learned that in the world of journalism, he could do more than describe. He could wrestle with justice and sometimes affect its course.

Justice in 1930s Algeria was French justice. From a strictly administrative point of view, Algeria was part of France. Colonized in 1830,
it was incorporated into the French administrative structures, with
three large "départements" (states): Algiers, Constantine, and Oran.
Algiers was France's fourth largest city, after Lyon. A popular guide
to Algeria vaunted a huge population explosion in its European
community over the course of the 1930s.[7] Statistics from the period
of Camus's young adulthood are biased, and should be taken with
a grain of salt. Of nearly 6.5 million people living in Algeria in 1931,
Europeans were said to represent 50 percent of the urban population of the four major cities.[8] In the rural areas, the so-called natives
or indigenous Arabs and Berbers represented 78 percent according
some accounts and 95 percent, according to others. Greater Algiers
had a population of 319,095 inhabitants—212,487 Europeans and
106,608 indigenous. What was certain was the huge difference between the urban and rural areas: In Algiers, you could be in a neighborhood like Hydra, in the heights of the city, and imagine you were
in any French metropolis. The Arab population was heavily con-
centrated in the Casbah, while the Europeans lived on boulevards
that looked exactly like Marseille or Paris. But in a rural area such
as Kabylia, the mountainous region east of Algiers, there was not a
European in sight.

On the docks and in Camus's working class neighborhood, Belcourt, the populations mixed. Linguistically, the separations between the European and native communities were both strict
and uneven. Europeans living under a French administration had
little reason to learn Arabic; Arabs working for Europeans neces-
sarily knew enough French to do their jobs—only a small elite read
and wrote French. The Arabic spoken in Algiers was a dialect, oral
rather than written, and the majority of the Arab population was
unschooled and illiterate. Arabic was not taught in French schools.
Camus didn't speak Algerian Arabic, but it was a language whose
sounds were familiar to him, and he would have known phrases—

how to ask for a cigarette, or shout down his opponents on the soccer field.[9]

All members of the society, Muslims, Jews, and Europeans, were subject to French law and French courts. Their status within those institutions was uneven. Algerian Jews, for example, most of whom were native to Algeria well before the European conquest, received full citizenship rights in 1870, separating them from their Muslim counterparts and pulling them toward European assimilation.[10] In a situation where Europeans and Jews had civil rights and an overwhelming majority of Arabs had none, the courts became a theater for the tensions and dramas of a society structured on inequality.

During the two-year life of *Alger-Républicain*, political trials gave Camus the opportunity to cover events over several weeks and earn a reputation as a troublemaker with the colonial government.[11] And this world-within-a-world served another more enduring purpose for the writer. At a time when *The Stranger* was barely a speck in his imagination, and *A Happy Death* definitively abandoned, Camus sat in closed courtrooms, hour by hour, discovering the well-oiled machinery of judicial plots, studying an extravagant cast of characters who were ready-made and waiting for a story teller's transpositions. In the long run, his time spent in court would allow him to plot *The Stranger* around a crime that grew out of ethnic tensions in Algerian society, and around a trial that made a mockery of the justice system.

In the very first trials he covered for the paper, Camus was both writer and a lobbyist for justice. A government agricultural agent, Michel Hodent, purchased wheat from Arab farmers and stockpiled it in order to regulate prices and prevent the kind of speculation that was rampant among rich landowners. Hodent was set up and imprisoned by the colonial government for embezzlement, with no proof. He wrote to *Alger- Républicain* for support. Camus took up his cause, and the case went to trial.

Camus had great characters to work with for his series of articles on the Hodent affair. The judge tried to prove Hodent's motive for embezzlement by suggesting that his honeymoon must have been expensive. No, Hodent retorted, he and his bride had gone camping. When Hodent's colleague defended him courageously, a lawyer named Navarro, representing the rich landowner in a civil case against Hodent, claimed that "people only defend their friends when they are guilty."[12] As Camus became familiar with the ways of the court, there was nothing he disliked more than lies clothed in judicial pretension—and he would make his impatience with the hypocrisy of the courts a cornerstone of *The Stranger*. He was becoming an expert at setting scenes and reporting dialogue with an economy of style, to give a sense of the here and now. Hodent was acquitted. It was a victory for the accused, and for the journalist who had taken up his cause. Camus wrote a quietly philosophical assessment. It would take Hodent a long time to get over what had happened to him, yet "there always comes a time when injustice is forgotten."[13] This gentle ending was modest, since Camus was in large part responsible for getting Hodent his day in court. It was also the kind of open ending that allows a reader to dream about a character's future—a writer's ending.

Camus's next series of articles covered a politically charged murder trial that galvanized the public and set religious and state institutions against one another. Many considered the Cheikh El Okbi trial an Algerian Dreyfus affair. Cheikh El Okbi, a theologian who believed in the modernization of Islam, had been lobbying the government for the extension of legal rights to Muslims. The conservative Mufti Kahoul, violently opposed to the reform, considered Okbi and his allies dangerous agitators. When the mufti was stabbed to death in broad daylight on the streets of Algiers, El Okbi was the first to be accused.

El Okbi and Camus had worked together in the French-Muslim Union and Cercle du Progrès—they were political allies on the Algiers left. Camus wrote Jean Grenier, who was curious about the case, that he had always respected El Okbi, but it was impossible to really know him: every time a rapprochement was possible, he acted in a way that Camus found strange.[14]

The issue in the trial was whether the murder was a set up. Had the colonial government ordered the murder of Kahoul and framed

El Okbi to destroy the reformist movement? Or did El Okbi order the murder? Speculation was rampant.

The young reporter sat in a criminal courtroom hour after hour and listened to voices. One of the key players in the trial was a garrulous man named Akacha, an Arabic speaker and ex-con whose initial accusation had led to El Okbi's arrest. "Akacha, when questioned, responds to the interpreter briefly, in his dull voice, with a rapid and confident flow of words. First he defends himself against charges that he was a drunk and a pimp, adding that he had been absent from Algiers for sixteen years. He also said, 'I have always worked.'"[15]

The El Okbi trial offered Camus an even larger parade of full-fledged characters than the Hodent case, beginning with the lower-class Akacha, who had no sooner retracted his accusation than he came under suspicion of murder himself. Even more perfect was the French magistrate, Louis Vaillant, who waved a crucifix at Akacha in court:

> M. Vaillant explains the figure of Christ that he shows the accused. He says to Akacha: "If you are religious, we can understand one another, I am a Christian. And I also believe in God. I have an image here that helps me when I turn to it." And showing [the crucifix] to him, he says to Akacha, "When you believe in God, how could you have killed a religious leader and want to send another religious leader to prison?" Akacha intervenes and declares: "No, I said I don't believe in God. He is too old. He needs to be changed."[16]

Some courtroom banter is as clever as fiction. Akacha's quip was well placed, since the court was supposed to be secular. Instead, in this highly publicized trial, a French judge brought Jesus into the courtroom in the form of a crucifix and tried to discuss his faith with the Muslim witness. For the judge, it was a gesture of empathy, but for Camus and *Alger-Républicain*, it was proselytizing, ridiculous and inappropriate. Camus wrote one of the strongest scenes in *The Stranger* using the dialogue between Akacha and Vaillant about the crucifix and transposing it to Meursault and the examining magistrate.

At the end of the theatrical trial, Akacha, not El Okbi, was condemned to life in prison. Although Camus admired and shared El Okbi's political views, he had doubts about who was responsible for the murder. Instead of the answers, which he didn't have, he concluded with a very literary scene that left the reader wondering:

> Akacha cries out ironically: "Long live French Justice." And he adds: "My conscience is clear." By a curious coincidence, at the moment the sentence is pronounced condemning Akacha, the bells of a neighboring church ring out and a cluster of pigeons fly off the wall we see from the window in the courtroom. Then Akacha is taken away, and with him goes the entire secret of the crime.[17]

Camus was already an artful journalist who knew how to build suspense through a few well-chosen details. On his walk from the newspaper to the Palais de Justice, he never failed to notice, at an angle behind the courthouse, the Église Saint-Augustin, which was named after the patron saint of Algeria but looked as if it had never left the French countryside. The ringing of those church bells was the perfect way for Camus to underline the intrusion of religion into a judgment that was supposed to be secular. When he wrote the verdict scene of *The Stranger*, he remembered that bell.

In July, Camus traveled to Philippeville in Eastern Algeria to report on a heartbreaking case. Twelve native farm workers who had fought for a pay raise were accused of setting fire to empty shacks. They were tortured in an attempt to extricate confessions, then condemned to forced labor. Camus covered the appeal of their sentence, which failed. Ahmed Boualeg, Mohammed Alimi, Mohammed Fisli, Amar Bettiche, Salah Sellaoui, Khemis Sadouni: he named them, calling them "innocent men condemned to forced labor and their families condemned to misery 'in the name of the French people.'"[18]

But there were other trials in the Algiers criminal court—stories of murder and petty violence that were just as likely, perhaps even more likely than the political cases, to nourish the imagination of a novelist in search of stories about colonial encounters. Violence in the bars and on the streets, especially during the hot Algerian summer, pitted native Muslim Algerians (referred to in the press as "indigènes") against Europeans. These stories got a few columns in the paper and were generally unsigned. Anyone on staff might have written them, and you'd have to conduct the literary equivalent of a DNA test to determine whether the sentences were written by Camus. Whether or not he wrote the stories, he certainly read them. He knew, in the spring and summer of 1939, that the narrator of his new novel was going to kill an Arab, and there was an abundance of material in the press about conflicts between Arabs and Europeans. In March and July of 1939, two murder cases reported in *Alger-Républicain* were suggestive, because they were so ordinary.

On March 4, 1939, the murder trial of Raphael Cozzolino packed the Algiers criminal court with Europeans and Muslims, most of them dockers.[19] Vaillant was once again the presiding judge. The case turned around an issue of self-defense: Toubal Salah, an angry unemployed Arab dockworker, had accosted Cozzolino, his union representative, in a bar. Cozzolino claimed that he saw Toubal Salah put his hand in his pocket, so he took out his gun and fired in self defense. The bullet struck Toubal Salah in the abdomen and he died in the hospital two days later.

The prosecution argued that Cozzolino did not appear to have been provoked. The defense countered, arguing that life for a man of the docks was a struggle, and that "the defensive gesture was a natural reflex" for Cozzolino. In his youth, Cozzolino had attacked a man to defend his sister—and had endured a prison sentence for that offense, which made him even more vigilant. The defense also argued that Toubal Salah was lazy, drunken, and quarrelsome. Whoever wrote the unsigned article took Cozzolino's side and expressed surprise—practically outrage—that the European union man was sentenced to seven years in a penal colony for the crime. He would be leaving Algiers for Cayenne. It wasn't a death sentence—for that he would most likely have to have committed several murders, or commit a felony murder involving several crimes—but it was one instance where a European suffered a serious legal consequence for killing an Arab.

That July an even stranger trial put a European named Billota on the stand for having shot his neighbor, an Arab named Belkacem ben Amar, who had chopped down a hedge dividing their property, then trespassed. Billota, who wept throughout the trial, was represented by the defense as "mentally diminished" by a workplace accident: "He was an instinctive man, without any culture, without any control over himself." Billota lacked, according to his defense lawyer, an "exact notion of social obligations." The case for self-defense was flimsy: Belkacem had punched Billota and thrown rocks at him, which hardly justified murder. The jury condemned Billota to two years in prison with a suspended sentence.[20] The sentence was laughable, and the defendant bizarre. For Camus, in search of a character, here was a man without social obligations who seemed to have gotten away with murder.

It was always the details that counted. In trial after trial, he observed how the prisoner waited inside a tiny room for the bell to ring before the gendarme escorted him to the stand, like someone throwing a bull into the corrida. He knew what to expect next. And he was keenly aware that the mechanisms of the court led inexorably to a sentence, which might or might not be just.

6

Any Person Condemned to Death Shall Have His Head Cut Off

LIKE MOST WRITERS with a novel on their minds, Camus carried his story around with him. And once he understood that Meursault would be condemned to death, he began to see death sentences everywhere.

An old family story made him especially sensitive to the issue, and it may have been the initial reason he ended his novel with the prospect of a guillotine. When he was a little boy, Camus's grandmother told him a story about his father. He listened with the rapt curiosity of a child who has never known his parent: Lucien Camus had died in World War I, when Camus was barely a year old. The story was gruesome. An agricultural worker had murdered an entire family in cold blood, and Lucien, shocked by news of the crime, decided to attend the execution. Camus couldn't leave the story alone. He made a place for the anecdote in *The Stranger* and in *The Plague*, but it is in a postwar essay, "Reflections on the Guillotine," that he describes his father's experience most powerfully, without the ornaments of fiction:

> What he saw that morning he never told anyone. He came rushing home, his face distorted, refused to talk, lay down for a moment on the bed, and began to vomit . . . Instead of thinking of the slaughtered children, he could think of nothing but that quivering body that had just been dropped onto a board to have its head cut off.[1]

The story had lodged itself in the writer's imagination with physical precision. When Camus described his father at the scene, he imagined that what must have captured his horrified attention was not the guillotine itself, but the body of the condemned man, quivering.

That an execution made Lucien Camus sick, that it filled him with such horror he couldn't speak, was really the only thing Albert Camus ever learned about his father. After his death, the military hospital sent Camus's mother a piece of the shrapnel that killed her husband, which she kept in a little box, the way other widows might keep a wedding band or a pair of cufflinks.[2] The execution story became, as the years passed, the son's special inheritance. As a boy, Camus would wake up in terror of being executed, and the fear got even worse when he came of age and came down with tuberculosis. He put the words in Patrice Mersault's mouth in his 1936 notebooks: a man condemned to death was living and breathing inside him.[3] As his new novel simmered, he watched and he listened for a way to tell the story his father had refused to tell. He didn't have to look hard for stories of capital punishment in those years leading up to World War II.

·

In the House Above the World, when he still had time to read at leisure, Camus was drawn, like most French intellectuals of his generation, to American crime fiction.[4] Not the staid British mystery novels based on clues and suppositions, reassuring puzzles resolved by aristocrats, but stories coming from mean streets, where the plots moved fast and the style didn't call attention to itself. Sartre rewrote *Nausea* after reading Dashiell Hammett. For Camus the model was James M. Cain's *The Postman Always Rings Twice*, which appeared in French translation in 1936. Several critics have speculated that this novel led Camus from the dead end of *A Happy Death* to *The Stranger*. Whenever anyone asked, Camus acknowledged its influence. What was he thinking when he read it for the first time?

The plot goes like this: Nick Papadakis runs a gas station and roadhouse twenty miles outside of Los Angeles. His wife, Cora, is a product of the Hollywood dream factory: she won a beauty contest in Iowa, came out to California, and failed to make it, so she settled for life with Nick instead. Everything changes when a handsome drifter named Frank Chambers shows up. Papadakis hires Frank to do odd jobs, and soon enough he and Cora are in the throes of a searing affair. In a first sex scene in the novel, Frank bites Cora's lip until it bleeds—it was enough to get the book banned in Boston. The adulterous couple decides to kill Nick and run off together, and from there ensues the infernal machinery of plot.

It wasn't the storyline—a classic adulterous triangle—that appealed to Camus, it was the way the story was told. Frank speaks right to the reader, in the first person, confessing as he waits for his punishment in the death house. The effect of this first-person narrator was the opposite of what Camus had achieved in the third person with the emotionally expansive Patrice Mersault. The sentences were short and taut and there was no rumination, no analysis, no deep inner self, just a very ordinary American voice—"a hobo with good grammar," as Cain called Frank.[5] "That night at supper, the Greek got sore at her for not giving me more fried potatoes. He wanted me to like it there, and not walk out on him like the others had." The first reviewers of the novel were impressed that Cain could achieve sensationalism though understatement.[6]

Cora and Frank are acquitted of Nick's murder for lack of proof, though the district attorney tries to set them up against each other. What happens next gives the ending of the novel a cruel twist. Cora, pregnant with Frank's child, takes ill on the beach, and in a loving scene, Frank rushes her to the hospital. He is so anxious to protect mother and unborn child that he races at top speed and crashes the car. Cora dies in the accident. Frank is then accused of murdering her, and a jury finds him guilty—he gets the death sentence. From a legal point of view, the ending is completely unrealistic, but philosophically, it's perfect: Frank gets away with the crime he actually committed—the murder of Nick Papadakis—but he will die for an act of love.

Frank finishes writing his long confession—the book we've just read—as he waits to be taken to the gas chamber: "Here they come. Father McConnell says prayers help. If you've got this far, send up one for me, and Cora, and make it that we're together, wherever that is."[7] It is an uplifting religious ending, a sentimental retreat that betrays the brutal core of the novel: Frank is going to be executed for the wrong reason. That was the logic Camus retained for his own novel.

Cain's crime novel had other appealing traits. First, the ethnic tensions in the California setting. When Frank speaks to Nick Papadakis directly, he calls him "Nick." But when Frank thinks about him or talks about him to Cora, it's always just "the Greek." Easier to talk about murdering the Greek than to contemplate killing a man with a name. "The Greek" sets the tone for other kinds of ethnic hatred. Cora is terrified she'll be taken for a Mexican because she's married to "a soft greasy guy with black kinky hair." The Greek makes her feel she isn't white. These California highways, so close to the Mexican border, were defined by the everyday racism and violence that Camus knew well, where, as he put it, just like in Africa, "people also live short and violent lives."[8] The crimes against Arabs that had come to trial in the Algerian courts—the Cozzolino case, the Billota case—offered up a gritty social reality that suited a hard-boiled approach. When Camus said *The Postman Always Rings Twice* inspired *The Stranger*, he didn't go into detail.[9] It is easy to imagine that when he observed the effect Cain got by using "the Greek" in place of a proper name, he realized he could create a similar effect by calling the murder victim in his own novel "the Arab." It was a way of describing prejudice without explaining it, by reducing a man to his ethnic label.

·

Clearly Camus couldn't get away from *The Stranger*, even on his day off, and what he retained from a popular 1938 movie called *Le Schpountz* becomes fundamental to *The Stranger*'s plot.[10]

"I am sure I have a gift," claims Irénée Fabre, the hero of *Le Schpountz*, to his disbelieving family of grocers in Provence.[11] He presents himself for judgment before the American movie moguls who happen to be passing through his village. They indulge him by offering him a screen test, but really they're toying with him. Behind his back they call him a schpountz, an easy mark. And in this most unlikely situation, the death penalty rears its head again, this time as pure comedy.

Le Schpountz opened at the Régent cinema on the rue d'Isly the week of November 22, 1938. Camus had been working as a journalist for a month with barely a break. His novel was on hold, and he didn't have a second to spare. But who could resist the French comic actor known simply as Fernandel? Ten years older than Camus, he was a box office comedy star, in part because no one could look at his horsey face and enormous smile without laughing.

This time, Fernandel's character was as ridiculous as ever — Irénée Fabre, trapped between the dried cod and the soggy Roquefort in his uncle's grocery, is convinced he has a god-given genius for acting and is bound to become a movie star, if he can only audition. Unlike Camus's Uncle Acault, a butcher who supported his intellectual life, Irénée's uncle doesn't understand his nephew.

The screen test is Irénée's big chance. He chooses to showcase his talents by repeating, in a series of distinct moods, Article 12 from the French penal code, which describes the death sentence: "Any person sentenced to death shall have his head cut off." As the cynical Parisian film crew cheers him on, Irénée performs the sentence in distinct moods: fearful, pitying, affirmative, thoughtful, comic. His face devours the screen as he moves from one exaggerated mood to another with overwrought passion. The filmmakers convince him he has a lead in an American film called *Le Schpountz*. They give him a fake contract, and off he goes to Paris.

For the reporter who was spending his days in the courthouse, *Le Schpountz* provided excellent comic release. In Fernandel's rubbery face, Camus could see a version of his own. And in the Mediterranean hick, Irénée, he saw another boy dreaming of glory as an actor, or a writer, in the metropolis. He had done every kind of theater, from the sublime to the ridiculous: Malraux, Aeschylus, Dostoyevsky, Gide, Rojas. In 1937, Camus toured with the popular Radio Algiers theater, playing comic roles. In Courteline's *Article 330*, he played Monsieur La Brige, who hangs his bare buttocks out the front window of his apartment to taunt the crowds at the World's Fair! There was also *A Happy Death*, put aside for now, and with it his dreams of success as a novelist. When the Schpountz sticks out his chest and proudly imitates a fearful, then thoughtful, then comic man, Camus could laugh at his own ambitions.

After a series of misadventures, Irénée Fabre triumphs. With the support of a good woman, Irénée's luck turns when he comes to understand that his face, his gestures, are perfect for comedy—not tragedy, as he once thought. He has to accept what he's good at to become a star. Then comes a true Hollywood ending. He returns to his hometown in an enormous car with a chauffeur, and the local children gather around in wonder while he embraces his family.

"I'm a mixture of Fernandel, Humphrey Bogart, and a Samurai," Camus is supposed to have quipped to friends, mocking his reputation as the handsome man-about-town.[12] Fernandel was Camus's alter ego—an idiotic part of himself, ambitious, grandiose, deluded. Without ever mentioning *Le Schpountz* in *The Stranger*, Camus would make a Fernandel film central to his plot, and to Meursault's destiny. You could even argue that Fernandel and his movie become the main cause of Meursault's demise.

A few hours in the meditative darkness of the Régent cinema, free from the pressures of the newsroom, had advanced his novel in the most unexpected way.

·

In *The Stranger*, Camus stopped short of portraying Meursault's execution. But as he was conceiving the novel, a murder trial in metropolitan France put the death sentence in international headlines.

The week the story came to a head, his thoughts were miles away. It was early June 1939, and Camus was in Kabylia. He had just finished the most intense assignment of his two years at the paper, a multipart investigative report on conditions in the mountainous region that tore at his heart. The Kabyle people traced their ancestry back before the Arab conquest; they spoke their own language and had their own forms of government. The French colonizers tended to romanticize them as a purer, more democratic people than the Arabs, but that didn't improve their commitment to the region. Neglectful policy, subsistence wages, children so hungry they ate the poisonous roots of plants: Camus saw in all of it the likelihood that France, without the most radical reforms, would lose Algeria.[13]

It is important in understanding Camus's reactions not to rush ahead to the Algerian revolution with its hard-and-fast opposition between revolutionary Arab nationalists and intransigent French colonizers. Even though Camus was appalled by colonial violence and deeply hostile to government policy, his point of view throughout the 1930s was French, and he saw his duty as a social critic to strengthen French humanistic values.

His idealism was repeatedly coming up against reality: reform was not working, at least not enough to address massive inequalities. Referring to France's generosity to its neighbors devastated by World War I, he contrasted the hypocrisy of colonial avarice: "We managed to come up with the money to give the countries of Europe nearly 400 billion francs, all of which is now gone forever. It seems unlikely that we cannot come up with one-hundredth that amount to improve the lot of people whom we have not yet made French, to be sure, but from whom we demand the sacrifices of French citizens."[14] France was willing to help out a neighboring country while it ignored the suffering in its own Algerian territories—ignored people who sacrificed their well-being in wartime and in peacetime in the service of France, without a living wage or the rights of citizenship. It was as if France were condemning the natives of Kabylia to a long, slow death sentence.

When Camus returned to Algiers from Kabylia on June 16, he was jolted out of one political despair into another, by way of a news story that brought his obsession with capital punishment to the fore. A Paris murder trial had preoccupied the public for weeks and was reaching its gruesome dénouement. The defendant, a German national named Eugen Weidmann, was condemned to death and scheduled to be guillotined on June 17. Weidmann had confessed to the murder of six people, including an American dancer, Jean De Koven, whom he trapped in a suburban villa and strangled. *Alger-Républicain* printed the wire service coverage, which included an enormous photo of the guillotine set up in front of the prison in Versailles, and a cameo of Weidmann's face in the upper left corner, staring impassively at the instrument of his death. The day after the execution, the papers announced that Weidmann had paid his debt to society. His lawyer, Vincent de Moro-Giafferi, said on record: "Everything was contradictory in this unhappy person: his crimes are monstrous; his death, saintly. All of us on his defense will remain profoundly convinced that we have just put to death an abnormal being. I've never felt such an emotion . . ."[15] Some people believed that the flamboyant lawyer had fallen in love with Weidmann.

What the June 17 report in *Alger-Républicain* didn't mention was that the execution in Versailles created a mob scene. The photo in the newspaper showed an empty courtyard, but in fact crowds had gathered around the city and people had rented out window space for viewing and for taking photos, since the seats in front of the guillotine were reserved for the press and for officials. French executions were always scheduled for dawn, but this one was delayed because of red tape. By the time Weidmann appeared, it was broad daylight and the execution was filmed. At least one account told how the executioner couldn't get Weidmann's head angled correctly, so the procedure took longer than it should have. Stories about the Weidmann execution escalated in the days following the event. Women had supposedly swarmed the guillotine and dipped their handkerchiefs in Weidmann's blood, as in the days of the Revolutionary terror. Shocked by the reports—fictional and real—the French prime minister declared that executions would no longer be public. As the armies of Europe were on alert and so many lives were about to be sacrificed, the people of France had enjoyed their last ritual execution. From then on, the guillotine would do its work inside the prison walls and any literary reference to a public execution in

France would date the setting before the summer of 1939—before Weidmann.

Though Camus wasn't at Versailles that June day, and though he had only the news stories and the rumors to go by, for months afterwards, he imagined, as Meursault would imagine, the gathering crowds and their cries of hatred. He thought about his father. He heard Frank Chambers speaking to him in his dull, neutral voice. And he laughed at the Schpountz's mad refrain: "Any person condemned to death shall have his head cut off."

7

The Absurd

JULY 1939, THE LAST MONTH of innocence. As July turned to August, the exhausted reporter spent "three marvelous days swimming, walking, and laughing" on the coast near Oran.[1] It was meager consolation for the trip he dreamed of making to Greece with Francine, which the tense international situation had now made impossible. Greek and Roman gods dominated his notebooks that summer: Minerva, Prometheus, Zeus.[2] Although still working in Algiers on *Alger-Républicain*, which was now struggling to say afloat, Camus found himself spending more and more time in Oran with Francine and her family and a widening circle of friends. He checked regularly on the Oran newspapers—in particular the right-wing *Écho d'Oran*, which supported Oran's fascist mayor and was reliably opposed to everything Camus believed.[3]

His everyday life provided the material for a send-up of Oran, an essay he decided to call "The Minotaur, or Stopping in Oran." But on one of his visits to Oran, as he was biding his time there, he heard a story that caught his imagination for a different purpose. Or at least that is how Camus's biographers, Herbert Lottman and Olivier Todd, reconstructed a sequence of events connected to *The Stranger*.[4] Lottman interviewed Pierre Galindo and Todd interviewed Raoul and Edgar Bensoussan, the three men who had been part of Camus's crowd in Oran before the war. The Bensoussans furnished Todd with a scene, a sequence, and a set of details: two Arabs had dared to use a beach reserved for Europeans, and one of them provoked a fight. The story has traveled well beyond Lottman's and Todd's biographies, since the locals still call that stretch of beach *la plage de L'Étranger* (*The Stranger*'s beach.)[5]

The trouble began, the story goes, because one of the Arabs stared intently at Raoul Bensoussan's wife, or girlfriend. Raoul Bensoussan and the Arab started to wrestle, and it looked as if Bensoussan would prevail, until the Arab took out a knife and slashed Raoul Bensoussan's biceps and cheek. Raoul retreated to a little beach house where his friends were preparing a picnic, and a doctor friend bandaged his wounds. After lunch, he went back to the beach, looking for revenge. He had a pistol in his pocket. He found the Arab and his friend, and a second fight ensued.

Many details, and especially the sequence of events, match in an uncanny way the story of Meursault's crime on the beach, with a few exceptions. First, Raoul Bensoussan never fired his weapon. The police came and arrested one of the two Arabs, but the Bensoussans didn't press charges. Second, the fact that Raoul Bensoussan was Jewish also made the fight different from the one Camus created in fiction. Raoul and Edgar were French citizens by virtue of the 1870 Crémieux decree, fully assimilated, but they were also natives. Jews and Arabs had spoken Algerian Arabic together for centuries. The fight would not have been silent. Unlike Meursault and the Arab, these men knew how to trade words.

.

This scuffle on the beach was soon dwarfed by news of a much bigger fight. Tension had been brewing for a long time, but those hot summer days of 1939 marked the official end of peace. Hitler had shown his colors in March when he invaded Czechoslovakia in violation of the Munich agreement. He invaded Poland on September 1 with Soviet complicity; two days later, France and England declared war on Germany.

The French declaration of war meant a massive mobilization of soldiers. They were sent to defend France's borders on the Maginot Line. The Germans, on the other side of the borders, defended their own Siegfried Line. Aside from an occasional skirmish, nothing happened. And so began the long wait, which a World War I novelist, Roland Dorgelès, described perfectly as the *drôle de guerre*—the phony war.[6]

On the literary front, Camus was hesitating. "I'm going to attack my novel," he wrote Francine on October 6, 1939, from his mother's apartment in Belcourt, where he had moved in September to keep her company after his brother was drafted: "I see the form and content around me in the poverty here, the simple people, and their resigned indifference. They give an image of a rather frightening world without tenderness." But he didn't attack the novel. By the next day he had changed his mind and decided instead to begin an essay on the Absurd, which became *The Myth of Sisyphus*. Three days later, he burned his correspondence.[7]

·

There were reasons for his literary agitation. The dwindling paper supply and meager resources convinced Pia to give *Alger-Républicain* a new format and a new name. *Le Soir Républicain* would be a two-page bulletin sold only in Algiers, by street vendors. It started publishing on October 4, with Camus listed on the masthead as the editor-in-chief. This meant that Camus was no longer traveling to get stories; he was busy putting out this new bare-bones paper, making do with reprints and ready-made articles. Because of the military draft, the staff was reduced to Camus, Pia, and a few others.

It was no longer peacetime, but it wasn't exactly wartime either. The wire service from metropolitan France no longer functioned, so for news, they transcribed what they were hearing on the BBC. The colonial government, ever vigilant, went after any form of criticism. Pia and Camus anticipated the censor by printing pieces that had already passed muster in mainland France. More often than not, the paper was full of big white squares where text should have been: "beautiful white spaces, as pure as a veil at first communion," as one of Camus's satirical articles described them.[8]

In his September 1939 notebook, he recorded the sparest of exchanges between a son and a mother, to show that the war was reaching everyone:

> A cold wind comes in through the window.
> Maman: The weather's starting to change.
> Yes.
> Will the streetlights be dimmed for the whole war?
> Yes probably.
> It's going to be a gloomy winter, then.
> Yes.[9]

The newspaper began a series, clearly inspired by Camus's own mother—called "Under the Streetlights of War." It included political essays by contemporaries like Huxley, pieces by old sages like Voltaire, and analyses of Nazi doctrine.[10] Camus regretted not being drafted—it was another reminder of his illness—but in *Le Soir-Républicain* he pointed to recent history to attack the principle of war, decrying the Versailles treaty and its errors and connecting the brutality of the Nazis to German national despair. He and Pia called for a truce as late as October 1939, after the Nazis had taken Poland. This was a period when pacifism was widespread on the left.[11] But even those who acknowledged the need for war lacked the fervent patriotism of 1914; they remembered the devastation of that first world war and acknowledged the likelihood that it would be repeated. It mattered that both Pia and Camus had lost their fathers in World War I. When they said that millions of lives that would be lost in a second world conflagration, they imagined families like their own, children like themselves. On the issue of war, as on so many other issues, Camus reasoned from the heart.

Then there was the game against the censors, with its own momentum. As the censors came down on the paper, *Le Soir Républicain* fought back with ever more sarcastic rebuttals. Anyone who had ever said anything against wars had their day in the paper, which became a collage of antiwar sentiment. They quoted with glee a pacifist statement from Jean Giraudoux, now minister of propaganda but famous for his antiwar play of 1935, *The Trojan War Will Not Take Place*.[12] They found critiques of war by Napoleon and Spinoza and Valéry; even God the Father had a column in *Le Soir Républicain*.[13] Giraudoux's dialogue was heavily cut, and on some days "Under the Streetlights of War" was completely blank. The papers' investors urged caution, and they were outraged both by the pacifist line and the risks that Camus and Pia were taking. Camus wrote his editorials under pseudonyms: he signed one article "Jean Mersault," using the last name of the main character in *A Happy Death*; he signed another article "Néron," after the emperor Caligula's nephew. Signing his journalism with names taken from his literary world was one more sign of Camus's growing understanding of himself as a creator of fictions. Always ready to joke at his own expense, he even signed one article "Irénée," surely a wink at Irénée Fabre, Fernandel's character in *Le Schpountz*.[14]

So it went until the new year. How do you send your readers the traditional New Year's greetings when the world is going to hell? The very last editorial of *Le Soir-Républicain*, dated January 1, 1940, tried this tack:

> . . . it is vain to wish for happiness this year, but essential to work to construct it. Wish for nothing, but accomplish something. Do not wait for a destiny built from start to finish by others, when that destiny is still in our hands. *Le Soir-Républicain* does not wish you happiness, since it knows that your body and spirits are battered. But it wants you to maintain the force and the lucidity necessary for forging your own well-being and dignity.

The French troops, who'd sat on the Maginot Line facing the Siegfried Line for four uneventful months, were indeed battered. They were pitifully battered by lassitude, boredom, and subzero weather. One soldier wrote home: "Nothing new here. I am bored to death. All we do is wait. But wait for what? This is the life of an imbecile and I am beginning to be completely fed up with it. Oh, let it end soon."[15] Meanwhile, on the radio, the civilians left at home could hum along to the hit song of the season: "We're going to hang our wash on the Siegfried Line."[16]

.

On January 10, 1940, the government officially ordered *Le Soir Républicain* to shut down. They might as well not have bothered: Camus and Pia had been planning a last issue on January 11, because they had exhausted their stock of paper. In the months that followed, they had to go to small claims court to get their back pay from the owners of the newspaper. Pascal Pia moved to Paris, where he was hired at the big daily *Paris-Soir*. Camus began to look for other work in Algiers.

Camus had asked his readers to go on and he asked the same of himself. What better time to return to *The Myth of Sisyphus*, the book on the Absurd that he began drafting in October, conceived as a philosophical companion piece to his novel. A man condemned by the gods to roll a rock up a hill reaches the top, but each time he does, he is condemned to watch the rock slide back down, and to start over again. Camus considered that moment of watching the rock slide back down the hill to be the best moment of human consciousness; the truest state of mind in which to observe the world without sentiment or false faith. He had models, or rather, anti-models. Jean-Paul Sartre's novel *Nausea*, which he had reviewed for *Alger-Républicain* in 1938, defined the absurd in a very different way.[17] Sartre's character Roquentin was haunted by an awareness that his existence was illogical and completely arbitrary, and so he was filled with dread. For Camus, the meaning of the absurd lay not in dreadful self-consciousness, but in a confrontation with the physical world—with the earth and its supreme indifference to mankind. He began *The Myth of Sisyphus* with an injunction: the only true philosophical question is whether to commit suicide in response to this indifferent universe, and the only viable answer is no. Furthermore, to live means to live as Sisyphus, and to imagine Sisyphus happy. The questions he asked were drawn from his everyday life: how to be happy even though you are bound to die, when you are tubercular and there is no cure, when the world is going to war and unimaginable suffering will follow? How to be happy when you love many women, and never quite find love? The coming war, he claimed, changed very little of this essential absurdity of life—it only rendered it "more immediate and more relevant."[18] In the play he drafted, the emperor Caligula murders his people and expects, from his power and freedom, nothing less than the moon. But he won't get it. His friend Cherea, a model of common sense and good values, explains that no one who pushes the absurd to its limits can be happy. Caligula dies at his hand. In *The Myth of Sisyphus*, Camus wanted to turn the negative power of the absurd in the opposite direction: to show that Sisyphus would fail at every task and rejoice in the effort.

The Myth of Sisyphus is a manual for living, an attempt to describe and to surmount the feeling of dread that comes over us when we face mortality. Camus wrote to his teacher Grenier that he had given up on making *Myth of Sisyphus* into a systematic thesis—it would be a personal essay. The book is filled with quotations from philosophers, but Camus insists that there is no such thing as absurd philosophy, only a feeling for the absurd. People live by forgetting they will die, because no one has ever experienced death. But inevitably there comes a time when we realize that the world is indifferent to our existence. Camus describes that moment as "strangeness,"—a terrifying moment, although there is also something beautiful and exalting about looking at the world and seeing how thoroughly it disregards us and our need for rationality:

> A step lower and strangeness creeps in: perceiving that the world is "dense," sensing to what a degree a stone is foreign and irreducible to us, with what intensity nature or a landscape can negate us. At the heart of all beauty lies something inhuman, and these hills, the softness of the sky the outline of these trees at this very minute lose the illusory meaning with which we had clothed them, henceforth more remote than a lost paradise. The primitive hostility of the world rises up to face us across millennia.[19]

A sense of the absurd can strike at any moment, even when nature is far away: while looking at a man talking on the phone, behind a glass partition, or seeing oneself as a stranger in the mirror (as Roquentin does in Sartre's *Nausea*). In a series of thematic treatments of the absurd, Camus expands the absurd sensibility to include Don Juan's endless search for love, and writers' impossible search for meaning in a world that has none.

Camus drafted a chapter of *The Myth of Sisyphus* in October, as *Alger-Républicain* gave way to *Le Soir Républicain*, but by late November he wrote Francine that he was having trouble sustaining a long argument. In early December he wrote her that he was putting *Sisyphus* aside for the time being.[20] With everything that was happening he was too agitated to write, and his essay had no momentum. Making an argument about the absurd was a strain. He had always preferred description to explanation and images to philosophy. What he had written in his 1936 notebook continued to nag at him: "We only think in images. If you want to be a philosopher, write novels."[21]

As 1939 turned to 1940, Camus may have been stumbling in his philosophical essay, but he was zeroing in on images for *The Stranger*. Under the heading "novel," he wrote in his notebook: "This story begins on a burning hot blue beach, in the tanned bodies of two young people—bathing in the ocean, playing games in the sea and sun."[22]

He was ready to begin. Of course life and work never travel to the same beat. Hadn't he failed to write *A Happy Death* in the House Above the World, where life was so good? Now as he moved closer and closer to *The Stranger*, his writing grew more certain and his life more difficult. In February he continued to look for work, to no avail. A local printer wanted to hire him to design a new magazine, until he got word from government officials, his biggest clients, that if he used Camus they would cancel their contracts.[23] In other words, he'd been blacklisted by the colonial government.

In March 1940, with nothing to keep him in Algiers, Camus moved to Oran, where he gave private lessons in philosophy and history. Because his divorce from Simone Hié wasn't yet final, he and Francine weren't married, but they were a couple, and he depended on Francine's family for support. When he was too tense to work or write, he went to the beaches, to Bouisseville, where Raoul Bensous-san had his altercation with the Arab, and Trouville. He wrote about the little beach houses with green and white fences and verandas, about the hard blue sky, the long hours in the sun, and the beauty and melancholy of being caught between life and death.[24]

8

A First Chapter

CAMUS DISLIKED ORAN, Francine Faure's home town, and yet it was in this dull, enervating place, in the first months of 1940, that *The Stranger* began to take shape.[1]

The port of Algiers accommodated entire worlds—a dance hall, a swimming pool, fish restaurants, warehouses transformed into theater space. In Oran, located on the same north coast of Algeria, looking out at the same Mediterranean Sea, 250 miles to the west, there was no seaside promenade at all, only a commercial port at the bottom of a steep seawall, inaccessible to walkers in the city. There had once been a city beach, at the old place Sainte Thérèse, but it was gobbled up by the port in 1936, a victim of the city's commercial soul. In Algiers, Camus could *se taper un bain* anytime he wanted (he liked the local expression , which means something like "take a dip"), but in Oran he had to travel by bus, five kilometers out of the city, to Mers-el-Kébir, Bouisseville, or Trouville, or on his good days, get on his bike. Once he got there, his sour attitude towards Oran fell by the wayside, and he opened his heart to the sea: "On these beaches in the province of Oran each summer morning feels like the world's first. Each dusk feels like the last, a solemn death proclaimed at sunset by a final light that deepens every shade. The sea is aquamarine, the road the color of dried blood, the beach yellow."[2]

Oran was reputedly the most European of any Algerian city. Unlike in Algiers, where the Casbah defined the center of the city, the "native" population of Oran was isolated in a district in the heights

known as the *village nègre*. In 1936, 76 percent of the Oran population was European (a figure that included Jews), while only 14 percent was Muslim—in dramatic contrast with the country as a whole
which was 86 percent "native" and 14 percent European.[3] Francine
lived on the rue d'Arzew, Oran's equivalent of the commercial rue
de Rivoli in the center of Paris—several blocks of shops and wide
sidewalks under connecting stone arches. Her grandfather had developed the stretch of commercial properties under the arcades,
though the family fortune was a thing of the past. Francine's father
had died in the same Battle of the Marne where Lucien Camus had
perished. Her widowed mother had gone back to work, rising in the
ranks of the civil service at the post office. Francine, whose great
love was the piano, had a job teaching math at Oran's lycée for girls.
Her sister Christiane, as domineering as Francine was delicate and
shy, was a litertature professor, a product of the prestigious École
Normale Supérieure in Paris. Camus felt scrutinized by this family of
disciplined, talented women. Christiane was not convinced that her
sister had found a suitable mate in the unemployed, ailing journalist
from Algiers. She told Francine he looked like a monkey. "The monkey is the closest mammal to man," Francine is supposed to have replied—and when she reported her comeback to Camus, his affection
for her deepened.[4]

In the winter of 1940, Camus was getting his mail at the Faure
apartment. He complained in letters to friends that he was suffocat-
ing. To distract himself, he continued working on his satirical essay,
"The Minotaur, or Stopping at Oran." He began with the idea that
Oran turned away from the sea, like a snail curving inward on itself.
The town was a labyrinth and the Minotaur within was boredom.
The downtown place d'Armes was decorated with bronze statues of
lions on squat legs: urban legend had it that they urinated on the
square by night. The boxy "Maison du Colon," built to celebrate a
hundred years of colonization, combined the worst of Byzantine,
Egyptian, and German grandiosity. Camus's Oran was a place where
the worst taste of Europe and the Orient met, a capital of dust and
stones.[5]

In early 1940, Camus went back and forth between Oran and Algiers, where a young woman named Yvonne Ducailar made him wonder if he was ready to marry Francine. He accumulated notes on future characters for his novel: "a old man and his dog, eight years of hatred" was the germ of his story about Meursault's neighbor Salamano and his mangy pet. He imagined another character who couldn't resist adding "I'd even say" to every sentence: "He was charming, I'd even say pleasant." He gave the tic to Raymond's friend Masson.[6] In a time of hesitation in all other realms, conceiving the first pages of *The Stranger* was an amusement and an unexpected anchor. His work-in-progress diaries included notes on the "burning blue beach" and two people playing in the water. That image stayed with him, but it wasn't his opening. Instead he started *The Stranger* with the paragraph he had jotted down back in August 1938: "Today, Maman died. Or perhaps yesterday, I don't know. I received a telegram from the home: 'Mother deceased. Funeral tomorrow. Our best regards.' That means nothing. It might have been yesterday."[7]

From the notebooks to the published novel, he altered not a single word of these confounding first sentences. He knew this was his beginning, and he stuck with it.

That first paragraph dictated the whole movement of chapter 1, and with it the temperament of his central character, Meursault. Camus took Meursault to the old people's home at Marengo, using his memories of the day he accompanied his brother Lucien to a funeral there. The director of the funeral home is the first person in the novel to utter the narrator's family name: "Madame Meursault came to us three years ago."

In the only surviving manuscript of the novel, housed today in the Camus archives in Aix-en-Provence, Camus still spells his narrator's last name "Mersault," identical to the hero of *A Happy Death*. Later, he would differentiate him from the main character of *A Happy Death*, by adding the "u" to Meursault's name. When you pronounce "Mersault" without the "u," it sounds ethnically Spanish, like "Merso"—a name that could have belonged to heavily Spanish ethnic Europeans who lived in Oran, or to someone who was kin to Camus's mother, Catherine Sintès. Where did the "u" come from? Some Camus experts claim he thought of the name change at a dinner party where he was served the delicious and expensive white Burgundy wine, Meursault. Whether or not the story about the Paris dinner party is true, there is something more expected about the way *Meur*-sault sounds to a French ear than *Mer*-sault, and the coincidence might have pleased Camus, since the extra "u"—signifying *meur* (death)—served his novelistic purposes in every other way. Which may be why, late in his process, Mersault/ Merso, a Spanish/Algerian sounding name, became quintessentially French: Meursault.

Openings set the tone, and *The Stranger* begins with an unsettling mix of the present, the past, and the future ("Today, Maman died. . . . I'll take the bus at two").[8] The narrator doesn't know, or seem to care, whether his mother died today or yesterday. After the opening paragraph, he recounts, in a flat, factual voice, how he took the bus downtown, ate at Céleste's, almost missed the bus to Marengo, arrived at the home, met with the director, attended the wake, and marched in the funeral procession under a blazing sun. While he sits with his mother's casket, he decides that the presence of her corpse means nothing to the old people around him. Then he adds, "But I believe now that it was a false impression." Where is he when he corrects himself? Camus does not explain when and where Meursault is when he tells his story. In one page, he solved the problem that made *A Happy Death* impossible to revise: he has endowed his narrative with momentum, with a mystery that needs to be resolved.

To position Meursault in time, Camus used one of the features that makes James M. Cain's *The Postman Always Rings Twice* so unsettling. The reader of Cain's novel will eventually discover that Frank Chambers is telling his story from his prison cell on death row—or he may be telling it after his own death, like one of those Hollywood movies narrated by a dead man who never explains how he can have a voice in the first place. That became Camus's plan for Meursault, and part of the magic of the first pages of *The Stranger* is that the story is told both in the moment, like a diary, and from a mysterious future beyond the grave. During the funeral, Meursault speaks in the present tense about the weather as if he were in the moment: "But today, with the sun bearing down, making the whole landscape shimmer with heat, it was inhuman and oppressive." He also recollects that day, or tries to recollect, as if it were long past: "After that, everything seemed to happen so fast, so deliberately, so naturally that I don't remember any of it anymore." Some sentences in the book suggest that the story is part of a diary he might have kept at the end of his life: "Several other images from that day have stuck in my mind."

Cain's Frank Chambers is a man with no real interior, recounting the most shocking events in a flat, neutral tone. As Camus adapted the flat American voice to his own story of a wake and a funeral in Marengo, he enabled Meursault to zero in on his surroundings more precisely than Frank Chambers had done. Meursault watches the world outside himself with painful clarity: he sees two hornets buzzing on the glass roof of the mortuary; he notices that the men's eyes were mere slivers of light in the middle of a nest of wrinkles; he observes that old women have huge stomachs.

The Postman Always Rings Twice was one inspiration for Meursault's voice. But Meursault evolved from something deeper—the conditions of Camus's own life. During his entire childhood and adolescence, until he moved to Uncle Gustave's, Albert Camus lived with a mother whose vocabulary amounted to 400 words and who had little language to give him beyond her gestures. Since his first, most intimate attempts at communication were defined by the absence of verbal understanding, the physical world became essential. To create Meursault, Camus drew on memories of his own attempts to live with a deaf mother and uncle. A concrete world, where objects come first, concepts last, and each sense is given its due. On the bus to Marengo, Meursault takes in "the bumpy ride, the smell of gasoline, and the glare of the sky and the road." In the old people's home in Marengo, Meursault sits with the casket in a whitewashed room and observes: "The furniture consisted of some chairs and some cross-shaped sawhorses. Two of them, in the middle of the room, were supporting a closed casket. All you could see were some shiny screws, not screwed down all the way, standing out against the walnut-stained planks."

Rather than making the coffin the center of the comparison and writing that "the casket was resting on two sawhorses," Camus gives the sawhorses a strange kind of agency in supporting the coffin ("two of them . . . were supporting a closed casket"). When the screws on the casket are tightened, Meursault notices.[9]

Camus lent Meursault's mother some of his own deaf mother's traits: "When she was at home with me," Meursault recalls, "Maman used to spend her time following me with her eyes, not saying a lot." In his debut collection of essays, *The Wrong Side and the Right Side*, Camus evoked a child's acute awareness of his deaf mother, and in his work-in-progress notebooks, he'd described a son whose bizarre feeling for his mother was his entire sensibility. He believed that writers have a very few things they want to express, that they end up writing the same book over and over again. But *how* they write that book is different every time. Meursault contains both Camus's mother—walled off from the world—and the son to that mother, hyperattentive to what he hears, as though he could compensate for her deafness by hearing for her.

Meursault often makes comments about people's voices and the way they speak. He notices that the nurse "had a peculiar voice that didn't match her face, a melodious, trembling voice." And while he is attuned to objects and to his senses, he is closed off from other people, reluctant to engage. On the bus to Marengo, he dozes off and wakes up slumped against a soldier who smiles at him and asks him if he's been traveling long: "I said 'Yes,'" Meursault reports, "just so I wouldn't have to say anything else."

Through the relentless gaze of his narrator, Camus orchestrates the funeral procession with strict precision. Meursault sees the people around him the same way he sees nature, as pure matter. And yet those people have their own subjectivity, emotions he observes without sharing them. Thomas Pérez, his mother's fiancé, appears, disappears, and reappears because he knows the shortcut to take on

the blistering hot day; he has taken that path many times on prome-
nades with Meursault's mother. Meursault's view of Pérez is synco-
pated, interrupted by the landscape and the funeral march itself. At
each glance, a different piece of Pérez comes to the fore: the soft felt
hat with the wide brim that he puts on and takes off when the casket
is near; his pants corkscrewed around his ankles; his thick red ears
sticking out through his wispy hair, his slight limp.

Then Camus goes a step further. He saves the most radical description of Pérez and marks it as a memory from the past: "Several other images from that day have stuck in my mind: for instance,
Pérez's face when he caught up with us for the last time, just outside
the village. Big tears of frustration and exhaustion were streaming
down his cheeks. But because of all the wrinkles, they weren't drip-
ping off. They spread out and ran together again, leaving a watery
film over his ruined face." The image of Pérez's frustration on the
wrinkled varnished surface of his face (the French is "a varnish of
water") is born of Camus's "sensibility of the absurd."

In the winter of 1940, Camus's future was uncertain, but that first
chapter was a promissory note: he knew that all he needed to keep
going was a place to write, and time. He had found in Meursault an
agent to transform his earliest perceptions of the world and to make
good on the challenge he had set himself: "The true work of art is the
one that says the least."[10] With this discovery that he didn't have to
be ornate to be a writer, that he could say "I" without confessing, he
had what he needed to continue with the rest of the novel.

Being laconic did not mean giving up on lyricism. It meant refusing to lend to the world a meaning it didn't have, and not reassuring
with false connections. The last sentence of the first chapter Camus
wrote is nearly a half-page long, an extended musical performance
of the absurd, juxtaposing flowers, earth, bodies, voices, and slid-
ing without warning into Meursault's fatigue and relief as he leaves
Marengo and returns to Algiers: "Then there was the church and the
villagers on the sidewalks, the red geraniums on the graves in the
cemetery, Pérez fainting (he crumpled like a rag doll), the blood-
red earth spilling over Maman's casket, the white flesh of the roots

mixed in with it, more people, voices, the village, waiting in front of a café, the incessant drone of the motor, and my joy when the bus entered the nest of lights that was Algiers and I knew I was going to go to bed and sleep for twelve hours."

Camus found his rhythm. When he was interviewed by a French professor about what made *The Stranger* work, he remembered how it happened: "once I discovered the trick, all I had to do was write."[11]

9

What He Carried

CAMUS SPENT TWO MONTHS in 1940 looking for work in two Algerian cities, subsisting on a pittance from his philosophy tutoring and some help from Francine's family who saw him as a ne'er-do-well. Then he boarded a ship. Francine had doubts about her fiancé, and in any case, she didn't want to accompany him to Paris as long as his divorce wasn't final. But he couldn't stay in Oran. If he could pay his transportation to Paris, there was a job waiting for him, thanks to Pia, as a layout editor at *Paris-Soir*, a big-circulation daily. It was only his second trip to the capital of France, the "metropolis."

He traveled thirty-eight hours from Oran to Marseille by boat; another nine hours from Marseille to Paris by train. The winter of 1940 had been particularly bitter in France; on March 15, the day Camus left Oran, the front page of *Paris-Soir* reported that hurricane-strength winds had toppled a church steeple in the western part of Paris. The storm cleared the air, and on March 16, the day Camus arrived, it warmed up to 70 degrees, but compared to what he was used to, the city seemed cold and gray. He brought his notebooks and the first chapter of *The Stranger* with him. Did he bring his press clippings from *Alger-Républicain*, in case he needed them for finding other work? Were there favorite books he couldn't leave behind? Whatever he packed, it couldn't have been much. His sense of separation from everyone he loved put him in a state of mind that was both painful and enabling.

•

Pascal Pia had booked Camus a room at L'Hôtel du Poirier on the rue Ravignan in Montmartre. For a romantic literary type, it was about as picturesque a place as Paris had to offer: on one side of a cobble-stone square with its own fountain, the little hotel stood directly across from the Bateau-Lavoir, a beehive of artist studios that spread out like a ship. On this vessel of high modernism, Picasso painted the *Demoiselles d'Avignon* in 1907. The glory days of the Bateau-Lavoir had ended after World War I, but it still exuded its bohemian aura. Montmartre, one of Paris's "buttes" or hills, crowned by the mammoth Sacré-Cœur cathedral, was proud of its cleaner air and lower rents. The district was an acquired taste, with its own diehard citizens—pimps and scoundrels, anarchists and poets, at least according to legend. Far from the business districts, Montmartre was still, in 1940, a neighborhood where an artist or writer could get by on almost nothing, practically a separate village. There were terraced steps, just as in the heights of Algiers, and there was even a vineyard next to the Lapin Agile cabaret.

Maybe Pia thought that Montmartre would be a familiar and welcoming spot for Camus, but it wasn't. Instead, for the exhausted young man far from home, the long Metro ride from *Paris-Soir* on the rue du Louvre in the center of Paris to the Abbesses stop in the north, the cramped elevator rising from the bowels of the Metro line to the surface, the walk up the windy hill in slippery March weather, only brought home how alienated he felt. His first notebook entries from Paris were much more confessional, less literary, than what he had been writing in Algeria: "What does this sudden awakening mean, in this dark room, with the sounds of a city that has suddenly become strange? And everything is strange to me, everything, without a single person who belongs to me, with no place to heal this wound. What am I doing here, what is the point of these smiles and gestures? I am not from here—not from anywhere else either. And the world has become merely an unknown landscape where my heart can lean on nothing." Then Camus adds a crucial sentence:

"A Stranger, who can know what this word means." In French, as in English, a stranger can mean a foreign national, an alienated outsider, an unfamiliar traveler.[1] He had already felt like a stranger in Oran; Paris only intensified the feelings he had been struggling with since January. In the next entry in his notebooks, he described the reaction to despair that always seemed to enable his best writing, and he began with that powerful, multivalent word: "Strange, admit that everything is strange to me. Now that everything is clear-cut, wait and spare nothing. At least work in a way that achieves both silence and creation. All the rest, all the rest, no matter what happens, is unimportant."[2]

He had an empty, dark hotel room, a table to write on, and a day job that paid 3,000 francs a month for five hours of work a day, all in an unfamiliar city.

When he wasn't writing, Camus was in charge of page four of *Paris-Soir*. Layout work at the popular daily had nothing in common with the political and cultural journalism he and Pia had done at *Alger-Républicain*, and he found the content distasteful. But he was only an editorial secretary, in charge of assembling the pieces of page four, the back page of the paper that looked like a jigsaw puzzle, with its tiny articles in different-sized boxes, combining a variety of styles and type fonts, all crowded onto a page called "Last Minute." On April 10, 1940, for example, page four reported that a philosophy professor named Bertrand Russell was denied a job at the City University of New York because he once managed a nudist colony. Last-minute news was often ridiculous, or forgettable.

The job was not without its rewards. Camus's work day at 37, rue du Louvre always ended on the third floor of the nine-story art deco building that housed *Paris-Soir*, supervising the "stone" (in French, *marbre*) where the lead type was arranged and corrected in its blocks, before the page went onto the linotype machines. He would proofread every word of every sentence and review the boxes and columns until the long page was ready to roll. He loved teamwork — the soccer teams of his childhood, the theater groups of his young adulthood — and now, working with union printers who oversaw the production of some 1.6 million newspapers a day, he entered a world with its own collective pleasures. It was, without his knowing, the most valuable preparation he could have had for the coming disaster.

Paris-Soir was not Paris's most intellectual newspaper, nor was it the scandal sheet for shopgirls that Camus deplored in his notebooks.[3] As the war intensified, its pages were given over more and more to European politics: Mussolini's alliance with Hitler; Germany's invasion of Norway and Denmark; Daladier's resignation as prime minister of France and his replacement by the supposedly more hawkish Reynaud. Camus felt the rising madness of war, and he wondered if he might be called up for the draft, and taken this time, despite his illness. But it didn't happen. He wrote to Grenier that what affected him most was not the prospect of dying, but the spectacle of hatred—as evident in civilian life as in the military.[4]

He began the second chapter of *The Stranger* almost immediately, and if there had been any doubt about the title, his Paris journal entries show that *The Stranger* was now firmly established in his mind.

Chapter 2 switches moods entirely: after his mother's funeral, Meursault returns to Algiers on a Friday, in time for the weekend. He sleeps for twelve straight hours. On Saturday morning he shaves and decides to go for a swim at the public beach: "In the water I ran into Marie Cardona, a former typist in our office whom I'd had a thing for at the time. She did too I think. But she'd left soon afterwards and we didn't have the time. I helped her onto a float and as I did, I brushed against her breasts." They play in the waves—just as Camus had imagined in his notebook entry about the tanned bodies under the burning sun. When Marie gets up on the float, Meursault rests his head on her stomach. To write the scene, Camus called on the palette of sky and sunshine in "Nuptials in Tipasa," a lush description of the fantastic Roman ruins along the sea outside Algiers that he had just published a year earlier, the most rhapsodic essay in the collection called *Nuptials*: "this sun, this sea, my heart leaping with youth, the salt taste of my body and this vast landscape in which tenderness and glory merge in yellow and blue."[5] Only here in the novel, the enthusiastic declarations of the Tipasa essay are toned down to telegraphic brevity. Meursault looks up from his nap and says, "I had the whole sky in my eyes and it was blue and gold."

Camus had a challenge: he wanted to establish in Meursault's character both the sensual connection to the world and a lack of connection to people. For sensuality a few words sufficed. For the lack of connection to people, he finds the perfect moment, in conversation, when Marie suggests to Meursault that they see a Fernandel comedy—she doesn't say which one—then observes that Meursault is wearing the traditional black mourning band on his shirt sleeve: "I told her Maman had died. She wanted to know how long ago, so I said, 'Yesterday.' She gave a little start but didn't say anything. I felt like telling her it wasn't my fault, but I stopped myself because I remembered that I'd already said that to my boss. Besides, you always feel a little guilty."

Here is the essence of Meursault in three sentences: an ineffectual straining for truth, and a sense of guilt even in the midst of pleasure. As for the Fernandel comedy, Meursault finds it "funny in parts, but otherwise just too stupid." Camus was preparing the "causes" of Meursault's fate in the most insignificant, ordinary details.

Camus had only been in Paris a week when he wrote to Francine to make sure she still had the manuscript of *A Happy Death*. He hadn't brought it with him, and now he needed it. There were a few pages he thought he could reuse in chapter 2: a scene where Mersault and Emmanuel chase after a truck on the docks; a second scene where Mersault looks out the balcony of his mother's apartment on a Sunday, following every passerby in rapt attention.

The apartment that was too big without Maman; the chair set on the balcony for viewing, just the way the tobacco merchant set his chair across the street; the passersby; the empty tram, the girl with the big bow and the patent leather shoes—these details, translated into the first person, gave a continuing sense of all that Meursault sees and notes outside himself. Most of all, the pages borrowed from *A Happy Death* convey the slowness of time in Meursault's world: "It occurred to me that anyway one more Sunday was over, that Maman was buried now, that I was going back to work, and that, really, nothing had changed."[6]

·

The manuscript pages arrived safely from Oran, and Camus brought chapter 2 to an end. He was writing well, but he was homesick in his empty room on the rue Ravignan. With his mother, who couldn't read a letter, his communication was inside him, in the memory of the glances they exchanged, their few words. Francine Faure was now his muse, the person to whom he could confide his ambitions, his doubts. One reason *A Happy Death* had failed, he had told her after they first met, was that he had written in fits and starts, always in a mood of exasperation. Although Christiane Galindo typed the manuscripts, and he was surrounded by the friends in the House Above the World, he told Francine that there had been no one to whom he could read a single line.[7] He had elected her, and he wanted her to feel chosen. In Paris he was even more alone, but the work at the newspaper demanded absolutely nothing of him intellectually, and when he got home from his shift, the novel was waiting for him like a dear friend. He shared with Francine his wavering sense of achievement, his excitement, and his doubts: "As I am writing I feel a great joy within me," he wrote on April 18, after a month in Paris. "I have never worked so much before. This room is miserable; I live alone, I am tired, but I don't know whether my troubles are the cause or the consequence of my fatigue. I write everything that I wanted to write and soon I shall be able to judge what I am worth and decide one way or another."[8]

He could work at the newspaper from 6:30 a.m. to 11:30 a.m. and have the rest of the day and night for his writing. Or he could take the night shift and write all day.

There were distractions. In April, Pascal Pia, who had a slightly more demanding job than Camus as an editor at *Paris-Soir*, took him to a special event. André Malraux was giving a private screening of *Sierra de Teruel*, the movie he had finished about the Civil War in Spain, only to have it censored by the government. After the screening, the three men went out for a meal. Camus wrote to two friends, Claude de Fréminville and Yvonne Ducailar, about a fascinating hour spent with Malraux, "a person full of tics, feverish and disorganized, but with an amazing intelligence."[9] His belief in Malraux hadn't faltered since the day in July 1935 when the writer-adventurer had spoken to a crowd in Belcourt about the dangers of fascism. Grenier had seen Malraux in Algiers that week, but he hadn't introduced him to his young student. Now, thanks to Pia, whose intellectual generosity was tremendous, Camus had a solid connection. Malraux would remember Pia's elegant young friend.

10

Writing Part I

FOR TWO MONTHS, Camus wrote, faithful to his ideal of silence and creation. His notebooks were good company: "Why is it that knowing how to remain alone in Paris for a year in a miserable room teaches a man more than a hundred literary salons and forty years' experience of 'Parisian life'? It is a hard, terrible, sometimes agonizing experience, always so close to madness. But left to his own company, a man's talents must be tested and affirmed—or perish. And if they perish, it's because they weren't strong enough to survive."[1]

In April 1940, a woman living on the floor above him in the Hôtel du Poirier committed suicide by jumping out the window, landing on the back courtyard of the hotel, and cracking open her forehead. Camus recorded the event. She was thirty-one years old, just five years older than he was.[2] In 1936, during Camus's lonely stay in Prague after his separation from Simone, a guest had died down the hall in his hotel—died of natural causes. Camus had felt the death within him, "Death in the Soul," as he called the chapter about Prague in *The Wrong Side and the Right Side*, and now he felt it even more acutely with this young woman's suicide.[3] *The Myth of Sisyphus* began with an idea she may have inspired, or confirmed: whether to commit suicide or go on living is the only truly serious philosophical question.

Camus went on, for his work sustained him. He liked finding simple truths and the right way to express them. In his notebooks, he practiced every kind of writing. He wrote about the black trees in the gray sky and the sky-colored pigeons, about seeing Paris from atop Montmartre, "a monstrous fog beneath the rain." He wrote about Catholicism in France, the way it dominated art and mood.[4] On his way to work at *Paris-Soir* on the rue du Louvre, next to the city market, Les Halles, he looked through foggy window panes at the vendors and the delivery men having their morning shot of calvados in hot coffee.

He continued to gather thoughts and phrases for *The Myth of Sisyphus*, which he had interrupted in Oran. In March 1940, there was an exhibit at the Galerie Mai on the rue Bonaparte; the paintings inspired Camus to add a passage to his manuscript about the way that colors create a metaphysics of matter.[5] An insight on painting was a useful addition to the thinking about novels and theater he had honed in his columns in *Alger-Républicain*, and other thoughts from his notebooks about what he was beginning to call "absurd creation": all of it would go, one way or another, into the patchwork of *The Myth of Sisyphus*. The novel, on the other hand, was so sharply delineated in his imagination he could write without any notes at all.

For two months, he worked on *The Stranger* every day and part of every night. He discovered that he could be in the middle of a paragraph, go off to work his shift at *Paris-Soir*, come back to the hotel room and pick up exactly where he had left off, with no difficulty. At *Alger-Republicain*, he developed speed and agility as a journalist, but he had never done creative work with so much ease, and certainly not fiction.[6]

He had his structure and soon had found the mold into which he could pour the pieces he had gathered. The novel would be in two parts, part I with six chapters, part II with five. The book hung on the last chapter in part I, where Meursault commits the crime that gets him condemned to death—a murder on the beach. By April, 1940, after two weeks living at the Hôtel du Poirier, Camus had chapters 1 and 2 on his table, and he started on chapter 3.

He began this chapter by borrowing more pages sent by Francine from *A Happy Death*, using the sequence where Patrice and his friend jump onto the back of a truck down at the port, jump off in Belcourt, and eat at Céleste's café. Céleste, with his big belly, white mustache, and apron, looked a lot like Camus's uncle Gustave Acault reigning over his butcher shop on the rue Michelet.

After lunch, Meursault goes back to work, and after work he goes home to boil some potatoes. But before he gets to his rooms he runs into old man Salamano insulting his mangy dog on the staircase, and then he meets Raymond Sintès, who is rumored to be a pimp but calls himself a warehouse guard.

Raymond invites Meursault for dinner. You can't say that Meursault decides to eat dinner with Raymond, any more than he decides to make love to Marie. He falls in with Raymond. The table is set with two plates of blood sausage and a full bottle of wine for each man, in a filthy apartment decorated with a pink-and-white plaster angel above the bed and pictures of famous athletes and naked women on the walls. Raymond has an agenda. He wants Meursault to ghostwrite a letter that will help him take further vengeance on his mistress; he has already beaten her badly because he is convinced that she is cheating on him.

Raymond's plan is to lure her back to him with the letter, get her into bed, then spit in her face "right at the last minute" and throw her out.

As he listens to his neighbor, Meursault drinks more and more of the red wine until his temples are about to burst. He agrees with everything Raymond says: that his plan for vengeance could work; more important, Meursault says he is willing to help by being Raymond's scribe.

"When he told me the woman's name, I realized she was Moorish." It isn't until Meursault sits down with the pen and ink provided by his host, that he understands this important detail about Raymond's mistress. *Mauresque*: in French it connotes a world of sexual exoticism, of courtesans in a colonial harem. It is also a decorous euphemism for "Arab." Meursault sounds polite as he takes on his new responsibility as ghostwriter for his friend.

It had been two years since Camus first tried out Raymond's voice in his notebooks ("I knew a lady"), and added in small letters "C'est une Arabe." Two years to think about what he would do with the Arab woman, and many options. He decided not to name her. Meursault, writing her a letter, knows her name, since Raymond has told him, but Camus won't tell, and all but says he won't tell.[7] It's a taunt by which she remains a type, rather than a person—*une Mauresque,* an exotic touch in a derelict setting that is anything but exotic.

From dereliction to dereliction: the setting for chapter 3 was Belcourt but the Montmartre hotel where he was writing gave Camus the dinginess he used to capture Meursault's world. After the meal with Raymond, the chapter ends in a series of simple sentences that show us Meursault, inert and already hung over, not knowing that his fate is set: "The house was quiet, and a breath of dark, dank air wafted up from deep in the stairwell. All I could hear was the blood pounding in my ears. I stood there, motionless. And in old Salamano's room, the dog whimpered softly."

In chapter 4, Raymond has sent the letter. Meursault takes Marie to the beach, and they return to make love in the apartment. Raymond and Salamano are woven into chapters 3 and 4—Salamano abusing his dog, Raymond abusing his mistress. A neighbor realizes there is a beating going on and brings a policeman to stop Raymond. Marie leaves. After Raymond's conversation with the police, he and Meursault go out for a drink. When they return, they find Salamano heartbroken because his dog has gotten free of his leash at the fairgrounds. It is a wrenching chapter, where, in a matter of minutes, love gives way to hate and hate to grief. Although the momentum of the novel is aimed at getting Meursault to the guillotine, Camus realizes that his plot can't be a fishing line: not every aspect can feed directly into Meursault's crime.[8] So he weaves in the story of Salamano and his dog. In this cameo of man and beast, Camus plays on all the themes of the book he is writing: life, death, ambivalent love. Salamano's frustration with his aging dog, his abuse, then his wild sense of loss are the violent tableau against which Meursault's indifference shows its fragility. "For some reason I thought of Maman," he confesses as he listens to Salamano crying in bed. It's one of the few places in part I of the novel where Camus brings Meursault close to a feeling, then jolts him back to indifference with a non sequitur: "But I had to get up early the next morning. I wasn't hungry, and I went to bed without any dinner."

In chapter 5, Marie asks Meursault if he loves her, and if he wants to get married, and he tells her it makes no difference one way or the other, but he will do it if she wants to. It was a conversational gambit he had already tried in *A Happy Death*, with Marthe and Patrice Mersault.[9] Here it was better matched to Meursault's personality, and his fate.

Next, Camus introduces a character whose presence in the novel seems purely accidental. The robot-like woman who sits down at Meursault's table at Céleste's restaurant has no function except to show how easily Meursault is distracted by the ridiculous show of life. She adds up the bill and assembles her money, checks a magazine for the entire week's radio programs, and puts on her jacket with the same jerky movements she used to take it off. Meursault follows her out of the restaurant, as "she made her way with incredible speed and assurance," but as soon as she disappears from sight, he forgets about her. She doesn't mean anything, though she provides a page-long distraction from the central drama of the novel about to unfold. Who is to say exactly what Camus intended—he believed that the best novelists worked from instinct.[10] Though certainly he was also discovering that by introducing cameos like Salamano and the woman at Celeste's, he could control the pace of his storytelling. He didn't want Meursault to meet his fate too fast.

Chapter 6 is the dead middle of *The Stranger*, its noontime sun. Camus borrowed elements from the Bouisseville brawl: Meursault and Marie spend a day at the beach with Raymond and his friend Masson—the man Camus imagined in his notebooks, who adds "I'd even say" to every sentence. Wandering along the water, Raymond and Meursault encounter the brother of Raymond's mistress, armed with a knife and seeking revenge. He wounds Raymond, and Raymond retreats to the cabana. After lunch, Meursault returns alone to the beach, carrying Raymond's gun. He hears the sound of a flute. He can barely see the Arab but he spots the sun glistening off his knife. Camus took Chekhov's famous advice to heart: "one must never place a loaded gun on the stage if it isn't going to go off." When he thinks the Arab is pulling a knife on him, Meursault fires once, then four more times. Camus uses one of the rare metaphors in the novel to end part I: "It was like knocking four quick knocks on the door of unhappiness." As though he were encouraging his reader to stop for a moment with Meursault, to stand at the threshold of his ruined life.

·

As Camus worked in the silence of his hotel room, he could hear as well as see his story: Raymond yelling at his mistress, Salamano yelling at his dog. For the scene at the beach, he described the sound of the water and the flute "within the silence and the heat," and of course the fatal gun shots: "the noise, sharp and deafening," shattering the quiet.

Camus stayed true to his plan to focus Meursault's attention on the physical world. As Meursault had noticed the sawhorses supporting his mother's casket, he now fixated on the Arab's knife, glistening in the sun. This was the beauty of a narrator with no interior life: the external world takes the place of rumination, analyses, feelings.

·

The work Camus was doing in that small hotel room would change the history of modern literature. He was giving a new energy to the novel, a form that had existed for centuries, by turning it outwards, simplifying its expression and deepening its purpose. Of course if he had had the slightest inkling that this was what he was achieving, grandiosity might have sabotaged his efforts. All he knew was that he had found his rhythm, like a long-distance swimmer riding a tide.

In *Distant Reading*, Franco Moretti argues that the novel has evolved by diverging: forms compete with one another, and the strongest, newest forms are selected to create new species, or sub-genres. Moretti's macro literary history is replete with analogies from evolutionary science, and although he doesn't mention Camus, *The Stranger* makes an excellent case for his theories. Moretti points out that thousands of novels disappear for every one that is remembered, but that certain books have set the novel on a new course.

There was a restlessness among novelists in the 1930s and 1940s, a sense that the European model was exhausted and needed a boost. No one expressed this sentiment better than Cyril Connolly, the preeminent Irish-English critic and magazine editor who specialized in sly and cunning maxims about writers and literature. In a 1944 collection called *The Unquiet Grave*, Connolly surveyed the territory and found it wanting. "Flaubert, Henry James, Proust, Joyce and Virginia Woolf have finished off the novel" he wrote, so that "novelists (. . .) can no longer develop character, situation or plot." As far as he was concerned, too much experimentation had flummoxed the form and made novels unreadable. Everything, he insisted, would have to be reinvented.[11]

He was expressing what many writers were feeling, and foremost among them the French. Sartre tried to invent a new form in *Nausea*, by combining philosophical thinking with hard-boiled detective prose. But Camus's specific combination of an Algerian setting with American *noir* produced a story that was less affected, truer to itself. Their contemporaries, European writers from Gide to Montherlant, had been drawn to North Africa as a setting for their immoralism, their exotic self-discovery. And in popular literature, Algeria had produced a tradition of folk tales featuring a character named "Cagayous." Camus knew the folk tales and the modernist exoticism inside out, but he kept both at arm's length in *The Stranger*. He was interested in working-class European Algiers, a place that was neither folkloric or exotic, and the techniques of American writers such as Hemingway and Steinbeck suited him. It wasn't an accident that the citizens of Oran—Camus delighted in the detail—called the slick young men who paraded down the boulevards "Clarques," after Clark Gable.[12]

·

The Stranger is not Camus's autobiography. If anything, what Camus was doing was reversing his life story: Camus's childish love for his deaf mother became Meursault's indifference. The silent world in which he had grown up became the noisy place where Meursault heard every sound. Camus's hatred of colonial violence expressed itself through Meursault's murder of an Arab. In the gloom of Paris, the writer purged the crude and heartless underside of every noble, uplifting sentiment he had ever had. Carl Jung gave a name and a theory to such investigations: Camus was looking for his shadow side to free him—but from what? From the darkness of Paris, from the blinding Algerian sun; from thoughtless violence and indifferent love? It was a strange literary beginning for a humanist.

In May, Camus wrote to Jean Grenier about his new life in Paris. With Francine he emphasized loneliness; with Grenier, he wrote with disdain about the futility of social life in the city. He found Paris repugnant, yet the capital was serving his purposes. He was seeing a lot of fancy people, most of whom disgusted him. He noticed in the *Nouvelle Revue Française* that Grenier was about to publish a book about the Mediterranean: he thought there was something good about a book that had nothing to do with the war. He was working hard, and he would soon have a new manuscript for Grenier to read, if he was willing.[13]

11

Already Traced within Me

IN PART II OF HIS NOVEL, Camus switched palette, from blue and yellow to gray, from burning beach to cold prison cell. If part I was animated by his memories of the streets and beaches of Algiers, part II was sustained by the isolating drabness of Montmartre. If he had been making a film, part I would have been in color, part II in black and white.

Part II of *The Stranger* is told from behind prison walls. It brings Meursault from his arrest to his incarceration and trial, into the justice system whose rituals had become so familiar to Camus during his months covering the courthouse for *Alger-Républicain.*

He remembered the ridiculous Judge Vaillant explaining Christ to the Arab Akacha in the El Okbi trial—a judge who was such a nervous wreck, he had finally taken early retirement.[1] Of course Akacha had refused to play the game, answering the judge's question about his beliefs with this retort: "I don't believe in God. He is too old. He needs to be changed."[2] In the novel, Camus wrote a similar dialogue from Meursault's point of view. Akacha was sarcastic and surly, but Meursault would be passive and infuriating. The judge brandishes a silver crucifix at Meursault, who can barely listen to what the judge says because he is distracted by a fly landing on his face. He manages to tell the judge he doesn't believe in God. The judge panics, and he tells Meursault that everyone believes in God. If that weren't the case, he adds, his own life would be meaningless.

Meursault tries to suggest that the judge's problem with faith is his alone: "But from across the table he had already thrust the crucifix in my face and was screaming irrationally, 'I am a Christian. I ask Him to forgive you your sins. How can you not believe that He suffered for you?' I was struck by how sincere he seemed, but I had had enough. It was getting hotter and hotter."[3]

In his fiction, Camus transforms Vaillant's behavior in the courtroom into something out of bounds of any expected behavior. The judge in the El Okbi trial was nervous and mildly inappropriate. In *The Stranger* he acts like a crazed priest.

·

In a novel full of sounds, Marie's visit to Meursault at the prison is the loudest scene. Sartre used a similar scene in *Nausea*. Roquentin, eating in a restaurant, gets distracted by the ridiculous conversations around him. It was an old trick used by Flaubert at the county fair in *Madame Bovary*: interweave the agricultural commissioner's speech with the repartee of two lovers, so that love and official discourse are set off against each other in a way that ridicules both ways of speaking. Meursault and Marie were never very good with words, but now there are so many clashing voices around them, they can no longer hear each other at all. Meursault is trapped on the other side of a wall of useless sound. He uses the same images in *The Myth of Sisyphus*, so many ordinary expressions of the absurd: the familiar loved one who suddenly becomes strange; the man talking on the phone behind a glass partition, his silly, meaningless gestures.[4]

Camus needed to show, in a very few pages, the infinite emptiness of Meursault's experience of time passing behind bars. From his hotel, Camus wrote to Francine that he was overwhelmed by memories of Algeria, especially on the "viscous rainy spring nights" in Paris.[5] That longing for home was a powerful inspiration when he portrayed Meursault lying in his cell, cataloging every object in every inch of his room.

To punctuate the emptiness of prison life, Camus introduced a found object into Meursault's cell, a torn, yellowed newspaper clipping about a man in some uncertain country—Meursault imagines it is Czechoslovakia—who returns home after many years to his mother's inn, only to be robbed and murdered by his mother and sister, who don't recognize him. Camus had seen the actual story in an Algiers newspaper in 1935, and he hadn't forgotten it. He uses it here in *The Stranger* and later makes it the center of his play *The Misunderstanding*.[6] The story hit a nerve, both because of his particular dread of exile and his guilt about leaving his mother behind when he left Algiers for Paris. But he needs to keep his narrator in character. Meursault has to be obsessed by the story and, at the same time, indifferent to it. A son is killed because his own mother doesn't recognize him. It is a situation full of psychological meaning for any reader, and especially for Camus, who wrote about the boy whose "entire sensibility" was defined by his relationship to his mother. But for Meursault, the story must be a pure distraction, a pastime. Meursault reads the clipping at least a thousand times, and concludes: "I thought the traveler pretty much deserved what he got and that you should never play games." Camus had created a protagonist incapable of empathy.

In chapter 3 of this second half, Camus moves Meursault more and more outside himself as his trial begins. Meursault approaches the event as though it were happening to someone else: "In a way, I was even interested in seeing a trial, I'd never had the chance before."

In the courtroom, Meursault sees a reporter with a slightly lopsided face and has the odd feeling of being watched by himself. Camus liked to say he had a lopsided face—like Fernandel—and he uses this uncanny moment to mark a solidarity between himself as the author and his main character. He and Meursault, with their family resemblance, might be brothers. Like those Renaissance artists who included a likeness of their patrons in a corner of their canvas, Camus is signaling gently that he is in charge of Meursault. He is attending to his fate.

·

Indeed, Camus might have been that reporter, sitting beneath the prosecutor on the benches of the legal correspondents, charged with recounting the trial. He knew exactly what the Algiers criminal court looked like. But to make his story believable, he had to forget what he knew and describe the scene from the point of view of Meursault the defendant, who is seeing a courtroom for the very first time:

> To my left I heard the sound of a chair being pulled out and I saw a tall, thin man dressed in red and wearing a pince-nez who was carefully folding his robe as he sat down. That was the prosecutor. A bailiff said, "All rise." At the same time two large fans started to whir. Three judges, two in black, the third in red, entered with files in hand and walked briskly to the rostrum which dominated the room. The man in the red gown sat on the chair in the middle, set his cap down in front of him, wiped his bald little head with a handkerchief, and announced that the court was now in session.[7]

When he covered El Okbi's trial for *Alger-Républicain*, Camus heard the church bell of the Église Saint-Augustin ring, just as the verdict was rendered. In the absurd, godless universe of *The Stranger*, Meursault is distracted from his lawyer's insipid defense speech by the honking horn of an ice cream truck. This detail says a lot about Camus's art. It wasn't in the reflection of a world, but in its transposition, in the metamorphosis of a church bell into the horn of an ice cream truck, that Camus defined his version of the absurd.

·

The last chapter of *The Stranger*, chapter 5 of part II, begins with a shift in time. Meursault, condemned to death by the court, is no longer recalling how the witnesses sounded, what the judge said, or what awaited him "back then" when he tried to fall asleep in his cell. Suddenly he speaks in the present, in real time—the time the reader has been waiting for throughout the entire novel: "For the third time I've refused to see the chaplain. I don't have anything to say to him." The fact that he is no longer remembering and reporting, but speaking in the here and now, makes him feel very near. He is close and he is brimming with emotions—with the sense of all he has lost, with the desire to live, with the knowledge of his imminent death. Gone throughout chapter 5 is the flat American affect of the rest of the novel, and in its place there's a tragic intensity. After several remarks in the present, Meursault reports on his last days of life from a future beyond death, and before it.

Soon he will be guillotined. He remembers seeing a guillotine in the newspaper, after "a highly publicized execution." Camus hadn't forgotten the photograph of Weidmann published in *Alger-Républicain*, and now it was useful, for with it he could enable Meursault to imagine the machinery of his death, "a precision instrument, perfect and gleaming."[8]

The chaplain's visit is a final joust with the inauthentic world of religion. Meursault reacts to the chaplain's consoling language with fury. After he sends the chaplain away, his anger is spent, and he remembers his mother taking a fiancé: "So close to death, Maman must have felt free then and ready to live it all again." Meursault is ready, too, but it is too late for him to live. When he rages at the magistrate who attacked him for not weeping at his mother's funeral, his love for his mother comes through at last: "Nobody, nobody had the right to cry over her."

Camus continued to write Meursault without the "u" in his handwritten manuscript of the novel—his character's name still sounded Spanish: "What did it matter if Marie gave her lips to a new Mersault?" With the "u" he added the French "I die" (*je meurs*) to Meursault's name. The fact that the "u" is missing from the only existing manuscript of the novel is a useful reminder to literary critics that much is unknowable about the art of fiction.

And so the story comes full circle. "As if that blind rage had washed me clean, rid me of hope; for the first time, in that night alive with stars, I opened myself to the tender indifference of the world. Finding it so much like myself—so like a brother, really—I felt that I had been happy and that I was happy again." To live without hope, to dissolve into nature, meant, in Camus's moral universe, to live authentically. Meursault had achieved enlightenment, and there was nothing left for him to do but look forward to dying: "For everything to be consummated, for me to feel less alone, I had only to wish that there be a large crowd of spectators the day of my execution and that they greet me with cries of hate."[9]

That last paragraph of *The Stranger* carries with it all the terror of a living nightmare. Was it Camus's own nightmare, a fear, as he finished so quickly, that he deserved to be punished for the novel that might finally succeed?[10] Or was he welcoming the death of the part of himself best left behind in Algeria, on the streets of Belcourt? Back in 1935, as he was completing his philosophy degree at the University of Algiers, he had written enviously to a high school friend who had made it to the capital: "I'm living right now for two things: the idea that in a month I can work whole heartedly on my book; the hope that in a year I will drop my little Algiers personality to lose myself in Paris."[11] Camus had dispatched Meursault, but *The Stranger* lived, and with it, the boy from the North African streets was safely confined between two covers.

". . . that they greet me with cries of hate." Under his last sentence, Camus drew a bar in black ink with a period before and after it. It was past midnight. He signed his name, Albert Camus, and added, "Paris, May 1940."

·

After signing his last page, Camus tried to stop writing. But he had so much excess nervous energy that he started a long letter to Francine. All his dreams for the novel are in the letter, and all his doubts:

I'm writing you in the middle of the night. I've just finished my novel and I'm too enervated to think about sleeping. Probably my work isn't finished. There are things I need to go back to, other things to add. But the fact is I've finished and I've traced the last sentence [. . .] This manuscript is sitting in front of me and I think about what it has cost me in effort and in will—how I have needed to be present to it, to sacrifice other thoughts, other desires, to stay in its atmosphere. I don't know what it's worth. At certain moments, these days, certain of its phrases, its tone, its truths, have shot through me like lightening. And I was terribly proud. But at other times, I see nothing but ashes and clumsiness. I'm too consumed with this story. I am going to put these papers in my drawer and start to work on my essay. In two weeks, I will take everything out and work on this novel again. Then I'll have it read. I don't want to spend much more time on it because really I've been carrying it with me for two years and I could see by the way I wrote it that it was already completely traced within me.[12]

It wasn't the work at *Paris-Soir* that was tiring him, it was the novel. The ease he felt writing was illusory, for the lure of *The Stranger* was so strong, it drew him into a constant effort and a focus that was exhausting. In his young life as a writer, he had never before had the sensation of a book "traced within him." You could say that *The Stranger*, compared to the other books he wrote in the 1930s—*The Wrong Side and The Right Side, Nuptials,* and *A Happy Death*—was a book he found in himself, rather than a book he wrote about himself. This idea of a fiction existing within the creator, waiting to be discovered, is an important part of a modernist credo in general, and of Camus's artistic values in particular. Proust, a writer at odds with Camus in so many other ways, explains the same idea very clearly in *Time Regained,* when he argues that a work of art is not an expression of the author's life, but something deeper: the work is there, inside the writer, waiting to be discovered. "The book whose characters are forged within us, rather than sketched by us, is the only book we have."[13]

·

Despite Camus's almost magical sense that *The Stranger* existed before he wrote it, he was uncertain about what he had accomplished.

Writing to Francine in the heat of the moment, he measured his contentment against his discontent. He knew he had done something important, but he was only twenty-six years old and, true to his youth, full of hesitations and questions:

> What's funny is that I don't even know if I am happy. Yet that is the only thing that can get me beyond myself and I believe that I will forgive everything in Paris for having allowed me to live locked up like this in what I was doing. Even if it didn't have value, the joy of the work itself has a value that no one can destroy and it is that joy I would feel tonight if I weren't so tired. I still imagine that the reader of this manuscript will be at least as fatigued as I am and I don't know if the continuous tension felt within it will not discourage many souls. But that isn't the question. I wanted this tension and I worked to transmit it. I know it is there. I don't know if it is beautiful.[14]

He shared a practical idea with Francine. Montherlant, who wrote him such an encouraging letter about *Nuptials*, mentioned him again to Jean Grenier, and asked what he was doing. Montherlant had made a name for himself in Paris as a virile dandy, a poet of Morocco and Algeria, and a consummate stylist. He was also a critic of colonialism. In 1938, Montherlant published *The September Equinox*, excoriating French weakness in the face of Nazism.[15] Camus wondered if Montherlant, with all his connections, might help him get *The Stranger* published, and *The Myth of Sisyphus* as well, when it was finished.[16]

What he couldn't know, that first day of May 1940, was that sides were being taken and a chasm of political difference would soon separate him from a writer he once admired. *The Stranger* would have to make other friends.

12

Exodus

ON MAY 1, 1940, after a sleepless night, Camus wrote in his notebook: "*The Stranger* is finished."[1] The pages were piled on his table, a manuscript to reread and revise. Calling the book by its title gave *The Stranger* a denser reality.

Appropriately enough, May 1 was France's Labor Day, and the twenty-six-year-old writer was exhausted. Albert Camus, in May 1940, was living his own myth of Sisyphus—pushing heavy boulders up hills and seeing them crash back down to earth. A life-threatening illness at seventeen, a painful separation at twenty-three, the loss of *Alger-Républicain* and exile to Paris, and the accelerating sense of political crisis throughout the 1930s defined his world. In politics and in life, appeasement had failed. Since September, his country was on high alert. Life was teaching Camus that the world could change, utterly, in a matter of days.

.

The war of waiting took a dreadful turn to action in April, when Hitler invaded Norway and Denmark. On May 10, 1940, the German army moved on to Belgium and the Netherlands, ever closer to France. On May 24, Camus wrote to his friend Yvonne Ducailar in Algiers that he had volunteered for ambulance duty in Paris; he hadn't been drafted, and he wanted to help. But nothing came of it. Belgium surrendered to the Nazis on the May 27, and on June 3 Paris experienced its first air raid of the war. When, only a few months later, the writer Irene Némirovsky sketched scenes of France in defeat, she began with that air raid.[2] She described the sandbags piled halfway up the important monuments, parents dressing their children by torch light as they prepared to flee the city, merchants abandoning their flower carts in the streets. Over two million Parisians left the city, joining masses of refugees from the north, in the course of the event that was dubbed, with biblical accuracy, the exodus.

The first day of the exodus coincided with a happy event for Albert Camus.[3] On June 4, he finally abandoned the dreary Hôtel du Poirier for the Hotel Madison, a more respectable lodging in the publishers' district of Paris. One wonders what the Metros were like that day or even how he was able to make his way from the hill of Montmartre in the 18th district of Paris to the boulevard Saint-Germain on the Left Bank of the Seine. Once installed in the Madison, he would have seen out his window the thick ribbons of cars, carts, and bicycles heading down the boulevard Saint-Germain towards the place de l'Odéon before making their way due south to the Porte d'Italie, one of the traditional gates of the city. In newsreels of the June days, traveling shots capture the endless lines of refugees making their way down country roads with all they could carry. The exodus itself was the most significant mass displacement, the longest traveling shot, in French history.

·

Camus saved up several thousand francs from his wages at *Paris-Soir* to leave the Hôtel du Poirier, and for the time being *Paris-Soir* continued to function. "Here the madness continues," Camus wrote Pascal Pia, who had been drafted, "I've been living for three days between two closed suitcases because *Paris-Soir* notified me that I had to leave for Nantes where part of the staff has already transferred to produce a newspaper for the provinces. Everyday, I'm supposed to leave the next day. Today, it's been decided—barring any change of plan!—that I will remain in Paris."[4]

The Hôtel Madison, sunnier and more expensive than the Poirier, stood right in the sweet spot of the neighborhood known as Saint-

Germain-des-Prés, across from the church. If Montmartre and its Bateau-Lavoir had been the center of artistic activity in the Belle Époque, the period from 1900 to the First World War, and Montparnasse the headquarters of the Jazz Age in the 1920s, Saint-Germain-des-Prés was quickly becoming the place to be for Camus's generation. Simone de Beauvoir and Sartre were among the first intellectuals to migrate from Montparnasse to Saint-Germain. By 1939 they were at the Café de Flore every day. For the foreseeable future, it was the place where they would eat, write, argue, and keep warm. In her memoir, *The Prime of Life*, Beauvoir paints an affectionate portrait of writers and filmmakers and photographers who gathered at the Flore. On a given day, she recalled, Picasso flirted with Dora Marr and their Afghan hound; Jacques Prévert, poet and songwriter, held forth at his table; a group of filmmakers argued loudly. In the chaos of June 1940, Sartre was taken prisoner of war, and the Flore became a shadow of its old self.

From the composing room at *Paris-Soir*, Camus followed the changing headlines, a daily lesson in false hope. June 7: "Our control points resist the enemy assault." June 8: "The Germans have deployed 2000 tanks but our troops have countered with a new strategy." June 9, a note of worry: "The enemy sends new masses into battle despite its losses." That week, all Parisians under the age of fourteen were ordered evacuated from the city. *Paris-Soir* couldn't remain unaffected. By June 8, the paper was reduced to a two-page bulletin. On June 10, the battle between the German and French armies spread to the Argonne Forest. On the 11th, *Paris-Soir*'s headline claimed "our troops resist with ardor and heroism." The battle continued.

Since the declaration of war in September 1939, France had secured its border with Germany at the Maginot Line of defense. The French military strategists were counting on the fact that the Ardennes Forest, along the border with Belgium, was unassailable, so little was done to secure the border with Luxembourg and Belgium. While the French army waited along the Maginot Line, the intrepid German tanks swept past the unprotected Belgian frontier.

As it turned out, the Ardennes Forest was passable if you had the right vehicles. Hitler's armies took Holland, then Belgium. They arrived in Paris on June 14, 1940.

On June 18, *Paris-Soir* was still looking for a ray of hope in the midst of defeat. The newspaper's headline read: "Hitler will pass. France will remain." For those two million Frenchmen leaving the city with as much as they could carry, braving fire from relentless German Stuka planes, nothing was less certain.

.

Paris-Soir responded to the German invasion by ordering its core staff to follow the French cabinet. That was no easy task, since the cabinet was having trouble finding a perch. Prime Minister Paul Reynaud's men went first to Tours, then to Bordeaux. Reynaud ceded his place as prime minister to Philippe Pétain. As the last prime minister of the Third Republic, the aged hero of Verdun negotiated an armistice with the Germans. Once it was clear that the Nazis would occupy Bordeaux, it was time to move again. Pétain took his cabinet members to central France, to Clermont-Ferrand. They spent twenty-four hours there, but had a better idea, so they moved on to the nearby town of Vichy. The numerous hotels in that spa-resort were easily transformed into ministries for a government claiming autonomy from the occupying forces. After the armistice, Vichy became the capital of what was called either the "free zone" or, less optimistically, the "unoccupied zone," and Pétain became head of state.

Paris-Soir followed the government—more or less. Camus, weary, wrote to Grenier that like everyone else, he had experienced both the retreat and the exodus twice, from Paris to Clermont-Ferrand and from Clermont-Ferrand to Bordeaux: "These are things you don't forget, but I don't want to talk about them. I'm in Clermont again."[5] In the midst of the upheaval, the owner of *Paris-Soir*, Jean Prouvost, was named minister of information at Vichy, and by the time *Paris-Soir* began publishing in Clermont-Ferrand, it took to lavishly praising Pétain, who had been voted full powers by the national assembly gathered at the Vichy Casino on July 10, 1940.[6] Pétain abolished the constitution and set up an authoritarian regime whose motto, "Work, family, fatherland," was designed to supplant the revolutionary "liberty, fraternity, equality" that had defined the aspirations of three French republics. Back in Paris, the Germans inaugurated their own *Paris-Soir*, which had nothing to do with the newspaper in Clermont-Ferrand. So *Paris-Soir* became the perfect embodiment of a country split into two uneven parts; one controlled by the reactionary Vichy government, the other by the Nazis. Reading the cool, impassive first chapters of *The Stranger*, it is easier to connect Camus's novel to the anxious boredom of the phony war than to the chaos and upheaval that followed.

·

Since he left his mother's apartment for his Uncle Acault's, Camus had been a free spirit with an ever-changing address; now his movements were dictated by political crisis. On June 10, after less than a week at the Madison, he was ordered with the reduced staff of *Paris-Soir* to leave for Clermont-Ferrand and put in charge of driving one of the *Paris-Soir* cars. Daniel Lenief, another editor at the paper, remembers: "Each of us was supposed to get to Clermont-Ferrand in the car given to him, since the regular drivers had almost all been drafted. We were the first to arrive and I can still picture Camus on the place de Jaude, exiting a car that had run out of gas, oil and water, its engine smoking. He turned pale, ran back to the trunk and took out his treasure, a manuscript he shoved in his pocket."[7]

He had driven by night to avoid the air attacks, with two passengers: his friend Rirette Maîtrejean, a copy editor at the newspaper with a glamorous anarchist past, and an editorial director whose tedious conversation made it difficult not to fall asleep at the wheel.[8] He reached Clermont-Ferrand after two nerve-wracking days, on June 12, 1940. If that sputtering, smoking car had exploded, Camus would have lost his only copy of *The Stranger*.

Camus lived in Clermont-Ferrand from June 12 until September 15, 1940. He would get together with his friends in a tiny room to share a meal; often, he was the one sent to brave one of the long lines for groceries, returning to regale his entourage with stories about what he saw.[9] He became fast friends with a staff member named Janine Thomasset, the secretary to Pierre Lazareff, editor-in-chief of the newspaper. Janine remembered Camus smoking cigarettes rolled in corn paper and admiring tweed jackets in shop windows. From time to time, during one of their evening get-togethers, he'd read his friends a passage from *The Stranger*. Georges Altschuler, the diplomatic correspondent at the paper, remembers Camus's muted delivery—the deliberate opposite of a theatrical reading.[10]

Camus's hotel was near a mental hospital, and he went to sleep at night hearing the screams of the patients, which he took as accurate expressions of the current reality: "the madman in the block who won't stop howling—earth on a small scale."[11] Camus's mood was bleak, even desperate. He couldn't get back to Algeria and to Francine, because there was no more civilian transportation. Francine was still unwilling join him in mainland France, as long as his divorce from Simone Hié wasn't final. He adopted a dog he named Blaise Blatin—Blaise after the philosopher Blaise Pascal and "Blatin," the name of the street in Clermont-Ferrand where his hotel and *Paris-Soir* were located. That August, instead of vacationing, he worked on *The Myth of Sisyphus*—the second piece of his absurd trilogy, with *Caligula* and *The Stranger*. Camus drafted a long section of the chapter he was calling "Absurd Freedom," on *Paris-Soir* letterhead with its Clermont-Ferrand address.[12]

His thinking about the absurd was evolving. After arguing that human life had no meaning, he was ready to take the next, positive step, and insist that life can be lived better once its meaninglessness is understood and accepted. The most affecting writing in the book is in this chapter, in sentences that sound sometimes like prose poems and sometimes like sermons: "If I were a tree among trees, a cat among animals, this life would have a meaning, or rather this problem would not arise, for I should belong to this world. I should *be* this world to which I am now opposed by my whole consciousness."[13] What was crucial, once you have the full consciousness of meaninglessness, is living "*without appeal.*" In *The Stranger*, Camus had put Meursault in a situation without appeal at the end of the novel, as he waited for the guillotine in his cell in Algiers. It was only his certain death that enabled Meursault to recognize at last the "tender indifference of the world" and to experience genuine emotion. "Without appeal" means without the help of religion, or schools of thought, without authorities or teachers. In *The Myth of Sisyphus*, there is exaltation in this discovery of living through meaninglessness, along with a refusal of passivity that the condemned prisoner Meursault will experience in his last, redemptive moments: "The certainty of a crushing fate, without the resignation that ought to accompany it."[14] We are all condemned to death, but some of us have more time than others.

In Camus's notebooks, descriptions of the German Occupation began to take on an allegorical edge. He told Grenier in June that he had no desire to speak of what was happening, and as the effects of the defeat intensified, he sought a way to write indirectly. He hadn't started revisions of *The Stranger*, but in the summer of 1940, he was already inching toward the theme of his next novel, *The Plague*: "The man who razes his house to the ground, burns his fields, and covers them with salt so as not to surrender them."[15] Perhaps he was thinking of himself when he wrote about a little man from the Bank of France, transferred to Clermont-Ferrand, "tries to keep the same habits. Almost succeeds. But is so very slightly off kilter."[16]

Time was counted in weeks, in days and hours, and October brought a final transfer of the newspaper, this time to Lyon. Communication was so bad that Camus wasn't sure whether his letters were reaching Francine in Algeria. One rumor had it that the only way to communicate was by telegram. Algeria, suddenly so distant, became an ideal for Camus, who wrote to Francine calling his homeland "the last French soil that is still free (without that ignoble thing called Occupation)."[17] He would soon learn otherwise.

13

Rue d'Arzew

FOR FOUR MONTHS, the manuscript of *The Stranger* accompanied Camus from Paris to Clermont-Ferrand, from Clermont-Ferrand to Bordeaux, from Bordeaux back to Clermont-Ferrand, and from Clermont-Ferrand to Lyon, where, in late September 1940, *Paris-Soir* set up shop for the duration of the German Occupation. During those months of wandering, the situation in a divided France went from bad to worse. Camus continued to work on *The Myth of Sisyphus* in Lyon, while the pages of his novel gathered dust in various drawers in a series of boardinghouses and hotel rooms. He wasn't ready to revise

In June, in the rush to leave Paris, he had left assorted clothes and papers at the Hotel Madison. When Pascal Pia passed through the capital on his way to Lyon after his release from the army, he tried to fetch the rest of Camus's things. All it took was a walk down the boulevard Saint-Germain for Pia to realize that the small hotel had been requisitioned by the Nazis. Legend has it that by the time Camus managed to get up to Paris with a *laissez-passer*, an interzone pass, the hotel clerk told him they had disposed of everything he had left behind—drafts and documents he had been using to write *The Stranger*.[1] Camus, as always, would make do with the bare minimum.

Two weeks after Camus arrived in Lyon, the government in Vichy passed a piece of legislation that set the tone for the horrors to come. On October 3, 1940, the first of two anti-Jewish statutes went into effect. They excluded all but a tiny quota of Jews from the professions, and excluded them altogether from public service, including the teaching corps. The statutes were immediately adopted in both the so-called free zone (Vichy), which included French Algeria, and in the occupied zone. In its eagerness to deal with "the Jewish question," Vichy had legislated in advance of its occupiers, judging that the "purification" of France from Jewish influence would ensure the moral recovery of the defeated nation. The Germans were only too happy to agree.

On October 20, 1940, *Paris-Soir* in Lyon published a front-page article illustrated with a genealogical chart to help its readers determine whether they were legally Jewish. Camus was working as a layout editor for a newspaper he had always disdained, and that now was acquiescing to a flagrant injustice—the legislation that would lead to the classification and deportation of 75,000 French Jews by 1944. Having three out of four Jewish grandparents made you a Jew, as did two Jewish grandparents and a Jewish spouse. You could have two Jewish grandparents on one side of the family, or one Jewish grandparent each on two sides of the family and still qualify as a non-Jew. Francine Faure had a Jewish grandmother, Clara Touboul, but this was not enough to make her Jewish under Vichy law.

In Lyon, continuing on staff at *Paris-Soir*, Camus boarded in a former brothel with red velvet décor and pictures of nudes on the wall. Finally his divorce from Simone Hié came through, and Francine agreed to join him. She arrived in this bizarre setting in the last days of November, and on December 3 the couple was married at city hall in the presence of Pascal Pia, Daniel Lenief, Camus's fellow editorial secretary, and four men who worked with them in the composing room. The atmosphere at *Paris-Soir* was changing. Many of the soldiers who had been drafted in the fall of 1939 were now back at work; the newspaper itself was reduced to four pages and constrained by shortages of all kinds. At the end of the month, Camus was laid off. He had worked at *Paris-Soir* for only ten months.

Unemployed once again, and with the new responsibilities of a married man, Albert Camus needed an income and housing; he needed stability in a climate that was anything but stable. He and

Francine saw only one solution: return to Algeria and lodge for free with Francine's family on the rue d'Arzew in Oran, a city Camus considered the capital of ennui.

·

In a letter home to Francine, Camus had imagined Algeria untouched by the occupation—as the only remaining free place—and it was true that the three Algerian departments were officially in the free zone and there were no Nazis in sight. But Vichy brought out the worst of the right-wing ideologues of Algeria, French fascists committed to anti-Semitism since the Dreyfus affair, who greeted the anti-Jewish statues with joy. Though there was never deportation to the death camps from Algeria, and no Algerian Jew wore a yellow star, one extension of the anti-Jewish legislation struck Algerian Jews at their core. The Crémieux decree of 1870 had given Jews in Algeria French citizenship, distinguishing them from Arab and Berber counterparts who had also lived in Algeria long before the French conquest of 1830. The day after the first anti-Jewish statute passed into law, an additional measure took French citizenship away from all Jews of Algeria, by abrogating the Crémieux decree.[2] While the Jews in metropolitan France lost their jobs and civil rights, the Jews of Algeria lost their rights as French citizens and were once again "indigenous" people, along with the Arab population. Ferhat Abbas, the Algerian nationalist, protested this "equality from below" vigorously, and in general the Muslims of Algeria were dismayed by the legislation, which made their own chances at citizenship even less likely.[3] The consequences were particularly dramatic in the French army, where Algerian Jewish officers were dismissed as of October.

Raoul Bensoussan, a protagonist of the Bouisseville beach story, is a good example. He had been called up for air force duty in 1939 and was demobilized in July 1940, following the defeat. Because he was stripped of his citizenship in October 1940, he became ineligible to reenlist.[4] The Allies invaded North Africa in November 1942, but General Giraud, the French military leader in charge of the liberated territory, refused to restore citizenship to Algerian Jews, in order to maintain what he called "equality" among the natives.[5] It was an added motivation for joining the Resistance, to act as a citizen patriot. In the spring of 1943, Raoul Bensoussan left for London to volunteer for the Free French Air Force. His brother, Edgar, also joined the Free French.

When Camus returned to Oran in January 1941, he was surrounded by people whose lives had been turned upside down by the anti-Jewish statutes and the loss of their citizenship. Many stories have come down from French writers who grew up in Algiers and Oran: Hélène Cixous's father, a doctor, was reduced to giving pedicures. Jacques Derrida, age ten in 1940, had to leave his school.[6]

Camus, who was denied a chance at the state teaching exam because of his tuberculosis, already knew a lot about exclusion. Among Camus's circle in both Algiers and Oran were Jewish teachers and students who could no longer pursue their advanced degrees and faculty members at lycées and universities who were ordered to leave their jobs by December 1940. Jewish primary- and secondary-school students, like Derrida, were forced to leave their schools en masse.

André Bénichou, who had studied with Camus in Algiers, was dismissed from Oran's Lycée Lamoricière, where he had taught philosophy. Camus had given private lessons in history and geography in Oran for a few months in 1940, before he went up to Paris. He began to teach again in a private school Bénichou opened for the Jewish students who could no longer attend public colleges and lycées. They met in makeshift classrooms in apartments around Oran, a few students at a time. Paul Benaïm, one of those students, remembers a dining room on the rue Etienne Eugène and a pale, serious man who rarely smiled, a teacher they would see in his worn-out trench coat, wandering the streets of Oran with a melancholy gait.[7]

Reduced to living with his in-laws and doing odd jobs, Camus never abandoned his work, the trilogy in progress he'd christened "my three Absurds." He produced a new version of *Caligula*, which he sent out to be typed. He finally finished *The Myth of Sisy-*

phus, using pieces from his notebooks, his critical essays at *Alger-Républicain*, and ideas generated by *The Stranger*.

In the final section of *The Myth of Sisyphus*, "Absurd Creation," Camus reflected upon what it meant to be a novelist of the absurd. "Absurd Creation" carries the mark of *The Stranger* without ever mentioning the novel. When he began *The Myth of Sisyphus*, *The Stranger* was still just a glimmer, but by the time he finished, his euphoria writing the first full draft of *The Stranger* was fresh. He still marveled at how the novel had come into being almost in spite of his efforts. That experience was exactly what he meant by absurd creation: the artist is placed *before* his work, which is concrete and carnal; he doesn't reason with it, but "becomes himself in his work."[8]

He marked the event in a notebook entry carefully dated "February 21, 1941"—and with a rare note of triumph: "Finished *Sisyphus*. The three Absurds are done. Beginnings of liberty."[9]

With the three manuscripts finished, he exalted. But "beginnings of liberty," creative liberty, was not liberty for the man. Camus was once again exhausted—indeed, he wrote Pia in March that the eleven-hour train trip from Oran to Algiers seemed too much to bear.[10] That's how Pia knew his friend's health was failing. At the very moment he finished *The Myth of Sisyphus* and was about to send *The Stranger* to trusted readers to see whether it merited publication, Camus had a relapse of his tuberculosis. His doctor, Henri Cohen, was Jewish and had been excluded from the medical profession, so Camus had to consult with him sub rosa, in the offices of a colleague who had slipped through the quota. Uncle Acault, who had supplied him with precious red meat the first time he took sick, was far away in Algiers. It was now left to Francine to comb the markets and shops of Oran for him.

14

A Jealous Teacher and a Generous Comrade

IN THE FIRST WEEK of April 1941, a weak, feverish Albert Camus mailed four manuscripts from Oran to two addresses in the unoccupied zone of mainland France. It is painful to imagine him making his way to the post office, gaunt and soaked in sweat, parting with the play and the novel in draft that had been his constant companions—sending them out in the hope that the sense of achievement he had nurtured in his Paris hotel room on the eve of the Nazi invasion would turn out to be more than a mirage.

To Pascal Pia, who was still working as an editor for *Paris-Soir* in Lyon, Camus sent *Caligula* and *The Stranger*—two out of three of his "Absurds." He sent duplicate copies of the same two manuscripts to Jean Grenier at his country retreat in Sisteron, high in the hills of Provence. Grenier, Pia, and Camus were all living in the official "free zone," and that was a good thing. Any mail that went across the demarcation line into occupied France had been reduced to fill-in-the-blank "interzone" postcards for family use only: "X has returned to ___"; "I am in good health/tired/wounded"; "I am without news of _____"; "X needs a supply of ___, ___, money." The previous January, Camus had sent one of the interzone cards to Grenier in Vanves, on the outskirts of Paris, but got no response. Grenier finally wrote to Camus to inform him that he had been transferred from Vanves to a lycée in Montpellier, in the unoccupied zone—which meant that Camus could write normally. It was as arbitrary as that: if Grenier hadn't been transferred from Vanves to Montpellier, he couldn't have read *The Stranger* in manuscript. Yet Paris was still the center of book publishing in France, and if Camus wanted to publish outside Algeria, he'd eventually have to find a way to get his manuscript to the capital.

For the time being, the mail service within the unoccupied zone, which included Algeria and large areas of southern France, served Camus's purpose and ran smoothly, even from one side of the Mediterranean to the other, on the big ferries that crossed several times a day.

·

The version of *The Stranger* that Camus sent to Pia and Grenier has not survived intact, and it is impossible to know for sure what it looked like. Opinions vary about whether it was typed or handwritten. "If they're typed, send me the three manuscripts you promised in your last letter, but to be safe, send them by registered mail," Pia wrote to Camus in March 1941.[1] Christiane Galindo had typed *A Happy Death* in the House Above the World. On the rue d'Arzew in Oran, Francine Faure Camus was in charge of preparing the typescripts of *The Stranger*—she may have prepared one copy for Grenier and one for Pia, or Camus may have sent a handwritten manuscript to his first readers and saved the typing for a later phase. Today, no writer would consider sending a handwritten manuscript out for a reading, and the art of penmanship is on the decline. But in 1941, Camus's loopy cursive wasn't so unusual—both Pia and Grenier were accustomed to reading him in longhand.

In sending *The Stranger* and *Caligula* to Grenier and Pia, Camus was seeking the approval and encouragement of the two men whose intellectual opinions he valued most—and whose sensibilities, literary and political, were vastly different. Jean Grenier, fifteen years older than Camus, his professor in both high school and university, had always hoped that his prize student would follow a career path similar to his own. He had been severe with Camus about the shortcomings of *A Happy Death*, and his criticism was largely responsible for Camus putting that novel aside. His letters to Camus continued to convey discouragement in the form of erudite critique. Pia, ten years older than Camus, was a colleague, someone with whom Camus had spent many late nights preparing the newspaper. Pia and Camus had plotted to keep *Alger-Républicain* alive, and when they failed, they had taken refuge together in the huge machinery of *Paris-Soir*. Pia was a comrade.

When Camus was laid off from *Paris-Soir* and retreated from Lyon to Oran, Pia remained in Lyon; the two friends corresponded regularly. Pia was on fire about a new literary magazine he wanted to launch. He was calling it *Prométhée*, and he sought Camus's help, as second in command, in a series of detailed letters. The idea was to found a Lyon-based publication with more autonomy than any of the literary and cultural magazines still operating in Paris. Pia was thinking most of all of the Éditions Gallimard's flagship *Nouvelle Revue Française*, which, after delicate negotiations to keep the publishing house open, was operating under the direction of the pro-Nazi intellectual Pierre Drieu la Rochelle.

Camus was enthusiastic about *Prométhée*, which had the potential to become a refuge for literature in a world where politics had turned toxic. Literature for Camus always meant freedom beyond politics, it meant going deeper; *Prométhée*, if it worked, would be a chance at making a literary community in a shattered world, at a time when it was most needed. On January 30, 1941, only a few weeks after returning to Oran, Camus asked Jean Grenier to send him an essay for the potential *Prométhée*, and tempted him by listing all the prominent writers who had agreed to contribute: Raymond Queneau, Jean Paulhan, André Malraux. . . . It was a role reversal, for now it would be Camus sitting in judgment on his teacher. Grenier sent Camus an essay for *Prométhée* on March 11, and on the 30th of the month, he wrote again to Camus to say how glad he was that Camus had liked his submission.

He added a request of his own: could Camus send him fresh dates from Algeria—they were so much less expensive than in France that it was worth it for him to pay the extra postage. Grenier had young children, and his children were hungry. All over France, occupied and unoccupied, people were looking to their friends and relatives in the country to fill their cupboards with butter and sugar and meat and fresh produce, all in short supply in stores and available only with special ration coupons on certain days: the idea of days "with" and days "without" became a regular part of everyday life. It was a good idea to stock up on those Algerian dates, which could give his children a boost of calories.

Please, Grenier added, if Camus sent his own manuscripts he should do so by registered mail. That was March 30. By April 19, twenty days later, Grenier had received those manuscripts, both the novel and the play from Camus, had read them, and had prepared and mailed a response.

·

Jean Grenier's letter in response to a draft of *The Stranger* has gone down in literary history as one of the great misunderstandings of a literary achievement. The letter, dated April 19, 1941, is worth quoting at length, both for what it acknowledges and doesn't acknowledge about the novel, and because it elicited such an important response from Camus. Grenier goes back and forth between enthusiasm and disapproval:

> I've read your manuscripts. *The Stranger* [is] very successful—especially the second part, despite the influence of Kafka, which bothers me; there are unforgettable pages on 1) the prison; the first [part] is very interesting but our attention lags—episodic characters most welcome (the man with the dog, the storekeeper, especially Marie who is very touching)—due to a certain lack of unity and sentences that are too short, a style in the beginning that becomes predictable: "I was happy . . ." for ex. But the impression is often intense. An idea shared with Kafka: the absurdity of the

world, the uselessness of revolt—though in your novel there are
the beginnings of a resistance against those who accuse your character of not having enough *heart*.[2]

He was not reading Camus so much as grading him, alternating
high marks and low marks and underlining his own knowledge of
Kafka. What could have been more discouraging for Camus than the
idea that he was merely walking in the footsteps of the greater writer,
Kafka? That his stylistic innovation was predictable—practically a
tic? That part I dragged, and that the sentences were too short? At
the same time, the manuscript was "very successful" and the effect
on Grenier was "intense."

Grenier found *Caligula* lively but had trouble imagining it on
stage. And in what was the lowest blow of his letter, he told Camus
that women's breasts were "a Freudian obsession" in both manuscripts: "wasn't there something sentimental and phony about this?"
(There are four references to Marie's breasts in the entire novel, but
there's nothing Freudian about any of them).[3] Finally, he couldn't
decide whether all the action in *Caligula* was an asset or a defect.

Camus's teacher then returned to his evaluation of *The Stranger*.
He was struck by Camus's use of the phrase "the indifference of the
world." He was referring to the beautiful last lines of the novel, already in place in this first draft, where Meursault confesses, as he
awaits death, that he has surrendered himself "to the tender indifference of the world." For someone who knew Camus's very early essays
as well as Grenier did, there would have been a lot to say about the
sentence. Camus had written a similar line in a far more joyous context in his "Nuptials at Tipasa": "I open my eyes and heart to the unbearable grandeur of this heat-soaked sky." Opening oneself: this is
the essential gesture in Camus, a brute confrontation between man
and the physical world, which differentiates him from an existentialist like Sartre, whose ideas were rooted in the social world, in the
confrontation of self and other.

Instead, the sentence reminded Grenier of his *own* œuvre: "I
should have sent you the twenty pages that I've written on this sub-

ject to ask you your opinion—or rather the whole of the manuscript which is rather short and focuses on the idea of the Absolute and the feeling of *indifference*." With false modesty—a request for Camus's opinion—it was a way of suggesting that he was the expert on matters of indifference, not his student.

His letter ends with an expression of praise tinged with condescension: "I thank you very sincerely for having sent me these two manuscripts. They represent a *decisive* progress with respect to what you've done thus far. You know that I was rather severe for certain things from your beginnings."[4]

"Was rather severe"—so severe that Camus had asked him, after the failure of *A Happy Death*, whether Grenier thought he should continue to write.[5] That the most beautiful sentence of Camus's novel, the emotional zenith, reminded Grenier of his own work, is certainly a competitive response, and a sign of narcissism—Grenier was responding to Camus's work by asking Camus to focus on his.

On April 28, Grenier followed up with another letter to Camus explaining that other friends had sent provisions and he had no more need for the shipment of dates. He suggested that Camus send his manuscripts to the publisher Gaston Gallimard, with whom Grenier was in regular contact. It was a generous offer, especially given his qualms. Gallimard, he explained, made regular visits to the Hotel Cavendish in Cannes, in the unoccupied zone. That was where to send them.

Pascal Pia also wanted to play the go-between, but his response to the novel and the actions he took were very different. Whereas Grenier told Camus to feel free to send his manuscript to Gallimard in Cannes, Pia simply took charge of representing the novel—he became the equivalent of a literary agent, and a very good one. Pia had always excelled at networking, and when it came to *The Stranger*, he would outdo himself in strategies, and in the energy he devoted to Camus's cause.

Pia wrote to Camus on March 16, 1941, worried about his health and eager to read *Caligula* and *The Stranger*. He suggested they might publish the novel in five or six installments in the first issues of *Pro-*

méthée. In other words, he was confident of the quality of Camus's fiction even before he had read it—which suggests he might have been one of the friends who heard Camus read aloud from the book in Lyon. Perhaps Camus had already shown him selections.

Pia acknowledged receipt of the manuscript on April 8 and responded in detail two weeks later. When Camus received Pia's letter in Oran, he had been living with Grenier's tepid response for a week. The novel astonished Pia:

Quite frankly, it has been a very long time since I have read something of this quality. I am convinced that sooner or later *The Stranger* will find its place, which will be at the top. The second part—the investigation, the trial, the cell—is a demonstration of the absurd, constructed like a perfect machine where nothing, however, discloses its craft. And the last fifteen pages are admirable. They are as good as the best pages of Kafka or Rudolf Kassner. I have every reason to believe that this will delight Malraux, to whom I shall send your two manuscripts [*The Stranger* and *Caligula*] once I have reread them. For anyone who knows that you have studied the philosophy of the absurd, the road taken is obvious. Sadly, it is rare that the University and the Sorbonne lead to a great book . . . frankly, I admire the mastery that allows you to explore Meursault's crime story and to write *Caligula*'s unhinged monologues.

What struck me also in *The Stranger* is the constant accuracy of the tone and, linked to that, the perfection of the images, as when you talk about the sweat and tears on old Pérez's face: "They spread out and ran together again, leaving a watery film over his ruined face."[6] This is of course only a detail, but it isn't negligible, for in general the "moralists"—if I dare use the term—and perhaps with the exception of Malraux—are either stripped bare to the end (like Vauvenargues, Sade, Benjamin Constant) or, on the contrary, are drowning in flowery rhetoric, like Gide before the last war.[7]

Was the reference to the Sorbonne rarely leading to a great book Pia's jab at Camus's philosophy teacher with his conventional academic trajectory? Or was Pia merely observing the literary world as he knew it?

Whatever his personal feelings about Camus's other mentor, Pia's response to *The Stranger* is a beautiful example of generous reading, of enablement, which stands in stark contrast to Grenier's response. Grenier is "bothered" by the echo of Kafka, while Pia finds *The Stranger* as good as Kafka's best pages. Beyond this one shared reference, the two men seem to have read entirely different books: Grenier sees a lack of unity and too obvious a style (the predictable short sentences); Pia sees a perfect construction that is never obvious. Pia appreciates the tone and the focus, and gives as a specific example, Camus's description of Thomas Pérez's face at Meursault's mother's funeral. Grenier quotes only a single line — "tender indifference" — and that in order to refer to his own work.

So while Grenier, despite his quibbles, offered to send the manuscript to Gaston Gallimard, Pia had a concrete plan. In May 1941, he sent *Caligula* and *The Stranger* to Roland Malraux, who was passing through Lyon and promised to give Camus's manuscripts to his brother André. Pia's dream of founding *Prométhée* would never materialize; he was unable to obtain the necessary authorizations from the Vichy government, which exercised a tight control over all publications. But *The Stranger* was on its way.

15

Resolve

CAMUS NEVER LOST HIS AFFECTION for Jean Grenier, the man who had made him dream of a life devoted to literature. But that affection was sorely tested at the very moment Camus was coming into his own as a writer. On May 5, 1941, two and a half weeks after Grenier's discouraging reading of *The Stranger* on April 19 and a week and a half after Pia's enthusiastic reading of April 25, Camus responded to Grenier with a letter designed both to honor his mentor and to mark his distance: "I'm glad you saw good things in *The Stranger* yet I have the sense that as a whole you don't completely like what I sent. It makes me a little uncertain. But I will not hesitate to continue everything I've undertaken. I waited for a long time to be able to write what you have read and what I have yet to do. Two or three years ago, it seemed that I could begin. Even if it is bad or not as good as I expected, I still know that it is mine now and I am willing to be judged on its merits."[1]

It was a polite but firm response. He had put the manuscript of *A Happy Death* aside in 1938 after Grenier's last critique and had even considered abandoning his aspirations as a writer, but this time around, Camus was not going to abandon *The Stranger*. "It is mine now": this was a leap into maturity, a decisive break with the anxiety and the doubts that had still dogged him in May.

There are three key moments in Camus's creation of *The Stranger*, three turning points that allowed him to bring the novel to fruition. First, the day in October 1939 when he burned his papers and with them an important chapter of his Algerian past, leaving for Paris in March 1940 with the sense of an unencumbered new start ("Two or three years ago, it seemed that I could begin"). Second, the last night of April 1940, six weeks before the Nazis marched down the Champs-Elysees, when he finished his first draft in the miserable Hôtel du Poirier in Montmartre and realized that the book he had written was completely different from his previous efforts. And now, the most important moment of all—this gentle revolt provoked by Grenier's misunderstanding of his work, and with it, the conviction that he had the right to continue without his teacher's approval, that he could be, as he described it in *The Myth of Sisyphus*, "an absurd creator," writing without appeal.[2]

Camus, whose own father had died when he was a year old, had been close to any number of father figures: his grade school teacher, Louis Germain, who encouraged him to continue his studies; his Uncle Acault, who had sheltered him when he was ill, and throughout his twenties; Grenier, who read everything he wrote. Now at age twenty-seven Camus was confident that what he had written was worth defending—and he defended it clearly before his closest and most respected critic.

Grenier's complaint that he was overly derivative of Kafka called for the strongest response, since it was at the heart of Camus's thinking about guilt and the absurd. The first draft of *Myth of Sisyphus* in February 1941 included an entire chapter on "Hope and the Absurd in the Work of Franz Kafka." Yet he didn't think his novel was derivative. In his letter of May 5 he explained:

> I asked myself if I was right to take up this theme of *The Trial*. It was distant from Kafka in my mind, but not in appearance. However, it was about an experience I knew well, that I had felt intensely (you know that I followed many trials in criminal court, including some great ones). I could not abandon it for the sake of just any concept in which my experience would play less of a role. So I decided to risk the same theme. But inasmuch as one can judge one's own influences, the characters and episodes of *The*

Stranger are too individualized, too everyday, to risk being associated with Kafka's symbols.

The Stranger, in other words, was not an allegory like *The Trial*. It
was set in the most recognizable, ordinary streets of Algiers. Meursault, heading home from work to boil potatoes, has little connection
to Kafka's realm of the symbolic, only to the banal, and the bizarre.

Camus remained even-tempered. He was happy to send figs and
dates any time Grenier wanted them, and was happy to read his
essay on the Absolute. Only the concluding paragraph of his letter
transmitted the sadness beneath his resolve:

> Yes, you have always been severe towards what I was doing. But
> I have never wanted it otherwise. You have helped me and I can't
> say as much about many men. This time though, your opinion has
> left me a bit melancholy. I put much hope in this current work. On
> what then should I place my hope?

It is possible that Grenier's qualms about *The Stranger* were a gift
that allowed Camus to break free of him. But freedom always has
its share of sorrow, and writing for himself would be a very different
activity than writing for approval, and would take getting used to.

After several exchanges of letters, the two men found a new equi-
librium. Grenier wrote on May 11 that he was taken aback by Camus's
May 5 letter, since he thought he had conveyed clearly that the two
manuscripts were very successful and somehow Camus had understood the opposite. (Which Camus might have taken as one more
insult—could he not even read a letter correctly?) Grenier wanted
to dissipate any misunderstanding. *The Stranger*, he insisted, was indeed excellent, expressing something profound and personal—"I
gave you my opinion with nuances, it's only natural, since without
that it wouldn't have had any value."

Grenier responded to Camus's claim that his characters were
much more everyday than Kafka's. "Your characters have an abstract
allure," Grenier insisted, based on individuals but transformed into

"actors who recite a role they don't understand." And—here he was responding with his own personal cultural references—"Maya," the Hindu god of illusions, "pushes them to the brink of despair." Alluding probably to Raymond Sintès and his tough-guy way of talking, Grenier flattered Camus by saying how much more interesting his characters were than Cagayous's, a working-class Algiers folk hero whose tales had been gathered in the 1930s by their friends Gabriel Audisio and Edmond Brua.[3]

Grenier's May 11 letter was an odd performance; he backpedaled and tried to recast his previous critique as praise. Always the professor, he supported his arguments with cultural allusions. He ended by encouraging Camus once again to write to Gaston Gallimard.

Camus, responding from Oran in early summer, bent over backwards with his own apology: "the misstep is mine—please excuse this misunderstanding."[4] At the same time, he let Grenier know that his criticism hadn't bothered him (literally, hadn't touched him)— he only found it "useful and usable." Then he explained that Pascal Pia had other plans for getting *The Stranger* and *Caligula* published. The message was clear: he had a supporter in another corner. It was conveyed delicately enough that Grenier would never have taken offense.

Was it before or after Camus's gentle declaration of independence that the young writer heard from Pia, who had amazing news? Pia wrote to say that he had received two letters from Jean Paulhan, the editor at the Gallimard publishing house in Paris. Paulhan had written on April 5 to say that he wanted to read the novel: "Try to get it to me [in Paris], I'll have it published by Gaston Gallimard." Then on April 14, Paulhan wrote to Pia again and announced: "It's all set for Camus. Gaston Gallimard will take it."[5] *The Stranger* was accepted unofficially before either Paulhan or Gallimard had read a single word of the novel.

These exchanges were so important for Camus's future that it is sometimes difficult to remember that his life in those months amounted to more than what was in his mail. Camus traveled regularly from Oran to Algiers, where he saw his friends in the House

Above the World. He also continued an intense but episodic love affair with Yvonne Ducailar, spending a week camping with her on the dunes outside Oran, to the great dismay of Francine's protective family. Everyone he knew was perfecting what the French call *système D* (short for *système débrouillard*): how to get along when the going is tough, whether this meant sharing food, responding to the anti-Jewish laws by raising money for unemployed friends, teaching students dismissed from public school, or sheltering refugees.

A friend of André Malraux's arrived in Algiers that April, an Italian analyst of politics and culture named Nicola Chiaromonte. Chiaromonte fled fascist Italy in 1934 on the threat of imprisonment; he served in Malraux's air squadron in the Spanish Civil War, escaped occupied Paris for Marseille in 1940, and in 1941 was making his way to the United States via Algeria. Camus became his protector and his friend. The House Above the World was Chiaromonte's safe house until he moved to Oran, where Francine's mother hid him in the apartment on the rue d'Arzew. Together Chiaromonte and Camus bicycled to the beaches beyond Mers-el-Kebir, to Bouisseville and Trouville. Chiaromonte took in the pleasures of the sun and water and relished their quiet solidarity, disturbed only by the horrible news that Hitler had invaded Greece. He couldn't shake the image of a swastika waving over the Acropolis, across the Mediterranean. When Chiaromonte left Algeria for Morocco and then New York, he felt an essential bond with Camus, the time-honored bond of stranger and host.[6] For his part, Camus's protection of Chiaromonte was a first brush with active resistance, a step beyond the refusal to conform that permeated *The Stranger*, toward a growing consciousness of revolt.

Back in Paris, writers had begun to organize, and to suffer. In early May 1941, Jean Paulhan, who would hold the fate of Camus's novel in his hands, was arrested by the Gestapo. He was a member of the Museum of Man network, a group of ethnographers and writers, and he had been hiding the printing press of their magazine, *Résistances*, in his house on the rue des Arènes. Paulhan was detained at the Santé prison and then at Fresnes, in the suburbs of Paris, for nearly two weeks. He was released on May 20 with a slap on the wrist. Drieu la Rochelle, the Nazi-approved editor of the *Nouvelle Revue Française*, had intervened on his behalf.

Pia referred to Paulhan's arrest in a May 31 letter to Camus. He wrote: "J.P. has just spent five days at the Santé prison—I don't know why."[7] In fact, he knew exactly why. *The Stranger* would be born a year later, into a world where more and more things could not be said.

16

The Malraux Factor

TRYING TO FOLLOW the manuscripts of *The Stranger* on their zig-zagging road from Paris to Algiers and back to Paris is like chasing several Minotaurs in a maze—the maze being occupied France. Camus sent separate manuscripts of *The Stranger* to Jean Grenier and Pascal Pia. Grenier, in Provence, sent his manuscript back to Camus in Oran, after his less-than-enthusiastic critique. Pia, in Lyon, gave his manuscript to Roland Malraux, who passed it on to his brother André Malraux in Cap d'Ail. After André Malraux finished reading, he passed that copy on to Roger Martin du Gard, the Nobel Prize–winning novelist who was living in nearby Nice. In Lyon, Pia discussed the murder scene in *The Stranger* with the poet Francis Ponge, who was working at the same time on a book of poetry called *The Voice of Things*—unexpected descriptions of pebbles, snails, cigarettes, candles. Sensitive to the way Camus and Ponge focused on objects, Pia recognized an affinity between the two writers.

The French literary world was a small network, and even with the country divided, word of an exciting manuscript traveled quickly. Enough writers hostile to the Nazi Occupation had retreated to the unoccupied zone that there was a critical mass of expert opinion from Lyon to Cannes, where Gaston Gallimard had set up a second unofficial office. In a matter of weeks, Pia had created what we now call a buzz about the novel among several key writers in the Galli-

Paths of *The Stranger* in Manuscript, 1940–1941

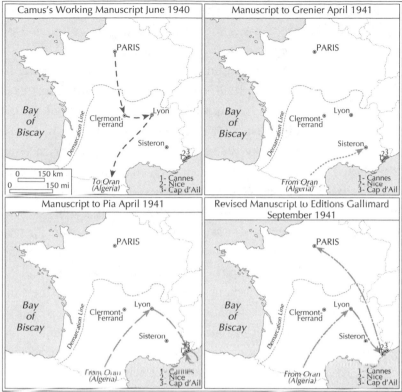

Paths of *The Stranger* in Manuscript (1940–1941). Courtesy of Dick Gilbreath, Gyula Pauer Center for Cartography and GIS, University of Kentucky.

mard/*NRF* stable before it even went to press. And the most important of those writers for the fate of *The Stranger* was André Malraux.

Malraux was by now even more glamorous a figure than he had been in 1933, with the success of *Man's Fate*. In the Spanish Civil War, he organized a French air squadron for the Republican cause, and that experience inspired a second novel on the human condition, called *Man's Hope*.

Malraux, who received his copy of Camus's manuscript from his brother in May 1941, was even more wildly enthusiastic about *The Stranger* than Pia had been, but wild enthusiasm was in his nature. It had been six years since he had swept down into Algiers on a hydro-plane and dazzled a twenty-two-year-old Camus with his call for antifascist action, and he was now going to apply his famous energy to his reading of *The Stranger*.

When Malraux first read Camus's manuscript, he was living in the art nouveau villa les Camélias in Cap d'Ail, a seaside resort near Monaco in the very southeastern corner of France. He had left his first wife Clara and his daughter Florence in Paris and set up house with Josette Clotis, a thirty-year-old journalist who had charmed literary Paris in the 1930s, and she had just given birth to their first son.

Malraux and Pia had been friends since they worked as young men for the same rare book dealer. Malraux knew Camus only as Pia's protégé, so he wrote to Pia and not directly to Camus. Pia was meticulous in reporting every detail of Malraux's letter in a letter he sent to Camus on May 27, 1941: "Here is what he tells me: '. . . *The Stranger* is obviously something important. The force and the simplicity of its means, the fact that it ends up compelling the reader to accept its main character's point of view, is even more remarkable because the fate of the book depends on whether or not it is convincing. And what Camus has to say, in convincing us, is not insignificant.'"[1]

It is odd that Pia went to so much trouble to transcribe and summarize Malraux's letter rather than enclosing it with his May 27 letter, but Malraux had not written an ordinary letter, and Pia, who was a collector, must have known that he held in his hands a significant piece of literary history.[2]

Malraux told Pia he had no desire to hold forth with intelligent or penetrating thoughts about the novel, he really only wanted to be useful, and if he sounded like a classroom monitor, too bad. In fact Malraux was a wonderful reader—practical, with specific advice, now relayed by Pia, for revisions and what difference they would make. Camus had already succeeded, he began. It was an excellent strategy for preparing a young author to accept criticism—the opposite of Grenier's tack. Nothing Malraux was about to say was meant to give Camus the idea that he had anything but a fully realized work on his hands.

"As for the details," Malraux wrote, "1. perhaps the sentence structure is a little too systematic: subject, verb, object, period. From time to time, it's too predictable. Very easy to fix by occasionally varying the punctuation."

Here in a nutshell was the difference between Grenier and Malraux. Grenier too had thought the sentences were too short in part I of the novel, but he stopped with the negative diagnosis: no suggested treatment, hence no cure. His criticism hadn't been, as Camus disingenuously put it, "useful and usable." Malraux put the same issue in perspective: those predictably short sentences were neither terribly important nor very hard to fix. All Camus had to do was to vary the punctuation of a few sentences. A small change in rhythm and construction here and there would make the prose less repetitive.

Malraux continued: "2. There is something to be gained by working on the scene with the chaplain. It isn't <u>clear</u>. What is said is clear, but what Camus means is only partially stated. And the scene is important. I know that this is very difficult. All the more reason, as the man says. 3. Same comment on the murder scene. It is good; it is not as convincing, to use this word again, as the rest of book."

Again, Malraux had a specific suggestion about improving the scene. What he understood is something the best writing teachers understand: that the smallest detail in a revision can make a world of difference, that going from mediocre to memorable in fiction can amount to a matter of a few words. It can be worse to do too much than to do nothing. Malraux suggested that all it might take was one more paragraph where Camus could insist on the link between the sun and the Arab's knife. In other words, Camus needed make the sun glint off that knife.

If several dated versions of the manuscript of *The Stranger* had survived, it would be possible to see exactly where Camus heeded Malraux's advice and where he didn't. In the only accessible manuscript of *The Stranger*, dated May 1940, with that date crossed out and replaced by a new date of February 1941—two months before Malraux's letter—the murder scene is handwritten in a smaller, condensed hand on unnumbered pages, as though Camus were responding to a critique.[3] It is conceivable that the extra pages were substituted well after February 1941, before the manuscript went to a typist or copy editor. As the occupation continued, paper had become more and more difficult to come by, and by the summer and fall of 1941 Camus's awareness of its scarcity makes the handwriting of his revisions smaller and even harder to decipher than the rest of the manuscript.

Camus worked on the murder scene and ended up with this:

> I knew that it was stupid, that I wouldn't get the sun off me by stepping forward. But I took a step, one step, forward. And this time, without getting up, the Arab drew his knife and held it up to me in the sun. The light shot off the steel and it was like a long flashing blade cutting at my forehead. At the same instant the sweat in my eyebrows dripped down over my eyelids all at once and covered them with a warm, thick film. My eyes were blinded behind the curtain of tears and salt. All I could feel were the cymbals of sunlight crashing on my forehead and, indistinctly, the dazzling sparks flying up from the knife in front of me. The scorching blade slashed at my eyelashes and stabbed at my stinging eyes. That's when everything began to reel.[4]

He had transformed writing that had been unconvincing into the most powerful physical scene in his book, a passage that sweats, then burns with its blinding light.

Malraux's fourth suggestion concerned Meursault's mother. Camus needed to tighten those passages. All the right accents were there and they were good ones, but there was "cotton" between them.

In addition to transmitting Malraux's good advice Pia analyzed the advice, and shared with Camus what he knew about his old friend's intellectual habits: "A.M. [André Malraux] is not in the habit of writing such long letters, and it's clear that your manuscripts shook him up. It is always this way with manuscripts he loves: he thinks about them for a long time, he thinks some more . . . and he proposes formal corrections." Pia had observed how closely Malraux had worked with Louis Guilloux on *Le Sang noir*, the great antiwar novel about a Breton town during World War I. The example was flattering, since Guilloux's novel had been a major event in Popular Front France.

Pia then stepped back from Malraux and gave Camus a sense of which suggestions seemed to him the most important. The dry style didn't bother him, it was a matter of taste. He noticed that the scene with the chaplain was incomplete, but so what? Camus would write other books, and he shouldn't throw this one out of balance by trying to exhaust every possibility. Pia agreed completely with Malraux about the murder scene. And as for the mother, nothing had bothered him when he read, so he would have to reread.

Malraux told Pia that he was going to give Camus's manuscript next to Roger Martin du Gard in Nice. Martin du Gard had won the Nobel Prize in Literature in 1937 for his *Thibault* cycle, a serial novel set around World War I about two brothers. At age sixty he was a decade older than Malraux and Pia, and like André Gide, he was a pillar of Gallimard's list, an elder statesman.

For all his enthusiasm, Malraux remained careful and politic. He asked Pia if Camus would want Martin du Gard to send the manuscript on to Gallimard. The only risk in seeking publication, he added, was that editors would compare Camus to his own bête noire, Sartre—but who gives a damn, he added, with his characteristic panache, and added: "Camus can be happy he's written this book."[5] It was Malraux's way of saying that anyone—he included— would be happy to have written it.

Pia concluded his report on Malraux's letter by explaining to Camus that Malraux obviously didn't understand that Gallimard had already accepted *The Stranger* on the strength of Pia's recommendation—Paulhan had already told him as much, twice over.

André Malraux, Roger Martin du Gard, Jean Paulhan, Jean Grenier: Camus was embraced by writers who believed that Gallimard and the *NRF* of the 1930s represented the best in French literary modernism. The publishers Grasset, Fayard, Stock, and Plon also had their stables of authors. Brasillach was at Plon; Mauriac and Giraudoux were at Grasset; and a few writers, like Montherlant, went back and forth between houses. But for Camus's mentors, there was no other house, no other literary address, than Gallimard.

·

After his success in placing the manuscript, Pia did not let up his efforts. As soon as Paulhan said yes to *The Stranger*, Pia wrote him back to find out whether Gallimard would be willing to publish the three Absurds simultaneously.[6] For a man who refused to have his own work published, it was a remarkable vote of confidence. Another person might have thought it was too soon, that Camus should be satisfied with a single triumph. Instead, Pia told Camus that if Malraux and Martin du Gard were equally enthusiastic about *Caligula* and the *Myth of Sisyphus*, the three publications could surely happen.[7] For Camus, who had never been published outside Algeria, the prospect of seeing not just one but all three Absurds published in Paris was nothing short of miraculous.

Once the publication of *The Stranger* was certain, except for formalities, and the other two Absurds were in the offing, Pascal Pia wrote Camus on May 31 to ask him to prepare new copies of *Caligula* and *The Stranger* and send them to him in Lyon along with *The Myth of Sisyphus*. In a world without photocopiers, where a manuscript took weeks to reproduce by hand or by typewriter, Pia would have to be patient until September.

Malraux received the manuscript of *The Myth of Sisyphus* from Pia at the end of October 1941. He wrote Camus directly this time, referring not to Camus's manuscripts or his books to come, but to his *œuvre*, the very word that Camus had used in his 1938 in a vow: "in two years, produce an *œuvre*." "Œuvre" in French implies a near canonical status, and it is a very deliberate word to use in communicating with a twenty-eight-year-old writer who, although he had published in Algiers, was from Malraux's Parisian point of view a first-time author. Reading *The Myth of Sisyphus* had shed a whole new light on *The Stranger*, and Malraux believed that "the essay gives the book its full meaning, and especially, changes what might have seemed in the novel to be a monochrome—practically impoverished—into an austerity that becomes positive, that takes on a primitive force." The essence of Malraux's belief in literature, which he would defend after the war in *The Imaginary Museum*, was that works don't exist in a vacuum; they illuminate one another. He had a quibble with the discussion of suicide at the beginning of *The Myth of Sisyphus*, which he found a little wobbly. But it didn't matter: "What matters is that with the two books together you take your place among the writers who exist—who have a voice, soon an audience and a presence. There aren't very many of them. Next begins their destiny, which is another story."[8]

At the same time, he wrote to Gallimard in Paris: "Have you read Camus's manuscripts? Watch out: this will be an *important* writer, in my opinion."[9] It was a grand welcome of Albert Camus into the republic of letters.

17

A Reader's Report

CAMUS WORKED ON the murder scene and the scene with the chaplain, just as Malraux had suggested the previous May. In September 1941 Pia was able to send Camus's new version of *The Stranger* to Raymond Gallimard in Cannes, asking him to transmit it to his brother, the publisher Gaston Gallimard, who traveled regularly between Cannes and Paris. Since it was still impossible to send mail from the unoccupied to the occupied zone, the best guess is that *The Stranger* finally crossed into the occupied zone in one of Gaston Gallimard's automobiles in late October 1941.

Gaston Gallimard wrote Malraux in November that he had read Camus's novel and had no hesitation to publish. But he had no idea where to send a contract; he didn't know Camus's address.

At this stage, with so many positive opinions in the air, the only figure who might have frustrated Camus's hopes at Gallimard was Jean Paulhan, the fifty-seven-year-old essayist and brain trust of the publishing house, the man who had edited the *Nouvelle Revue Française* before passing it along to Drieu la Rochelle, and still the man in charge of the publisher's literary acquisitions. He had accepted the novel in principle the previous April, yet the specific fate of *The Stranger*—the attention given to it, the hope invested in it and in Camus's other books— all depended upon his reading. Paulhan soon had Gallimard's copy of the manuscript in hand, and he wrote to Pia on November 10, 1941, that he had read *The Stranger* in one sitting: "It is very beautiful, frankly very beautiful. . . . Yes, *The Stranger* is seriously good. And the way the story within is transferred at certain moments into the events themselves, is surprisingly natural, and serious." He and his wife found it gripping.[1]

When the editorial board met at Éditions Gallimard, a secretary named Janine Gallimard took the minutes. She thought she recognized the man she had worked with at *Paris-Soir*, her friend from Paris and Clermont-Ferrand and Lyon. Could it be the same Albert Camus? Janine Thomasset was now Janine Gallimard, the wife of Gaston Gallimard's nephew.

Paulhan wrote the official reader's report:

M. Mersault learns of his mother's death; she had been living in an old peoples' home. He is sad about it (moderately so); travels to the home, attends the funeral, goes back to Algiers, meets Marie (or rather, meets up with her again) the next day, and that night, after having taken her to a Fernandel movie, sleeps with her.

Mersault gets to know one of his neighbors who seems to be some kind of pimp, and he does him the favor of writing a letter for him whose purpose is to set up the fellow's mistress in an ambush. The ambush works. His mistress's brother wants to avenge his sister, wounds the pimp; Mersault, a moment later, thinks he's being threatened and kills the brother mechanically (He's an Arab).

Mersault is indicted; the public prosecutor argues his inhumane character (his indifference to his mother's funeral) and obtains a death sentence.

Truly he is *inhuman* (hence the title). To the extent of welcoming, by any means, with the same curious indifference, without ever taking *sides*, life and death, love, social conventions, and all the rest.

That a novel whose subject is more or less "M. is executed for having gone to the movies the day after his mother dies" is credible, and, if that were not enough, *fascinating*, is sufficient. This is a first rate novel which begins like Sartre and ends like Ponson du Terrail. Accept without hesitation.[2]

A first-rate novel—"Un roman de grande classe"—he meant a world-class novel. Paulhan was a writer usually given to ambiguity. He liked and specialized in circuitous sentences that carried several meanings. His reading of Camus's manuscript resembled him, for it emphasized all that was paradoxical and incongruous about *The Stranger's* pull on the reader. How can indifference be fascinating? What he doesn't say is also revealing of a mental universe—European and modernist—that would define the terms for readers of *The Stranger* for decades to come. Paulhan himself was no stranger to the French colonies—he had lived and taught in Madagascar, and his literary career began with the translation of Malagasy poetry—but only Meursault's mental state mattered to him. There is no mention in his report of the setting of the novel—either the city of Algiers or the beach. Sun and water—the essential ingredients of Camus's universe—are absent. The murder victim gets a parenthetical phrase "(He's an Arab)." Paulhan's reading of *The Stranger* is cerebral: he locates the meaning of the novel in the hypocrisy of the court, which condemns Meursault for going to the movies after his mother's funeral—an absurd, unjust condemnation. And he insists on Meursault's flat affect, his inhuman indifference. He inserts a final comment with an arrow and a bubble; after "grande classe," he adds that Camus has written a novel that "begins like Jean-Paul Sartre and ends like Ponson du Terrail." He was showing off, entertaining the editorial board with this outlandish combination of Sartre's *Nausea* with a popular nineteenth-century writer of action-packed adventures. But his sense of a dramatic change of tone between part I and part II of the book was accurate. For some readers, the emotional ending was a sign that Camus had backed off from his commitment to indifference; to others, it was a necessary catharsis.

There is a final mystery in Paulhan's report that may never be solved. He spells the narrator's name "Mersault" without the "u"—just as it is spelled in the only surviving manuscript of the novel dated May 1940/February 1941. Was it only a slip of the pen—did the manuscript he read actually say Meursault? It is always possible that the "u," the fateful letter that took Mersault into the symbolic universe of death, and transformed a Spanish-sounding name into a fine French wine, was only made on the publisher's page proofs.

André Abbou, the leading authority on manuscripts of *The Stranger*, discovered an advertisement in a 1937 issue of *L'Écho d'Alger* announcing a literary prize of 3,000 bottles of Meursault wine to be given annually to a book celebrating the glory of the land. Could it have given Camus the idea for a new name?[3] The surviving manuscript of *L'Étranger*, seventy-two handwritten pages and fourteen typed pages, doesn't clarify anything.[4] With different sized handwriting and corrections by the author, it appears to represent an amalgam of several versions, rather than the final manuscript that Paulhan vetted in 1942. The pages of the murder scene are not numbered—as though a rewrite had been substituted for the first draft, following Malraux's advice. Page 20 to page 30 of the manuscript are missing: they represent chapter 3 in part I of the novel, which begins with a passage borrowed from *A Happy Death* and includes Meursault's encounters with Salamano and with Raymond Sintès. On the final pages of this manuscript, Meursault is still spelled MERsault.[5]

18

Gallimard's War

PAULHAN WAS ONE LINK in a chain of powerful readers bringing the manuscript from an unknown writer's desk in Oran to a publishing house in Paris. From Pia to Malraux, from Malraux to Gallimard, and from Gallimard to Paulhan and the members of the editorial board, the manuscript traveled with remarkable efficiency. In ordinary times, a relay such as this one would have been impressive but not unheard of. Given the circumstances of war and occupation, *The Stranger's* journey was already a feat, but Paris was only the first stop in an even more challenging process. There was no roadmap for the writers and publishers stuck in occupied France. It was clear after 1940 that the country would go on publishing, but the process was going to be unpredictable and politically fraught. Acquiescing to censorship, skirting issues with German approval in mind, publishing in the free or the occupied zone, not publishing at all—writers and their publishers were making compromises for which they would one day be accountable. Camus was caught in this system, and so was Gaston Gallimard.

Camus was in Oran when he received Gallimard's official letter of acceptance on December 8, 1941. The publisher of Proust, Malraux, and Gide found *The Stranger* outstanding, and was happy to publish it as soon as possible. He was offering what he was calling the standard royalty terms: 10 percent of the list price on the first 10,000 copies, 12 percent on subsequent copies sold, and an advance against future royalties of 5,000 francs—the equivalent of $200 dollars in

1941. (Pia had warned Camus that the amount would be small and he should take his time accepting.[1]) Gallimard asked for first refusal on Camus's next ten books—a standard clause that must have delighted the young author.

The offer might have looked standard on paper, but in practice it wasn't. Gallimard was asking for Camus's approval so that he could send the manuscript into production before a contract was even prepared, let alone signed. Gallimard was at his brother Raymond's home in Cannes, in the unoccupied zone, and traveled to occupied Paris only once a month; the contract itself, Gallimard reported, would take weeks to put together. Camus responded to this request on December 12 with an authorization he never would have given in ordinary times: he released *The Stranger* for publication before he had signed a contract. He reminded Galllimard that he would like to see *The Myth of Sisyphus* in print as well. That manuscript was with Jean Paulhan, along with Camus's play, *Caligula*.[2]

.

Behind Gallimard's seemingly offhand comment about contract delays was a saga that had begun two years earlier, taking Gallimard from one end of the country to the other, threatening the life of his publishing house, and forcing his hand. When the phony war was declared in 1939, Gallimard temporarily closed his offices on the rue Sebastien Bottin and moved operations and staff to the family compound at Sartilly, near Mont Saint-Michel, Normandy. When France fell to the Germans after the disastrous six-week campaign of June 1940, Normandy and the other strategic coastal regions were the first to be occupied. Gallimard was one of millions who took to the roads in a massive exodus from the north. Even before Camus evacuated Paris with the staff of *Paris-Soir*, Gallimard headed south from Sartilly.

Gallimard's group of thirteen relatives and employees made its way in two vehicles: a massive, fast-moving Citroen *Traction-Avant* and a truck. Jean Paulhan was in the group. So were André Gide, the celebrated Gallimard author whom Camus had read as an adolescent, and Julien Benda, an essayist and favorite target of the anti-Semitic far right. They headed southwest, towards the medieval fortress town of Carcassonne.

One can imagine the kind of planning that must have gone on in Carcassonne and the extent of the anxiety, not just about the business of publishing, but about loved ones whose fate in the Battle of France was uncertain. Gallimard was still without news of his son Claude, who'd been taken prisoner—one of nearly two million French soldiers captured by the Germans in the June days. France was defeated and occupied and no one knew how long the occupation would last or what the future would hold for France in what was, for the time being, Hitler's Europe. An apocryphal sentence attributed to Otto Abetz, the Reich's ambassador to France, is often quoted in an attempt to represent the occupiers' state of mind on French culture: "There are three institutions to control by all means: the Bank of France, the Communist Party, and the *NRF*. Start with the *NRF*." Whether or not Abetz actually said this to his colleagues, the gist of it was true, and it applied to all of Éditions Gallimard. The publishing house was so strongly identified with the magazine that many people referred it as "the *NRF*," rather than by the family name Gallimard, and indeed all of Gallimard's books carried the *NRF* logo. The *Nouvelle Revue Française* was not only the in-house magazine at the Éditions Gallimard, it was the birthplace of French literary modernism, which, for Abetz and his men, fell under the category of Communist, "Jewified" culture.[3]

The effect of the German presence on all of French literature was immediate and devastating. Censorship, pillage, and "Aryanization" would swiftly become the laws of the land: in the occupied zone, all books by English, American, and Jewish writers were taken off the shelves of bookstores and libraries. The so-called Otto List of censored books was named after Abetz, who in his dubious role as "ambassador" to occupied Paris served as an enforcer of the Nazis' cultural politics in France. Bookstores were closely monitored, and libraries were ordered to remove titles from their card catalogs and shelves; 700,000 books were confiscated and taken to an enormous warehouse on the avenue de la Grande Armée, near the Porte Maillot—the literary equivalent of the Nazi plunder of works of art that belonged to Jewish collectors. The anti-Jewish statutes that were passed into law by the Vichy government in October 1940 had sweeping consequences for the role of Jews in business, including the book business. Publishing houses were "Aryanized," which meant eradicating any traces of non-Aryan culture or ownership. The Éditions Calmann-Lévy, for example, became the Éditions Balzac, under new management.

When Gallimard returned to Paris after leaving Carcassonne, he began to negotiate with the occupying authorities to keep his business afloat. He transferred the in-house editorship of the *NRF* from Jean Paulhan to Gallimard author Pierre Drieu la Rochelle, a World War I veteran and former surrealist who had evolved into a flamboyant fascist. Drieu la Rochelle was close to both Malraux and Aragon, but in the mid 1930s he promoted what he called a "fascist socialism." His 1939 novel *Gilles*, an autobiographical portrait of a young French convert to fascism, indicted France for its mediocrity and decadence. Under his leadership, Gallimard's *NRF* was authorized to be published, becoming the first literary magazine in the occupied zone to obtain official approval. Meanwhile, the Nazi occupiers' overzealous police force, ignorant of negotiations by their colleagues in the German Propaganda-Staffel, put the publisher's headquarters on the rue Sébastien-Bottin under lock and key just as an agreement had been reached. Drieu la Rochelle, whose editorship had just been announced, had to intervene.[4]

With Drieu la Rochelle in charge, the *NRF* began to publish champions of the Collaboration. Henry de Montherlant was one of them; he had been critical of France's soft response to Hitler in 1936, but now he came out swinging even harder against French decadence after the defeat, putting his faith in the virile German army.[5] This shift baffled Camus, who had been grateful for Montherlant's letter of praise about *Nuptials*. Camus wrote to Jean Grenier from Lyon,

"Montherlant is publishing a lot and I'm not sure his articles are op-portune. I suppose he has his reasons but I would like to know what they are."[6]

Writers were watching one another warily as they took positions, published, or remained silent. The *NRF* became a test case. Drieu la Rochelle managed, at least in the beginning, to hang on to the maga-zine's mainstream writers (Gide and Valéry), and bring in a few un-expected figures such as the Breton Louis Guilloux, a pillar of the French left. This was in part thanks to Paulhan, who played a double game. Working daily in an office next to the *NRF* office at Gallimard, Paulhan recruited writers to submit articles for the magazine he no longer edited, and at the same time, in secret, he was active in the publishing arm of the Musée de l'Homme Resistance network. His friendship with Drieu la Rochelle would save him when the Gestapo arrested him in May 1941.

The Gallimard house continued to publish novels, but only in small print runs, because paper was in such short supply. But Gaston Gallimard had a policy that set him apart from other publishers and served him well during the Occupation. He had always refused to re-mainder or shred excess copies of his books. Now the business made do in large part by selling off the remaining copies of the Gallimard backlist—novels and nonfiction that had accumulated in its ware-houses since the company was founded in 1911, and for which there was a new demand in book-starved France.[7]

To say that the very existence of *The Stranger* was threatened by the material conditions of the war is no exaggeration, since paper supplies were becoming more and more precious. It looked at one point as if Camus would have to supply his own paper stock!

Malraux wrote to him on December 15, 1941, a week after Gal-limard's acceptance letter had arrived in Oran and three days after Camus had declared himself a Gallimard author, to ask how much it would cost to get five tons of the highly desirable alfa paper stock to Paris. (Alfa bushes grew in abundance on the high plains of Algeria.) How complicated would export be, including transport by train, then by boat? Camus responded on January 6, 1942: a ton of alfa would cost between 370 and 400 francs and could be delivered in compact balls—a train car would hold six to ten tons. There would be no problem transporting by boat as long as they were in no hurry. But getting the merchandise to the boat was another story, involving fuel and tires, both available only by special authorization of the governor general of Algeria to the local mayor. Camus was optimistic: Algeria had an unlimited supply of the essential prime ingredient for paper. "Don't hesitate to call on me. I've made contact with the right people. For one thing, they're quite picturesque and for another, I want nothing more than to be helpful."[8]

Of course Camus was enthusiastic about helping the man who was now his publisher come up with the raw material needed to produce *The Stranger*. Malraux was grateful. In January he encouraged Camus to push for a bigger advance on royalties and offered to mediate. By April, Malraux informed Camus, with no explanation, that the paper supply was no longer an issue, but that Gallimard was appreciative of his efforts on the paper front and would certainly look favorably on a request for further funds that might help him weather the difficult period in Oran. After the paper query, Malraux wrote with a surprising personal request: he wanted Camus to look into sending him a handmade rug from Tlemcen and wondered how much this would cost. Camus answered with just as much care. Way too much, it turned out, 800 to 1,000 francs a square meter and export was illegal without an importer's permit. Inflation was out of control.[9] Malraux cheerfully abandoned the plan.

·

In this world of fractured economies and black markets where nothing could be taken for granted, publishing houses were as vulnerable as the more obviously political newspapers and magazines. As early as 1940, in what looked like a declaration of new affinities, Grasset published a polemical diary entitled *À La Recherche de la France*, inviting French writers and editors to return to occupied Paris, where benevolent occupiers allowed the true heart of France to go on beating.[10] Denoël inaugurated a new series, "Jews in France," to showcase anti-Semitic writing. Collaborationist publishers crafted new names to insist they were French ("Les Éditions de France"; "Nouvelles Éditions Françaises") as they courted Nazi ideologies. Gallimard, never an ideological anti-Semite or a Vichy apologist, adjusted to the Aryanization requirements. In 1940, he successfully fought off an attempt to turn over 51 percent of his business to a German publisher. Drieu la Rochelle, the newly appointed editor of the *NRF*, was on hand to lead the negotiations. As for the requirement that Gallimard dismiss its Jewish employees, the publisher took different tacks with different people. Louis-Daniel Hirsch, Gallimard's close friend and business manager, was officially dismissed but continued to receive a paycheck under the table. Julien Benda was told that he could no longer publish articles in the *NRF*. The most poignant story was Jacques Schiffrin's. Schiffrin, founder of the Pléiade collection at Gallimard, was dismissed with a curt note in November 1940; he escaped to New York with his family and set up a new publishing house, Pantheon Books. The Pléiade collection continued under Paulhan's direction. After the war was over, Schiffrin got a license from Gallimard to publish a New York Pantheon edition of *The Stranger* in French. The cover of the Pantheon's *L'Étranger* was black, with the title and author in red and white. It was the exact negative of one of Gallimard's traditional white covers, an homage to *L'Étranger's* birthright that dressed the book in postwar mourning.[11]

But in 1941 a future in which Jacques Schiffrin could publish his own edition of *The Stranger* would have seemed preposterous. Schiffrin struggled to reach New York, traveling via Marseille, Casablanca, and Lisbon with financial help from André Gide. Meanwhile, what mattered for Gallimard was that publishing could go on. In the course of eighteen months, a lot had happened, and the man who negotiated a contract with young Albert Camus in 1941 could say that he was doing what was needed to continue to publish the best in French literature, and that his publishing house would survive.

·

As a first-time Gallimard author and an outsider from Algeria, Albert Camus, in that first full year of German occupation, had to make his own fraught political choices as he prepared to publish *The Stranger*. Pia had wanted to feature *The Stranger* in the new magazine *Prométhée*, but that project never came to fruition. Paulhan had asked Pascal Pia in his first enthusiastic letter about *The Stranger* whether his protégé would be interested in publishing an excerpt, either in Drieu la Rochelle's *NRF*, or in *Comœdia*, another German-authorized cultural magazine in the occupied zone, which could offer Camus 5,000 to 6,000 francs. It was a chance to double the advance that Gallimard offered him in December. Pia advised Camus in no uncertain terms: "I do not think you would seriously contemplate signing your name to this magazine [the *NRF*]. The place is more putrid than ever."[12] He reassured him, too, that refusing Drieu la Rochelle would have no negative effect on the publication of his books: "If Gallimard had to blush or get excited every time an author disdained his review, he'd have died of shame or rage some months ago."[13]

Camus said no to excerpts in *Comœdia* and the *NRF*, but he never questioned the idea of publishing his novel in occupied Paris itself, nor did Pia or Grenier ever suggest he should. In *The Stranger*, Camus makes Meursault unambitious and indifferent to a chance to move to the capital. Indeed, Meursault's immunity to the longing for Paris that men and women in the provinces have demonstrated since Balzac's Rastignac is the ultimate demonstration of his strangeness. Camus, unlike his character, understood that publication in Paris was an absolute requirement for literary success.[14] He was an unemployed journalist, not yet thirty years old; he'd been making ends meet by tutoring in Oran and living with his in-laws. If he had turned down Gallimard on principle, no one would have noticed. Since Pia had sent around his manuscript, he had received praise and advice from the best-known literary figures in France—Malraux and Paulhan and Roger Martin du Gard. There was now a chance he would be noticed—a chance that he might live to see a future where his every ethical and literary position would matter. This future was closer than he knew.

There was one more difficult step before *The Stranger* could go into production. Gallimard needed German approval—indeed the cultural branch of the occupying forces determined the fate of every new book by veto, by censor, or by an allocation of paper for a few, or many copies. Books in favor of the Nazi regime or supportive of German culture and works of propaganda got first priority.

Gerhard Heller, head of the German Propaganda-Staffel, wrote many years later that when he received the manuscript of *The Stranger* from Gaston Gallimard's secretary, he stayed up all night reading it and endorsed it immediately. There was no need for censorship, he said, since the book was "asocial" and "apolitical." What did Heller mean by asocial and apolitical? Did he understand the book as purely philosophical? Did he believe that Meursault's refusal to conform to society's conventions had nothing to do with political resistance? Did he assume that a story about a Frenchman killing an Arab in a colonial setting was politically insignificant, or routine?

It's doubtful that Heller would have given the novel that much thought. A book had to have a straightforward anti-Nazi, pro-Ally message to be censored, or it had to be by a Jewish author. Reading for subtleties was not on the censors' agenda, but Gaston Gallimard anticipated trouble with *The Myth of Sisyphus*, which he wanted to publish next. On February 5, 1942, as *The Stranger* was going into production, he wrote to Camus to explain that *Sisyphus* would never get past the censor unless the chapter on Kafka were cut. He didn't need to specify the reason: Kafka was Jewish.[15] Camus agreed, and substituted an essay on Dostoyevsky. The altered *Myth of Sisyphus* appeared in October 1942, six months after *The Stranger*. But Camus didn't abandon the chapter on Kafka. He sent it to *L'Arbalète*, one of the brave little magazines in the Vichy zone that regularly skirted the censor. It appeared in the summer of 1943 alongside essays by Sartre and D. H. Lawrence.[16] After the war, Gallimard added the Kafka essay to its edition of *The Myth of Sisyphus*.

But this is to get ahead of the story of *The Stranger*. In the winter of 1942, *The Stranger* had no such problems, though there were enough practical difficulties with communication between Algeria and Paris that the months between acceptance in December and publication in April were nerve-wracking, full of worrisome silences and crossed messages. At the very last minute, there was a mix-up about which of the circulating manuscripts was the final version. Raymond Queneau, the Gallimard writer-editor who was ushering the book into publication, sent word to Pia to clarify which manuscript of *The Stranger*—two were in circulation—was the one to send to the printer. Camus wrote to Queneau that *only* the manuscript that Pascal Pia had transmitted to Paulhan was the definitive version—the last chapter of part I consisted of typed pages with different margins than the rest of the manuscript, and the very last chapter of the novel was eighteen instead of sixteen pages long.[17] Pia, too, wrote to Queneau to let him know that Malraux's manuscript of *The Stranger* was not the final version, and that the manuscript that needed to go into production was the one that he, Pia, had sent to Gallimard in Cannes along with *Caligula* and *The Myth of Sisyphus*.

These mix-ups were not the biggest obstacle to publication. Camus was now dealing with something worse than anxiety over his manuscript: his tuberculosis returned in the winter of 1942. It was his worst relapse ever, shattering his hope that the bout in 1941 had been his last. He informed Gallimard on February 12, 1942, that he was in very bad shape and needed to leave the details of the brief biographical sketch to Pascal Pia or Jean Grenier. Pia humored him: "Don't worry, I'll be discreet. However, if you think I should present you as a Hindu Prince, or a high ranking military officer, or a defrocked priest, I can send kilos of fantastical references to Paris."[18]

Camus was not strong enough to proofread his pages, and besides, it would have been impossible for the publisher to get them to Oran and back to Paris without delaying publication for months. Given his state of health, Camus was perfectly willing to let Gallimard correct the proofs in-house, and he had only two requests: could they please get rid of the word "but," second-to-last line of chapter 6; and eliminate the word "the" at the start of the third line of page 54. That was all.[19]

Jean Paulhan oversaw the correction of the last set of proofs, and Camus was spared the process that so many writers dread—the last-ditch search for mistakes, the very last chance to eliminate an excess word or change a sentence. *The Stranger* went to the printer on April 1, 1942, but by the first of May Camus had seen neither a copy of the book nor his contract.

19

The Stranger Is Born

THE STRANGER BEGAN ITS LIFE as a book the day the printers assembled its 159 printed pages and folded them into "signatures" (in French, "*cahiers*"), which they then stacked, aligned, and pasted by their spines onto a soft cream-colored cover. The author's name appeared in black and the title in large blood-red letters: the classic "*NRF* white edition" that had distinguished Gallimard's novels since 1911.

On April 21, 1942, the last pages of a first edition of 4,400 copies of *The Stranger* rolled off the Chantenay printing presses at 15, rue de l'Abbé Grégoire, only a few blocks south of the Gallimard bookstore on the boulevard Raspail, where it went on sale for 25 francs a copy—about $4.00 in today's money.[1] In April 1942, the month that the first copies of *The Stranger* were printed, the Vichy government set up yet another hurdle to publishing in occupied France: a watchdog organization called the *Commission de contrôle du papier d'Édition du gouvernement de Vichy* (The Vichy Government Commission for the control of paper).[2] *The Stranger* sailed through the system with the approval of Gerhard Heller from the Propaganda-Staffel, and the book skirted the new protocol by a matter of days.

Camus was in Oran, still suffering from the relapse of his illness, and still without news of *The Stranger*. In the third week of May, he finally received a single copy of his novel, along with two contracts and a wire draft of 10,000 francs to his bank account at the Société

Générale, representing a customary first-time author's advances for both *The Stranger* and *The Myth of Sisyphus*.[3] For reasons no one could explain, the contracts had languished in an office in Vichy for two months.

Camus wrote affectionately to Malraux on May 25: "I thought of you when I received *The Stranger*. It owes you so much. I am waiting for my author's copies to send it to you. You will see that I took all your criticism to heart. Tell me if the chapter on the murder and the scene with the priest, completely rewritten, seem better to you."[4] He had his one author's copy, but no extra copies to give his closest friends and the people who supported him.[5]

The Stranger was ready for the Paris bookstores by May, but it would take two more months for the novel to appear in the unoccupied zone. On June 27, a stylish ad appeared in *Le Figaro's* literary section, announcing Gallimard's newest releases: Camus's *The Stranger*, a reprint of Stendhal's letters, a Finnish war novel, and poems by Francis Ponge.[6] Because Gallimard relied on its backlist, new publications like those of Ponge and Camus were a rarity, and Camus's novel had pride of place on the list.

·

For writers, a powerful sensation of loss almost always accompanies the publication of a book. It's a cliché to talk about an author's postpartum blues. Mourning might be a more exact term: mourning for the loss of the book project, the closing of the opened-ended work-in-progress, and therefore, though it may seem strange, mourning one's own death—the death of the author—as the primary mover of the book. In 1942, there was more to mourn than usual. Publishing in the French-speaking world had always been centered in Paris, and authors could follow the fate of their books on the Paris scene as the works were printed, sold, and reviewed in a small community of interlocking publishers, bookstores, and newspapers. With the capital occupied by the enemy and cut off from the rest of France, with so many literary magazines and critics having fled the city, all normal circuits of conversation and publicity were disturbed.[7] Camus, in

Oran, was even further removed than his friends in southern France; he had no access to the few publications that reappeared in Paris after the German takeover. Malraux, Grenier, and Pia, all living in the unoccupied zone in the south, kept in touch with Camus as the first reviews appeared in both the occupied north and unoccupied south, and they helped him digest the good with the bad.

Waiting for his first reviews was all the more nerve-wracking because Camus had almost no experience with being reviewed, even though he had already published two books in Algiers. His *The Wrong Side and the Right Side*, published in a minuscule print run of 350, had no press coverage in Paris and only one review, written by a friend, that appeared in *Oran Républicain*.[8] *Nuptials*, published two years later, was reviewed by a writer in Camus's intellectual circle—that was it.[9] Camus had every reason to believe that *The Stranger* would enjoy a much different reception. Like any new author, he waited to be vindicated, or shamed, or—worst of all—ignored.

.

"We saw: Paul Eluard, Germaine and Jean Paulhan, Gaston Gallimard (very pleased about his newest young writer, Albert Camus, author of *The Stranger*), Jean Grenier, Raymond Queneau. . . . etc. etc.": The first mention of *The Stranger* in the French press was hidden inside a chatty article by Adrienne Monnier, reviewing an exhibit of paintings at the Galerie de L'Abbaye.[10] Gallimard had singled out his favorite new author to Monnier, a woman of letters who could ensure the success of a book through her Left Bank bookstore and library, La Maison des Amis du Livre. Malraux sent Camus the clipping—a sign, he said, that Gaston was supporting *The Stranger* in public, as well as talking it up among his close friends. Camus wrote back that the tone of the article was a little too "Deux Magots" (the name of the café next to the Flore, whose customers were old school), but the intention was good.[11]

Those were the first trickles of publicity. On July 13, Camus received even better news. Jean Grenier wrote that he had just left Marcel Arland in the offices of *Comœdia* and he was very happy with what he'd read. Marcel Arland's July 11 review of the *Stranger* is full of praise, but it is certainly one of the most curious articles ever written about the novel.

Arland, a Gallimard regular with a close relationship to Jean Paulhan, was in charge of the book pages at *Comœdia*. It featured major writers unstained by intellectual collaboration—Sartre, Beauvoir, Valéry—and regularly, as though it were paying a toll, it published articles that praised German culture and "the new [i.e. Hitler's] Europe." No Jewish writer was mentioned in its pages. Not marked as collaborationist but supported by the German Institute, the embassy's cultural service, it was given a healthy requisition of paper. The magazine existed thanks to a delicate pas de deux between the editor and the occupying authorities.

Arland was a freewheeling critic who appeared to have no concern about length—another indication that *Comœdia* had all the paper it needed. He could not resist quoting Camus: thirteen lines from the first page of the novel and another equally long quotation from the funeral procession at Marengo. Arland praised Camus for "this cynical candor, this minute and even detail, even in relating dramatic events." He admired Camus for establishing and maintaining throughout the novel an "indifference often more poignant than revolt."[12] Unlike his friend Paulhan, Arland was acutely aware that the Algerian setting made the book successful: "I do not think that the inhuman violence of the Algerian summer has ever been rendered in a more sober, stronger manner." He was most enthusiastic about part II, the trial scenes and the perverse condemnation of Meursault for not crying at his mother's funeral. In fact Arland was so enthusiastic in taking Meursault's side against society that something strange happened to his writing. He began to channel Meursault, putting words in his mouth to explain and justify his burst of emotion in the final pages: "I didn't lie to myself, I mistreated no one. With my death a few days away, I am accepting myself completely and committing to life, to my life, my only possession, fragile but unique."[13] And so Arland continued for eight more lines, seeming to quote Meursault, though not a word of the material he quotes in this part of the review appears in the novel itself. Arland was quoting his own fantasy of what Meursault was thinking. He concluded that Meursault speaks for Camus in the book's final pages—when really it was Arland who elected himself the uninvited mouthpiece for Meursault, transforming the narrator's lonely freedom in the face of death into a psychological triumph.

On July 25, Camus had still not read Arland's article. It is easy to imagine him bristling at the liberties taken with his novel when he finally received the issue of *Comœdia* that Grenier asked the magazine to send to him in August.[14] But he couldn't argue with Arland's conclusion: "We recognize . . . in *The Stranger*, a genuine writer." This "election" to the world of true writers was surely what Grenier meant when he said he was happy with the article: for a writer with an ambitious plan for future works, the label was what counted.

But nothing went the way Camus might have predicted. This first review from the occupied zone was hugely enthusiastic, while the second review, from the unoccupied zone, was harsh and disapproving. This came as a bad surprise. André Rousseaux reviewed *The Stranger* for *Le Figaro*, in Lyon, on July 19, 1942. A week later, Camus wrote to Grenier to tell him that he felt mistreated—morally at least—by reviewers in the unoccupied zone.[15] What was most galling to Camus was that Rousseaux, a conservative Catholic critic with a fine sense of literary form, understood exactly what Camus was doing. He just didn't like it. It was worse than if he had missed the point or distorted the novel. Rousseaux described "a precise, concise sentence, whose brevity has something naturally cruel about it, a simplicity that seems made to open directly onto inexorable truths. . . ." Camus, who followed the literary press, probably remembered that in 1938 Rousseaux had admired Sartre's *Nausea* despite its excess of intellectualism; he had praised Sartre for conveying the depth of one man's struggle with solitude.[16] But now Rousseaux showed no sympathy for Meursault, who, in his opinion, was simply inhuman. As Rousseaux saw it, Camus's talent made his narrator's inhumanity all the more despicable.

Despite his horror at the novel, Rousseaux was forced, at every step of his analysis, to praise Camus's formal achievement—and this forced praise gives his review a fascinating tension. The courtroom scene was remarkable, the construction clever, all designed to make Meursault a "stranger" to society's body—a foreign element that must be repulsed. Then Rousseaux, like Arland before him, but without Arland's enthusiasm, put words in Meursault's mouth: "The poor fellow declares that 'he never dominated his natural feelings.'" What Camus wrote was of completely different order, devoid of moral judgment: Meursault explains to his lawyer that "my nature was such that my physical needs often got in the way of my feelings."[17] In creating Meursault, Camus was inspired by Vincent the swimmer, a man he describes in *Nuptials* as living solely through his body. Camus was also inspired by his deaf uncle Étienne, whom he admired for his sensual simplicity. Vincent and Étienne were the opposite of painfully self-conscious characters like Michel, the narrator of Gide's *Immoralist*, to whom Rousseaux now compared Meursault. A final low blow in *Le Figaro*: Rousseaux, as a fervent Catholic, admitted in his review that he was going to ignore the scene with the chaplain where Meursault explains his absence of faith in God. Rather than objecting to Meursault's atheism, he had decided simply to ignore it.

What Camus wrote in his notebook could have referred to either Arland's or Rousseaux's review: "Three years to create a book. Five lines to ridicule it, with false quotations." He then composed a long letter, addressed to Rousseaux, which he confined to his notebook, specifying "destined never to be sent."[18] He was galled by Rousseaux's reference, at the start of his review, to the decadence of the contemporary novel, in contrast to the nobility of poetry. No critic, Camus argued, had the right to judge whether a work of art serves the national interest. He was outraged by Rousseaux's casual admission that he was going to ignore the scene between Meursault and the chaplain. And he was furious that Rousseaux misquoted him.

This anger was productive, for in pushing back against Rousseaux's criticism, Camus came to a sharper understanding of a novel that seemed to have come to him out of nowhere with a result he didn't entirely grasp. By reacting to Rousseaux, he began to construct his own account of what he had accomplished in *The Stranger*. Meursault only answers the questions asked of him, Camus wrote; he affirms nothing. Contrary to what Rousseaux claimed, he, Camus, was not writing simply as a realist. What he had given of Meursault was "a photographic negative" of real life.[19]

·

In August, Camus left Oran for vacation in the beachside village of Aïn-el-Turck. He was surrounded by friends, and it was a good place to relax as he waited for a medical authorization to leave for France with Francine, to seek a new round of tuberculosis treatments in the Massif Central. On August 8, Gaston Gallimard sent Camus a consoling message making light of the mixed reviews: "the criticism of the novel is indeed absurd."[20]

There were good surprises, too. On August 19, 1942, back in Paris, Maurice Blanchot, a young critic close to the *NRF*, and one of the right-wing, antiparliamentary "anticonformists" of the 1930s, published a review in the ancient *Journal des Débats politiques et littéraires*, where he contributed a regular book column. Blanchot was trenchant and precise, describing so succinctly what Camus was doing that a decade later, when Camus talked about his technique, he used Blanchot's formulation almost word for word: "The first-person narrative," Blanchot wrote, "usually used for confessions and interior monologue, interminable descriptions from the inside, is used by M. Albert Camus to keep any analysis of states of the soul, any possibility of dreaming at bay, and it serves even more to create an insurmountable distance between human reality and the forms revealed by events and facts."[21] Blanchot wished Camus had stuck to his cool narration through the novel, and unlike Marcel Arland, who had been swept away by the emotional ending, Blanchot was bothered by the change in tone in part II. He set Camus up against the Americans: if only Camus could have achieved the kind of crushing silence in the face of justice that Faulkner had achieved in *Sanctuary*! Nor did Blanchot appreciate the mechanism of the trial, which Pia had so admired. He found it overly constructed and artificial.

Pia enclosed the clipping in a September letter to his friend: "I'm sending you an important piece by Blanchot on *The Stranger*. I believe it is the most intelligent piece on the book so far. Which doesn't prevent him from getting it wrong when he says the staging of the trial is artificial. It's curious that there are so many reasonable people who haven't recognized the demented nature of justice and the unbelievable silliness of its apparatus: judges, lawyers, witnesses, etc."[22] Pia didn't mention another small mistake, which indicated an astonishing obliviousness on the part of the Parisian critic, both of the Algerian setting and the meaning of the sea and the sun in the novel. Blanchot described Meursault, the day after his mother's funeral, as "going to the swimming pool."

Camus wrote to another friend on September 6, reiterating what he had said to Grenier several months earlier: "The criticism: mediocre in the free zone, excellent in Paris. Finally it's all based on misunderstandings. Better to close one's ears and work."[23] To Malraux, the same week, he sent the identical complaint, with a small ray of hope: "The stir created by *The Stranger* was provoked by thick-headed misunderstandings. The publication of *Sisyphus* will avoid my giving explanations that, in any case, I wouldn't have given. Besides, all of this is quite puerile. I've discovered this: the critics don't like literature. This is clear from the way they praise and the way they blame."[24]

His hope was dashed. By the time Émile Henriot's review appeared in *Le Temps*, in November 1942, the *Myth of Sisyphus* was also in the bookstores, and this final review of the fall 1942 season took on both works. Far from fulfilling Camus's wish that his essay would help explain his novel, Henriot merely set the two books against each other, comparing the novel unfavorably to the lucid, energetic essay. Thank goodness most people don't think like Meursault! was the gist of Henriot's argument. To him, Meursault was a sad kind of hero. Henriot didn't understand the logic of the book—how Meursault could have written this entire confession in his cell. Henriot, a master of the unflattering comparison, argues that Dostoyevsky makes us feel pity for his idiots, his possessed, while Camus's criminal is unworthy of any pity. Henriot is so appalled by Meursault's behavior that he compresses the character's actions: "The very same day as the funeral, he takes a mistress and spends the evening at the movies." How Meursault could have gotten to Marengo and back and still had time to swim in daylight and go out in the evening stretches the imagination. Henriot made Meursault even more indifferent than he is in the novel.

Despite Henriot's negative review, *The Stranger* sold out its first print run that November and went back to press for a second printing of 4,400 copies. There would be a third printing in April 1943. The reviews were mixed, but the negative reviews were fiercely negative, and this energy, along with the praise, propelled the novel into the hands of readers. Pascal Pia had the last word on November 4:

> I'm sending you the article that appeared yesterday afternoon in *Le Temps*. I've always known that M. Henriot was an ass. He has managed to confirm my opinion. Besides that, what he says is rather encouraging, since after having read him one is left with the feeling it would have been a shame for *The Stranger* to get his vote of confidence. From Roussseaux to Henriot, we see the audience Meursault expected at his execution. I am tempted to write to the Minister of Justice to advise him to include these two critics on the summons for jury duty, in case they aren't already listed.[25]

20

Recovery

CAMUS WAS SETTLED in France by the time he read Pia's letter, a welcome comic relief for an ailing writer who felt that his bid for a literary public was proving less gloriously successful than he had hoped. His authorization to travel had finally come through, and he and Francine were staying in August 1942 in a boarding house run by Francine's aunt in a hamlet called Le Panelier, near Chambon-sur-Lignon, high in the Massif Central. As usual, Pia had tried to prepare the way by finding opportunities for Camus; in Grenoble he could have written for a small newspaper and worked as a forest agent—a kind of park ranger, one of Vichy's initiatives in support of the good French soil.[1] But his health wasn't good enough for strenuous work.

Every week, Camus would take the local train from Chambon-sur-Lignon to the city of Saint-Étienne for his insufflation treatments: a special gas was blown into the infected lung. Red meat and cold air, the so-called open air therapy, were supposed to do the rest. In early October, Francine left to resume her classes at the Oran lycée, where she was teaching mathematics, and Camus continued his cure alone.

During his fourteen months at Le Panelier, from August 1942 to October 1943, Camus did everything except recover. He worked on plays, essays, and a new novel; he bonded with a network of Resistance intellectuals and with Francis Ponge, the Communist poet whose *Voice of Things* was published the same month as *The Stranger*.

He had freed his imagination sufficiently from both *The Stranger* and *The Myth of Sisyphus* to take on new projects. In Le Panelier,

Camus started work on a play he called *The Misunderstanding*, based on the same newspaper clipping that Meursault discovers in his prison mattress. He was attracted to a tragedy of pure situation: the son who returns home incognito, only to be robbed and murdered by his mother and sister.

He returned to the first of his "three Absurds," his draft of *Caligula*. It was clear that whenever the war would end, however it would end, no theatergoer would be able to look at Caligula without thinking of Hitler. The selfish, mad emperor he had imagined in 1939 was easy enough to mold into a deadly practitioner of absolute power. So he revised, but he still wasn't ready to publish the play.

An essay he had written in Oran turned out to be the germ of a new novel. "The Minotaur, Or Stopping in Oran," which Edmond Charlot wanted to publish as a small pamphlet, was rejected by the censors in Algeria, who were favoring patriotic material for their diminishing paper supply. But the satirical essay fed into a story about Oran beset by plague. He had been gathering information on plagues throughout history, but there was a much more immediate source to draw on, a typhus epidemic in the Oran region. The wife of his friend Emmanuel Roblès had fallen ill with typhus in the village of Lalla Marnia, and from Roblès he got a firsthand account of the quarantine, the camps for the infected, the victims' symptoms, and the desperate wait for vaccines.[2] Still ailing himself and sometimes confined to bed, he drew on his memories of boredom in Oran to launch his novel *The Plague*: "The unusual events described in this chronicle occurred in 194_ in Oran. Everyone agreed that considering their somewhat extraordinary character, they were out of place there. For its ordinariness is what strikes one first about the town of Oran, which is merely a large French port on the Algerian coast. . . ."[3]

The Plague was an entirely different animal from *The Stranger*. Written on the move, in fits and starts, between 1942 and 1947, it was as difficult to construct as *A Happy Death*, and often just as frustrating. The novel begins with descriptions of the first rats dying in the city, and with a narrator who does not want to say his name, because he speaks for a community in crisis. The "194_" was a signal to the reader, on page one of the novel, that "the plague" was inspired by the 1940s—i.e. by the Nazi occupation. *The Plague* used the story of a city beset by disease to express a vision beyond the absurd: the possibility of solidarity in the struggle against evil, the power of friendship and community.[4] The kind of story that would establish Camus as a great humanist.

Camus's writing was becoming more markedly political, and his work in Le Panelier had powerful consequences for the way people read *The Stranger*. Would this shift have happened if Camus had returned to Algeria when his treatment ended? The plan was for him to join Francine, and ordinary life. He didn't want to return to their shared quarters with Francine's family on the rue d'Arzew in Oran: he longed to rent a beautiful spot in the heights of Algiers—in El Biar or Bouzareah, where Roblès had an apartment.[5] But as his dreams began to take shape, the world flipped on him again.

·

On November 8, 1942, the Allied forces put into motion their African landing. Operation Torch sent 60,000 soldiers to nine different beaches and ports on the North African coast, including Sidi-Ferruch beach in Algiers and the Andalouses, outside Oran, down the coast from Bouisseville.[6] After only a few hours of fighting at Aïn-el-Turck, the local Vichy forces ceded. Algeria and Morocco, under Allied administration, were officially liberated.

Back in metropolitan France, Hitler's armed forces retaliated. On November 11, they crossed the line of demarcation established by the 1940 armistice, the artificial border that had split the country into occupied and unoccupied zones. The Nazis occupied all of France, making the so-called autonomous Vichy government in the southern zone more of a fiction than ever. By February 1943, there was no more demarcation line, and the paradoxical result was that France regained its unity. You could now travel and send mail back and forth, from Lyon and Cannes to Paris. But it was a unity of subjugation rather than freedom. The newspapers that had set up free-zone headquarters in Lyon—*Le Temps, Paris-Soir, Le Figaro* suspended publication. Pia, too, was now out of work. Camus's immediate problem was that Algeria, now under Allied control, was completely cut off from Europe. He'd missed the last boat home. He was trapped, with so many others. "Like rats," he wrote in his notebook.[7] Even mail service was canceled. Camus used his sense of isolation and panic to continue his work on *The Plague*. The main characters in his novel—a doctor and a journalist—were quarantined in Oran, just as he was stuck in France.

In December 1942 Camus had been without news of Francine for a month. From his retreat, he sent Pascal Pia three pounds of dried mushrooms with cooking instructions.[8] He read two novels by Maurice Blanchot, who had reviewed *The Stranger* so intensely. The mountain air was not helping him, and he was losing weight again. Work was a consolation, but when he finished a first draft of *The Plague*, he wrote Pia that the novel was ungainly.[9] He was considering a new title: *The Separated*.[10]

.

During this period of solitude and literary production, both *The Stranger* and its author began to garner a new level of respect from the critics, and this respect would carry novel and novelist triumphantly towards the end of war.

In the summer of 1942, Henri Hell praised *The Stranger* in *Fontaine*, an Algiers literary magazine.[11] It was an inside job: Hell was the pen name of José-Henri Lasry, who had acted in Camus's plays and reviewed *The Wrong Side and the Right Side* in 1937. The review did have a critical angle. Hell hesitated about whether what he called a "stiff and stilted quality in Camus's writing" wasn't too obvious a sign of "the willful intelligence driving the novel."[12] But he concluded on a high note, declaring *The Stranger* a "classic in the best French tradition, achieved through a technique that was anything but classic."[13] Grenier wrote Camus that it was the best piece written on the *Stranger* so far.[14]

Six months later, an article appeared that would become required reading for anyone interested in *The Stranger*. Jean-Paul Sartre's *"The*

Stranger Explained" was a turning point. The novel might have faded into the background of the literary landscape after its initial reviews, but an essay by Sartre, already an important philosopher and novelist, imposed Camus's work on intellectual France. The attention he paid to Camus, the seriousness of his analysis, defined *The Stranger* as an essential contemporary novel. Once Sartre had spoken, the *Stranger*'s future was all but guaranteed.

The choice of Sartre as a reviewer for *The Stranger* was a foregone conclusion. Malraux, who never much liked the man, wrote to Pia before the manuscript made its way to Paris that there was a danger Camus's novel would be compared to Sartre's *Nausea*. Indeed, Jean Paulhan then described *The Stranger* in his reader's report as "a first rate novel which begins like Sartre. . . ." And in *Le Figaro*, André Rousseaux found Meursault lacking the qualities of Roquentin, the antihero of *Nausea*. All that remained was for Sartre to pronounce on the book that many readers took to be *Nausea*'s child.

Sartre's "*The Stranger* Explained" appeared in February 1943 in the *Cahiers du Sud*, a literary magazine published in Marseille. He used the same vocabulary in the winter of 1943 that Henri Hell had used in the fall of 1942. Sartre wrote, "*The Stranger* is a classical work, a work of order, written about the absurd and against the absurd."[15] But what he meant by "classical" was different than what Hell meant: Sartre's praise was double-edged.

Camus's *Myth of Sisyphus* had appeared in October, and Sartre played the philosophical essay off against *The Stranger*—though more charitably than Henriot had done in *Le Temps* the previous November. Sartre may have been dealing Camus a counterjab, since Camus had reviewed *Nausea* in 1938 in *Alger-Républican*. (Though *Alger-Républicain* was a distant, small-circulation newspaper, Sartre's publisher would certainly have sent him Camus's review with the rest of his press clippings.) Camus had argued that Sartre was a better philosopher than a novelist, and that *Nausea* was driven too much by ideas and not enough by images. Now in his review of *The Stranger*, Sartre pronounced Camus a much better novelist than a philosopher, launching a critique that has stuck with Camus to this day. (Sartre's major philosophical work, *Being and Nothingness*, was on the verge of being published that coming June.)

Sartre described *The Myth of Sisyphus* as overly talkative, while he praised *The Stranger* for using words almost miraculously to produce a sensation of silence. *The Myth of Sisyphus*, he wrote, was full of pretentious allusions to Jaspers, Heidegger, and Kierkegaard—thinkers Camus didn't really seem to understand. It was a high-handed and stinging indictment; the Paris intellectual was giving lessons to the man who had written from Algeria, that is, from the outer reaches of provincial France.

But when it came to the language of *The Stranger*, Sartre was enchanted and insightful. He said that each sentence of the novel was like an island, separated from the next sentence by a sense of nothingness. He had a theory about how Camus achieved this effect: first, by using an ordinary compound past tense made with an auxiliary verb and a past participle ("il s'est promené") instead of the simpler literary past tense ("il se promena"). The distinction doesn't exist in English, but even if you don't know French you can understand what Sartre meant when he said that Camus favored verbs that were "shattered"—split into two parts: *Il s'est promené. Je l'ai aimée.*[16] And the kind of past tense he used was meant to target a specific moment in the past, not to describe an ongoing past. Meursault desired Marie in the moment but not for any duration. Sartre quoted the salient passage: "Un moment après, elle m'a demandé si je l'aimais. *Je lui ai répondu que cela ne voulait rien dire, mais qu'il me semblait que non.* Elle a eu l'air triste. Mais en préparant le déjeuner, et à propos de rien, elle a encore ri de telle façon que je l'ai embrassée. C'est à ce moment que les bruits d'une dispute ont éclaté chez Raymond" [Sartre's emphasis]. Mathew Ward rendered this as: "A minute later she asked me if I loved her. I told her it didn't mean anything but that I didn't think so. She looked sad. But as we were fixing lunch, and for no apparent reason, she laughed in such a way that I kissed her. It was then that we heard what sounded like a fight break out in Raymond's room."[17]

Even before Meursault was condemned to death, Camus created

a world for him in which nothing lasted. Camus emphasized this feeling by refusing cause and effect, using linking words to connect thoughts in a way that makes Meursault's "between" reasoning feel more artificial, more arbitrary ("but I didn't think so"). Sartre had no access to the manuscript, but if he had, he would have seen the places where Camus revised to get exactly the style he described— changing a verb tense here, adding "but" or "and" or "finally" there.[18]

Literature was Jean-Paul Sartre's playground; he knew the history of the French novel, writer by writer and sentence by sentence. He suggested that a nineteenth-century naturalist would have written "a bridge spanned the river," while Camus preferred a sentence like "Over the river there was a bridge." Camus would want the simple verb "to be" to express this bridge in all its passivity, its raw being. Sartre found plenty of examples of the same effect on a single page of *The Stranger*: "there were four men wearing black in the room"; "a woman I didn't know was standing by the door"; "outside the gate stood the hearse"; "next to it was the funeral director."

Deprived of causality and agency, sentences such as these created a world of things in themselves, "passive, impenetrable, incommunicable, sparkling," Sartre concluded.[19] He knew absolutely nothing about Camus's life in 1942 and 1943 when he was drafting his essay; the two men had never met. He couldn't have known that Camus grew up in a silent household with a deaf mother and uncle, but he intuited in the sentences of the novel a relationship to language, and to things, that Camus had absorbed from his family, whose limited language favored a world of objects rather than abstractions. Sartre's "*The Stranger* Explained" is proof that it's unnecessary to know anything about an author's life in order to understand a work of literature. But you would have to add that a knowledge of Camus's silent childhood makes Sartre's critical intuitions even more impressive.

Sartre was alert to the Algerian setting of *The Stranger* without knowing quite what to say about it. He scarcely mentions the Arab victim of Meursault's crime except to repeat the absurd premise: that the sun made Meursault kill. He classifies *The Stranger* as a work that comes from across the sea; an outsider novel, interested neither in burying the ancien régime one more time nor in indulging in self-loathing—two commonplaces of the modern French novel. In short, Sartre added, *The Stranger* was a welcome reminder, in a terribly political moment, that a novel could exist with nothing to prove. When you start reading, Sartre said, it feels at first as if you are listening to a monotonous chanting, to the nasal singing of an Arab; then the structure of the work emerges, and you realize there isn't a single useless detail, that everything is as it needs to be. It was an odd and indirect reference to the sound of a flute Meursault hears on the beach coming from the menacing Arabs—and one of the least convincing comments in an essay where nearly every observation rings true. *The Stranger*, Sartre claimed, was not exactly a novel, more like a succession of inert moments in the present.

Finally, Sartre was not buying what people were saying about the book, that it was, as he put, "Kafka written by Hemingway." Kafka, he argued, had created a world of symbols, while Camus's world was down to earth. As for Hemingway, Sartre thought that Camus may have borrowed his short, direct sentences, but he saw this as a technique rather than an influence. Sartre didn't make much of the standard comparisons: "despite what it takes from the German existentialists and the American novelists, [it] remains ultimately very close to one of Voltaire's tales."[20] Sartre considered *The Stranger* a classic because it reminded him of the neat little tales crafted by the eighteenth-century moralists. Yet he had just said that the novel diverged from the mainstream of French literature, that it was unconcerned with the modern imperative to bury the ancien régime. Now Sartre contradicted himself. He put Camus back on the map of French literature, because in the end his perspective was bound by his own literary education. He made a flattering comparison to a high moment in French letters, but it was a paradoxical compliment that undercut the shock of the new and the uniqueness of Camus's Algerian setting, kicking the novel back into the traditional literary realm.

Camus wrote to Jean Grenier in March that Sartre's essay was a model of literary dissection but that Sartre didn't acknowledge how much of literary creation was instinctive—how much of the book had simply come to him: "Intelligence doesn't play such a big part." Sure, Sartre's criticism was mostly valid, even enlightening, "but why the acid tone?"

As for the philosophical references Sartre ridiculed in *The Myth of Sisyphus*, Camus told Grenier that his origins—his childhood poverty—ensured that he could never become a dilettante. Grenier didn't understand why Camus took offense: "Sartre's article was excellent; I don't find the acid tone you're objecting to. Obviously he analyses you in terms of himself—this is natural!"[21] (Grenier had done the same thing!) Grenier, a creature of the Parisian intellectual world, could see more clearly than Camus the prestige that Sartre's voice brought to his novel.

Other debates about *The Stranger* were taking place behind the scenes. Jean Paulhan, perhaps measuring the new status that Sartre's review had conferred, recommended *The Stranger* to François Mauriac for the French Academy's prize for best novel in 1943. He tried to appeal to Mauriac's religious views in a way that must have seemed blatantly manipulative to the devout and perceptive Catholic writer: *The Stranger*, Paulhan claimed, is a novel that asks "how can I love (my mother or my wife) if I don't start by loving God?" Mauriac was unconvinced: "I have no taste for [*The Stranger*], but strictly for technical reasons; I find its style too derivative. In novels by young men I want a sense of deliverance, a naïve, spontaneous manner of giving oneself away. . . . I find those who imitate America irritating. The slightest artistic arrangement becomes a recipe for them. I might be wrong, I'm only sharing my impressions."[22] The private exchange gives a quick sketch of two very important personalities on the literary scene: Paulhan, the strategist, with his bald appeal to Mauriac's religiosity, and Mauriac, mocking his own erotic proclivities and taunting Paulhan by saying he wanted his young male novelists to "give themselves away." Camus remained in the dark about the exchange.

Throughout the winter of 1943, Camus took his time to think through Sartre's argument. He wasn't going to draft an angry letter such as the one he never sent to André Rousseaux, the critic for *Le Figaro* who had written such a hostile analysis of *The Stranger*. Instead he waited for the perfect occasion, which came in the form of an invitation to contribute to a prestigious magazine. Six months after the *Cahiers du Sud* published Sartre's "*The Stranger* Explained," *Confluences*, the literary magazine in Lyon that was inching its way from polite support of Vichy to fervent resistance, published a special issue entitled "Problems of the Novel." The issue, composed of statements on the novel by leading writers and critics, set the terms of literary debate for a new generation; it was the event of the season. Marcel Arland, the reviewer from *Comœdia* who had channeled Meursault, contributed an article, as did André Rousseaux. What was remarkable was that only a year and a half after the publication of his first novel, Camus's book was already an obligatory reference in a special issue taking stock of the entire history of the genre: Tavernier, the editor, mentioned Camus in the introduction, alongside Kafka, as the best example of fiction that transforms itself in tune with psychological structures of society.[23] Alain Borne's article cited Camus as "one of the great names" of the contemporary novel."[24] *The Stranger* had arrived.

For his own essay in *Confluences*, "Intelligence and the Scaffold," Camus took up the idea of what a "classic" work might mean in the French tradition, and what literary "intelligence" is made of.[25] Sartre considered him a classic moralist, and Hell had referred to his "willful intelligence" in constructing his novel. Camus responded, putting his pride and his intellectual curiosity to work, with a witty and tightly constructed argument designed to show the Sartres of the world, in case they doubted it, that he could hold his own as a literary critic.

Camus began with three literary examples through which he demonstrated the perfectly controlled construction of the classic French novel: everything in *The Princess of Cleves* (the first novel in the French canon) is designed to get the princess to her nunnery; everything in *The Red and the Black* is designed to get Julien Sorel to the scaffold, and everything in Proust's *In Search of Lost Time* is designed to get the narrator to the party in the Guermantes' salon. Except that all of those books reached their end points through a series of artful zigzags. Camus didn't mention his own novel, but anyone who had read *The Stranger* knew that he had done his own version of the zigzag, in the form of cameos: the story of Salamano and his dog; the robot-like woman in the restaurant; the newspaper clipping about the traveling salesman killed by his mother and sister; the slices of life admired by the reviewers that seemed perfectly integrated into the novel's sense of the absurd without pointing to themselves as morals or lessons. Sartre had mapped *The Stranger* onto Voltaire's morality tales. Without rebuking, Camus replied. He looked to the history of the French novel not for morality tales but for a sense of the inevitable, for a struggle to the death between passion and control, and for the deep necessity that had haunted the writing of *The Stranger*. As long he was being assigned a place in the history of the novel, he wanted his say about the genre, about its powers and its particular forms of intelligence.

·

Among the positive reviews of 1943, the most gratifying came from Jean Grenier. He remained Camus's faithful correspondent, but in 1943 he began to write with authority about Camus. It was the start of a lifetime of reflection on his best student and close friend. Grenier reviewed *The Stranger* in the same issue of *Cahiers du Sud* that included Sartre's essay—a much shorter piece than Sartre's, in the book review section of the magazine. His is a tender, lyrical appreciation. It is also a very public apology, recognizable only to Camus, for doubts he had expressed in previous letters, point by point. Grenier quoted the now canonical first sentence with approval: "Aujourd'hui, maman est morte." Camus begins his novel like a great pianist, Grenier writes, diving into his music with so much confidence that there are no nuances, no precautions. (Gone is the complaint that the sentences are too short). Camus is the first writer born in Algiers able to portray life in that city without resorting to folklore (just as he had written Camus in May 1941, but softening his original qualms about the book).[26] Grenier did not agree with Camus's notion of "the tender indifference of the world," but saw that its expression in the novel was so strong and so sincere that any reader would be moved to take a position. *The Stranger*, he concluded, was a work into which a man has put all of himself, acknowledging what Camus meant when he told Grenier he was going ahead with the book despite his teacher's critique. *The Stranger* "revealed a great artist."[27]

Grenier's letters to Camus during the period when the writer was stuck in Le Panelier had been especially affectionate. Shortly after Camus arrived in his mountain village, Grenier reminded him it had been ten years since he made his way to the modest apartment on the rue de Lyon: "I remember my visit to your place in Belcourt. . . . I represented, in your eyes, SOCIETY, but for me you were never 'The Stranger.'"[28]

21

From the Absurd to Revolt

HOW DID *THE STRANGER* become a book people wanted to read to unlock the keys to Camus's character? The first building block of Camus's literary celebrity was set into place in 1943 by a prominent Russian-French writer named Elsa Triolet. She hadn't read *The Stranger*—she couldn't find a copy—but she decided to feature the novel in the title of a short story, "Who is this Stranger Who Isn't from Here or The Myth of the Baroness Mélanie." She created a character she called "the Stranger," who was not Meursault (about whom she knew nothing), but a generic, heroic Camus-like figure.

Triolet was was well known in Paris circles as the wife of the writer Louis Aragon and as an influential translator and writer who had recently left the Russian language definitively for French. She was Jewish, a Communist intellectual from a great literary family, and she had her own notions of what being a stranger meant. By 1943 she was on the run from Paris, staying in Lyon at the home of *Confluences* publisher René Tavernier, who maintained an informal safe house. During Camus's stay at Le Panelier, he often traveled to Lyon, where Pia introduced him to the crowd of French writers in exile. Camus met Aragon, then Triolet, who took an immediate shine to the man and his work. She wrote "Who is this Stranger Who Isn't from Here or The Myth of the Baroness Mélanie" in part as a flirtation, but she also wrote in response to *The Myth of Sisyphus*, whose emphasis on suicide provoked her: wasn't the fundamental mystery of life not suicide, but aging?

Triolet's short story appeared in *Poésie 43*, another Lyon literary magazine that had been publishing writers from both occupied and unoccupied zones since 1940.[1] The main character is Baroness Mélanie d'Aubrey, an old woman who grows younger by the year, until a handsome young man with rippling muscles beneath his silk shirt is suddenly no longer much older than she, and it is no longer strange to see them together. (Triolet was fifteen years older than Camus.) Triolet quotes Camus in her conclusion, making her Stranger speak lines from *The Myth of Sisyphus*, such as "the illusions of the everyday or of the idea [that] all these screens hide the absurd" and "The creature is my native land. This is why I have chosen this absurd and ineffectual effort." In the last paragraph of her story, she drops her allusions to the generic fictional Stranger and refers directly to Albert Camus, the real man: "'Who is this foreigner who is not from here?' asked the residents of the little hamlet where Albert Camus of Algiers, taken by surprise in France by the American landing [in North Africa], sought refuge. Perhaps these people with their vigorous vital instincts could sense that The Stranger was a magnificent myth, a philosophical contribution, a stimulus for the intellect, actually as incredible as the burlesque myth of Mélanie d'Aubrey."[2]

Dropping the mask of fiction, she identified Albert Camus, the refugee from Algeria who was living in the hamlet that insiders would have recognized as Le Panelier. Triolet started a trend for the coming era of existential stars, when Camus was considered as glamorous as his writing. The fact that she hadn't read *The Stranger* didn't stop her from seeing Camus in his title, as if it had flown loose from the book and fixed itself on the man. She anticipated the legend by several years.

In private correspondence, Triolet chided Camus for not answering her declarations: "I have the slight impression of having made a declaration of love to which you have responded, 'I love you like a brother!'"[3] Triolet was flamboyant and insistent, but behind her worry about friendship was genuine panic. She had been on the run, with and without Aragon, since the 1940 exodus; she had already been arrested once and released, during a brief foray to Paris in 1941.

After the Nazis invaded the free zone in November 1943, Triolet was on the run again, and her Resistance activity intensified. If you looked closely at her rambling story, there is fear behind the bravura.

Camus, in his mountain boarding house, was safer than Triolet, yet the danger around him was palpable. The next village over, Chambon-sur-Lignon, long a Protestant stronghold, had become a rescue center for Jewish children under the auspices of Pastor André Trocmé, and when Camus was finally able to communicate with Francine, via Morocco, he wrote in the coded language he had perfected: he had spent the summer "mostly with children, big groups of children."[4] He helped a farm family send a package with a false bottom to their uncle in a prisoner-of-war camp; in the bottom were papers that allowed him to escape. Triolet's biographer reports that Pia and Camus arranged fake identification papers for Triolet and Aragon. Throughout 1943, everyday generosity and tragedy were bringing him closer and closer to active resistance.[5]

·

In January and June of 1943, Janine Gallimard, Camus's closest contact at his publisher's, arranged for two travel passes so that the author could come to Paris—two short but productive trips during which he expanded his intellectual network. Literary Paris was eager to meet the author of *The Stranger*. A highlight of the trip in June was the opening of Jean-Paul Sartre's *The Flies* at what was now called the Théâtre de la Cité (which Parisians defiantly referred to by its real name, the Théâtre Sarah Bernhardt, after the great French Jewish actress.) In the lobby of the theater, Camus introduced himself to Sartre, and the two men shook hands.

Life on the mountain wasn't good for Camus. "This country is weighing on me," he wrote Grenier on April 15, 1943. "When I'll be able to run on the beaches again, I'll be too old." In October 1943 Camus got another official pass that allowed him to leave Le Panelier for a hotel in Paris. Pia had negotiated with Paulhan to get him a monthly stipend of 2,500 francs, an advance on future royalties, and he had a steady job reading manuscripts at Gallimard for 4,000 francs a month. It was just enough to get by. He was immediately chosen to serve on a panel of judges for a new literary prize, the Prix de la Pléiade, with writers who had reviewed him and others to whom he had been compared: Jean Grenier, Maurice Blanchot, Marcel Arland, André Malraux, Jean Paulhan, Jean-Paul Sartre. He went to the Flore, drank coffee with Sartre and Beauvoir, and smoked the only cigarettes available—horrible imitations filled with eucalyptus instead of tobacco.[6] The threesome talked shop and discovered they shared an admiration for Ponge's *The Voice of Things*.[7]

As far as anyone knew, Albert Camus was a writer and an editor, living at the Hotel Minerve on the rue de la Chaise and going to work every day on the rue Sebastien Bottin, where he shared an office with another editor, Jacques Lemarchand, who happened to have published in one of the most virulently anti-Semitic and collaborationist newspapers in Paris, *La Gerbe*.[8] Despite the ideological gulf between them, they shared a love of the theater, and they became fast friends. That kind of friendship was a luxury that people in the armed Resistance didn't have.

As 1943 drew to a close, reprisals for resistance were becoming more and more deadly, and executions more frequent, but life in Paris could be glamorous: Sartre asked Camus to play Garcin in his new play, *No Exit*, and they rehearsed in hotel rooms until the lead actress was arrested on suspicion of active resistance. Sartre dropped the project and later produced the play with professional actors. Camus was now at the heart of things. When Michel and Louise Leiris organized a reading of Picasso's spoof of a play, "Desire Caught by the Tail," Camus was there. In a historic photo by Brassaï, with Sartre, Queneau, Beauvoir, Lacan, and Maria Casarès, Camus is front and center, kneeling in front of Picasso with a hand on one knee, more interested in the Afghan hound Kabek than in the others—the jovial Sartre, to his right, and a mournful Leiris, to his left.[9]

Behind the worldliness, Camus's counterlife was beginning. Just as Pascal Pia had brought him to *Alger-Républicain* and shepherded his first novel at Gallimard, the seasoned newspaper editor brought Camus onto the editorial staff of *Combat*, an underground newspaper prepared in tiny studio apartments and maids' rooms in Paris and produced on a secret printing press in Lyon. The team was small, but politically *Combat* was more important than anything he had known, and the work changed him. Camus acquired a false identification card that gave his name as Albert Mathé, and a fake birth certificate to go with it. The comrades called him "Beauchard" (no one used their real name). When Pia took on other Resistance activity, Camus replaced him as editor-in-chief of a newspaper that by 1944 was publishing every three weeks and had a circulation of 250,000. His skill at organizing a team, at setting type, at articulating a political position—everything he had learned in the past six years about how to make a newspaper work—came into play. The small, courageous team that produced *Combat* considered his arrival as a benediction, especially Jacqueline Bernard, general secretary of the *Combat* movement.[10]

In 1941, Pia had promised Camus he would have plenty of opportunities in the future to develop the feelings he had explored in the scene where Meursault rages against the chaplain.[11] A short story he devised in 1943 as one of his "Letters to a German Friend," first published underground in *Cahiers de la Libération*, features a hypocritical Nazi clergyman in league with a murderous state, and ends with a French priest in the Resistance. The art is very much Camus's, but the very different portrayal of the clergy shows how far he had come from the rage against religion in *The Stranger*.

The story begins with eleven French hostages riding in a truck en route to the cemetery where they will be executed. Four or five of them have committed minor acts of resistance, distributing leaflets or attending meetings. The others have done nothing. One of these is a sixteen-year-old boy. Seated next to the boy in the back of the truck is a Nazi chaplain who tells him he must prepare to die, that God will be near, and that he, the chaplain, is a friend.

As the truck continues towards its destination, with the hostages seated in the back, the boy sees an opening in the canvas flap of the truck and seizes his chance. He opens the flap and jumps. In one fateful instant the chaplain must decide: is he with the henchmen or the martyrs? He raps on the front of the truck to alert the soldiers, enabling them to capture the boy and carry him back to his moving prison.

Camus next exercised his habitual power of discretion. Just as he left the scene of the guillotine out of *The Stranger*, he doesn't take this story all the way to the firing squad; that will be his reader's burden. In a conclusion, he speaks directly to his German friend, the recipient of his fictional letter:

> I am sure you can very well imagine the rest. But it is important for you to know who told me this story. It was a French priest. He said to me, 'I am ashamed for this man, and I am pleased to think that no French priest would have been willing to make his god abet murder.' . . . In your country, even the Gods are drafted.[12]

Here a man of the cloth can be a force for evil or a force for good in the Resistance. The German Chaplain is not a hypocrite by virtue of his situation, as in *The Stranger*. He is a human like any other, with a political choice to make.

In April 1944, when the Waffen-SS massacred eighty-six men in Ascq, one of several murderous reprisals for Resistance activity, it was Camus, drawing on the techniques of a fiction writer, who found a way to make the readers of *Combat* feel part of history, and understand the tragedy that might have been theirs. In an underground editorial, he wrote:

> Eighty-six men just like you, the readers of this newspaper, passed before the German guns. Eighty-six men: enough to fill three or four rooms the size of the room you're sitting in. Eighty-six faces, drawn or defiant, eighty-six faces overwhelmed by horror or by hatred. The slaughter continued for three hours, a little more than two minutes for each victim. Three hours, the amount of time that some of you will have spent that day at dinner or talking quietly with friends, while elsewhere people watched a film

and laughed at made-up adventures. For three hours, minute after minute, without letup, without a pause, in a single French village, shots were fired one after another and bodies fell writhing to the ground.[13]

Camus brought to his Resistance editorials the strength of simplicity, an ability to make a life-and-death situation real on the page. In 1944, his writing had a sense of contemporary struggle that was as compelling as the more private concerns that drove his fiction.

A series of tragedies in his own network made the high stakes of resistance clear to Camus. The poet René Leynaud, operating under his code name "Clair" was the head of the *Combat* movement in the Lyon region. In May 1944, he was arrested and executed by firing squad. In July 1944, Jacqueline Bernard, who worked closely with Camus in *Combat*'s underground newspaper, was arrested and deported to Ravensbrück. *Combat*'s printer in Lyon, with the code name "Vélin," was hunted down by the Gestapo and killed. Camus understood the danger and left Paris in early July. He took refuge in Verdelot, in a house belonging to Brice Parain, a fellow Gallimard author. The Allies had landed in Normandy on June 6 and were making their way towards Paris—Camus and the rest of the *Combat* movement knew that the liberation was near, that it was a matter of surviving for a few more weeks.

During that tragic month of July, Camus spent an unusual afternoon with Josette Clotis, Malraux's companion, in a house in Neuilly, on the outskirts of Paris. He had learned that his novel was gaining value among bibliophiles, and he saw an opportunity. Clotis read to him, from beginning to end, each familiar sentence of *The Stranger*. It had been a little over four years since he had written from his hotel in Montmartre that the novel seemed to have been etched within him. As Clotis read, Camus wrote, creating a fake manuscript. It was in his handwriting, but he went further, making it look like an early draft, with sentences crossed out here and there, and variations on the published novel that would surely appeal to collectors. He drew a sun in the margins, and a guillotine, and sawhorses supporting a casket. When he was done he scattered the papers on the floor and rubbed them into the ground with his shoe so they looked old and worn.[14] There was laughter and delight in the roguish work, and also a sense of reprieve. The counterfeiting scene perfectly captured Camus at age thirty, irreverent toward the literary world that claimed him as its newest star and scornful of critics who didn't like literature. He was happy to have arrived, but he would always remain independent, and irritated by fame. Besides, in this era of black markets and false papers and with his life on the line, creating this fake manuscript must have seemed a harmless enough way to supplement his income.

In a letter to Jean Grenier, Camus described the contradictions of those years of occupation and struggle: "History has been turned upside down, yet we go on with our little lives."[15]

22

Above Ground

ON AUGUST 21, 1944, the long ordeal was nearly over. A popular insurrection and the arrival of General Leclerc and his Allied troops made Paris a free city in a country still at war. Paris, wrote Camus, was "liberated from her shame," liberated from the German street signs, from the Nazi flags, from the Wehrmacht and the Gestapo in the finest hotels and government offices in the city—ready to raise the tricolor flag and restore the Republic.[1] Albert Camus emerged from his underground life that week in the most public way possible: he read his first "above ground" editorial for *Combat* on the newly liberated French national radio.[2] When, in October 1944, Francine finally got safe passage from Algeria to Paris, she realized instantly that her husband was a national and international spokesperson for the spirit of the French Resistance.

Combat's impact was immediate. Crowds gathered every day on the rue Réaumur in front of the building that housed the newspaper along with several other new publications, in the former headquarters of the *Pariser Zeitung*, the German daily doomed by the Liberation of Paris. Newspapers that had compromised themselves by publishing under Vichy were banned from publishing. The field was brand new. Paper was still in short supply, so the latest issue of *Combat* was always exhibited in a glass case outside the building. The editorials weren't signed, but everyone knew they were written by Camus, or by one of Camus's colleagues wanting to sound like

Camus. He warned about the dangers of an atomic world after Hiroshima. He reported on injustice in eastern Algeria, where there had just been a tragic massacre of Muslim veterans by the colonial government. He measured the trauma France had endured and set standards for his country's reconstruction, physical and moral. Camus butted heads with François Mauriac, the leading editorialist for *Le Figaro* and the voice of left Catholicism, over whether collaborators should be treated with charity, or whether justice called for the harshest punishment.[3]

In the early months of *Combat*, Camus took a hard line, arguing that collaborators should be eliminated for the good of the body politic, like rotten branches that must be chopped off to save a tree.[4] But when Robert Brasillach, a writer and editor at the fascist newspaper *Je Suis Partout*, who represented the very spirit of collaboration with the Nazis, was tried and condemned to death in January 1945 by a special court, Camus agreed to join Mauriac in signing a petition to spare Brasillach's life. He made it clear that he was signing as a matter of principle and not out of any admiration for Brasillach, whom he loathed, for he was sure that if the tables were turned, Brasillach would not have lifted a finger for the intellectuals in the Resistance who were murdered by the Gestapo.[5] He was suspicious of Mauriac's call for charity, with its religious overtones, but, as he once remarked, writers return again and again to the same few themes, and Camus returned once again to his own degree zero: the same horror of a state-inflicted death sentence that drives the story of Meursault. In the long run, he decided that Mauriac was right.

The first months of 1945 were violent ones. Brasillach was executed by firing squad on February 6, sending a warning to the intellectual community of Paris that they needed to take to heart their responsibility as writers. Words counted. Drieu la Rochelle, the fascist who had played the go-between with Gallimard and the Nazis at the *Nouvelle Revue Française*, committed suicide before he could be summoned to court. Publishers who had "Aryanized," including Gaston Gallimard, were brought before purge commissions. Camus was on hand to defend his publisher, along with Malraux and Sartre, and the Éditions Gallimard moved into the postwar era without sanctions.[6]

A group of Camus's friends from Algeria came up to Paris in those early days after the war, riding the wave of his success: Edmond Charlot decided to start a publishing house on the rue de Verneuil; Claude de Fréminville began a career in radio; Emmanuel Roblès, fresh from his experience as a war correspondent, visited regularly for the production of his plays. Max-Pol Fouchet, Camus's former rival in love, brought his magazine *Fontaine* to Paris. Sartre was impressed by Camus's Spanish and Algerian cronies, and he enjoyed how funny and crude Camus could be in those early days of their friendship—really very funny, he remembered. The director of *Combat* spoke with an Algerian accent, which sounded Provençal. Camus's "Algerian persona" amused and fascinated Sartre.[7]

In the offices of *Combat* was one man, seated at a desk, who seemed to be doing nothing. People would point to him and whisper, "He's the model for *The Stranger*!"[8] Pierre Galindo, the brother of Christiane, Camus's lover from the House Above the World, also moved to Paris and took a nominal job at the paper, thanks to Camus. He had been with the Bensoussan brothers at Bouisseville, a witness to the legendary fight on the beach. For Camus, he was a reminder of a lost world. When people asked, Camus liked to say that there were three models for *The Stranger*: "two men (including myself) and a woman"—referring to Galindo and his old girlfriend Yvonne Ducailar. He was probably kidding.[9]

Camus and Pia had put together a team of young reporters at *Combat*, just as Pia had done at *Alger-Républicain*—inexperienced, enthusiastic writers, most of them former devotees of the French Resistance, whom they could train. Roger Grenier, twenty-six years old in 1945 and no relation to Jean Grenier, worked for a smaller newspaper at 100, rue Réaumur, called *Libertés*. He admired *Combat*, the most prestigious of all the postwar newspapers, whose offices were upstairs. He had found a copy of *The Stranger* in a bookstall on the rue Mouffetard in January 1944. A friend in the Resistance in Clermont-Ferrand filled him in about the author: "He's a guy who's planning a newspaper for after the Liberation."[10]

When Camus was attacked by the Christian Democrats of L'Aube as an existentialist indebted to Heidegger's Nazi thinking, Roger Grenier was outraged, and he published an article in Libertés in support of Camus.[11] Camus thanked him and asked him if he wanted to write theater reviews for Combat.[12] So Grenier entered Camus's world and soon began covering the trials of collaborators at the Cour de Justice de la Seine. In a famous photo of the newspaper staff taken on New Year's Day, 1945, he is the bright-eyed young man with the black-framed glasses staring straight at the camera with an air of calm intelligence. Camus had learned his mentoring skills from a master, and he was as loyal to Roger Grenier as Pia had been to him. He was true to his word, editing Grenier at the newspaper and then at Gallimard, where Grenier published a book on the purge trials, and where Camus's editorial responsibilities had grown.[13] Camus would read his manuscripts and give comments: "You've used the word absurd four times—that's enough!"

When Combat first went above ground, Camus chose its motto: "From Resistance to Revolution." "Revolution" in this case did not mean a Marxist revolution, but rather a revolution in values, a commitment to carrying the spirit and leadership of the Resistance into peacetime. Since their days at Alger-Républicain, Pia and Camus had shared a fundamental suspicion of the state, and in the patriotic climate of 1945 they positioned Combat as a watchdog for democracy and social justice, to the left of de Gaulle and to the right of the Communist party. They would attempt to create a "reasonable" newspaper, Pia told the staff, but since the world was absurd, they would surely fail.[14] Their idealism was difficult to maintain, as bickering among Gaullists, Communists, and Christian Democrats soon replaced the politics of Resistance in the dawning Fourth Republic. Even Pia and Camus began to disagree. Camus, despite his affection for the team he had assembled at the paper, was at his wit's end. In the fall of 1945 he took time off from Combat to concentrate his energies on his own writing. He was thirty-one years old, and successful enough now to begin worrying in his notebook about the corrupting effects of privilege, money, and the constant distractions of being in demand.[15] He was also a new father—on September 5, 1945, Francine gave birth to twins, Jean and Catherine.

On March 10, 1946, Camus boarded a cargo ship, the *Oregon*, for New York. Claude Lévi-Strauss, the cultural attaché at the French Embassy, had invited Camus on an official tour of the United States. It would be an occasion for the writer to speak about the atmosphere in liberated France and to launch the first American edition of *The Stranger*.[16] Stuart Gilbert's translation of the novel was about to be published by Knopf, and the match of publisher and author could not have been better, since Knopf, which had been in business roughly the same number of years as Gallimard and had a similar aura, published the books that mattered most to Camus, among them James M. Cain's *The Postman Always Rings Twice* (1934) and Kafka's *The Trial* (1937). Camus was eagerly awaited as a spokesperson for the French Resistance and, whether he liked it or not, the representative of a new movement called "Existentialism."

23

Existentialist Twins

ALTHOUGH FEW AMERICANS had read *The Stranger* in French—it had been hard enough to find a copy in wartime France—word of the novel had crossed the ocean. Blanche Knopf had founded the US publishing house Alfred A. Knopf, Inc., with her husband Alfred in 1915, and she had a special interest in publishing English translations of contemporary European literature. She had been cut off from France for the duration of the war, but by February 1945 she was back in touch with Jenny Bradley, Knopf's agent in Paris. Sartre had lauded a new Camus novel, still in manuscript, called *The Plague*, in a lecture he gave at Harvard, and Blanche Knopf cabled Bradley, asking to see the proofs.[1] *The Plague*, with its link to the suffering and heroism of France during the German occupation, was bound to make a splash, and she understood that Knopf might also have to buy *The Stranger* in order to get it. Alfred Knopf cabled Bradley in February, eager to acquire *The Plague*, although Camus hadn't yet finished it, but he was still hesitating about *The Stranger*. In March 1945, he made up his mind and offered $350 for it.

Meanwhile, in England, Cyril Connolly (editor of the influential literary magazine *Horizon*), who had castigated the European novel for its tired ways, saw a whole new start in what Camus had written. He brought *The Stranger* to the attention of publisher Jamie Hamilton, who purchased British rights in February 1945, with an advance of 75 pounds. He asked Connolly to write an introduction. Hamilton chose the translator, Stuart Gilbert, a friend of James Joyce who had translations of works by Roger Martin du Gard and André Malraux to his credit. Knopf and Hamilton shared translation costs.[2]

In June, Blanche Knopf made her first postwar trip to Paris and finally met Camus in person, in her old spot at the Ritz Hotel on the place Vendôme. She liked to meet authors early in the day, smoking Chesterfields on a couch in the hotel's vast corridor, a space that remained quiet until afternoon tea was served. She would ask for information about up-and-coming French writers and was known to say "That's not good enough for America!" when she didn't like a suggestion.[3] With Camus, however, she let down her guard and listened. It was the beginning of a long and devoted literary friendship.[4]

Stuart Gilbert worked fast. By September 1945, he'd sent his complete manuscript to Knopf and Hamilton with instructions and a title, *The Stranger*.[5] On January 10, 1946, Jamie Hamilton sent corrected galleys of the translation to Blanche Knopf in New York. There was a bombshell in his letter, a fait accompli: "I send you herewith a set of corrected galleys of Camus's L'ETRANGER, which we have decided to call THE OUTSIDER, both because we consider this a more striking and appropriate title than THE STRANGER, and because Hutchinson's recently called one of their Russian novels THE STRANGER."[6]

In fact it was *Cudzoziemka*, a Polish novel by Maria Kuncewiczowa, which had just appeared in an English translation with the unfortunate title *The Stranger*. Hamilton feared that Camus's book might be confused with it. On the New York end it was too late to switch to *The Outsider*. Hamilton's galleys were as unexpected as the title change, for Knopf had already typeset the book so that it could be available for Camus's visit to New York. Blanche Knopf responded tersely to Hamilton's announcement: "I had assumed when I received the manuscript, because it had instructions on it from Stuart Gilbert, it was setting copy, we read it very carefully and made any necessary corrections. Certainly if I had known there was a chance of corrected galleys, I would not have set, and wish you might have cabled me the new title, which I can well understand your using."[7]

Hamilton hadn't cabled; nor had he telephoned. It hadn't occurred to him that Knopf would go ahead and typeset the book separately without waiting for his galleys.[8]

Not an ideological or interpretive divide, not even an aesthetic quarrel, but rather a question of timing and marketing explains why *L'Étranger* and *The Outsider* were born into the English language as fraternal twins — same text, different typography, covers, and titles. The doubling has continued to this day, even as new translations have replaced Gilbert's: no matter who is translating, the British edition is called *The Outsider*, the American edition *The Stranger*. Books about *The Stranger/The Outsider*, when they're published in both the United States and England, have to keep the titles straight for each country or risk disorienting readers. If you ask someone, English or American, which title they prefer, chances are they will answer: "the one I'm used to."

In England, Jamie Hamilton was certain he had a bestseller on his hands, and he planned a first print run of 10,000 copies — over twice Gallimard's wartime print run of 4,400. At Knopf, there was much more hesitation. In-house readers' reports were less than stellar.

Herbert Weinstock, a specialist in nineteenth-century opera and a Knopf advisor, had this to say about the novel: "This extended short story (the translation does not exceed 30,000 words) is pleasant, unexciting reading. It seems to me neither very important nor very memorable — and it also seems to me to be padded with extraneous detail." He attributed the piling up of details, the flat tone, and what he called "deliberate artlessness" to "a philosophic theory called existentialism," of which *The Stranger* could be considered a demonstration: "My best guess is that it will appeal to very few readers and produce something less than a sensation."[9]

Knopf's publicists had a formidable task. As *The Stranger* was about to go on sale in American bookstores, the publisher placed a full-page advertisement in *Publishers Weekly* (an American trade magazine for publishers, librarians, booksellers, and literary agents). It was signed by Blanche Knopf and entitled "On the New Literature of France." Jamie Hamilton referred to it "Blanche's 'existentialist' ad."[10] She was going to do everything possible to make *The Stranger* accessible and exciting.

The advertisement began by sympathizing with the average reader's dilemma: "There is no use trying to talk about new French literature unless you are willing to tackle 'existentialism.' Now this is a frightening word. . . . Everyone likes to show that he can pronounce it, but no one enjoys undertaking to define it. Well, here goes."

Existentialism, the ad continued, is the notion that a consciousness of the universe's meaninglessness can make us free. Passing mention was then made of the fact that Camus, whose somber countenance gazed out from the upper right of the page, refused to be classified with the existentialists, because their emphasis on meaninglessness was at odds with his belief in political justice. The author of *The Stranger* was introduced as a man who had lived a double life during the Occupation—publishing with the approval of the Nazi censor while editing a Resistance newspaper underground. *The Stranger* was then presented in a few words—a novel as simple and straightforward as John Steinbeck's *Of Mice and Men*.

Pitching *The Stranger* as both a lofty existentialist work and a straightforward populist novel was clever, since reviewers could take up either strand, high or low. Pitching Camus as an existentialist and a champion for social justice was also a good idea—here was an author both intelligent and heroic. After a month of what Blanche Knopf considered "fantastic" press, 2,500 copies of the novel had sold. In 1946, *The Stranger* was not yet a bestseller.[11] In the long run, the ad accomplished something more important than immediate sales: it introduced Camus to American magazine and newspaper publishers as a leading figure of a school of French literature called "existentialist," and it established that school as the most important new intellectual current coming out of France.

You would have to read the advertisement in *Publishers Weekly* more than once to glean that Camus disavowed the existentialist label, and that in fact he detested it. He joked in an interview with a French magazine that he and Sartre decided they ought to put out their own ad "stating that the undersigned have nothing in common and refuse to respond to any debts they might have incurred mutually."[12] Yet it was Sartre who prepared the way for Camus's New York welcome.

New York had been a privileged refuge for exiled intellectuals during the Occupation years, and as of 1945, when travel became possible once again on the big liberty and cargo ships, Sartre, Camus, and Beauvoir all made the trip. Sartre was first. In spring 1945, he filed stories from New York for both *Combat* and *Le Figaro*, and he returned in 1946 to speak to American universities about the literary scene in Paris.

In *Vogue* magazine, in 1945, Sartre described Camus as *the* emblematic writer to emerge from the Resistance—the only writer who corresponded to his theory of a "committed literature" essential to France's renewal. Sartre had read an early version of Camus's forthcoming novel, *The Plague*, in manuscript, and he was ready to vouch that the world was about to see a new Camus: the absurdity of the world in *The Stranger* and *The Myth of Sisyphus* gave way in this new work to positive revolt and struggle. *The Plague*, based on Camus's own commitment to the Resistance, demonstrated that the human spirit could come to rule over "the absurd world." Sartre described, as he had done in the *Cahiers du Sud* essay in 1943, Camus's somberness and his debt to the classical moralists, though now he underlined the potential of those qualities for a literature to come: "It is likely that in the somber, pure work of Camus are discernible the principal traits of the French letters of the future."[13]

For Sartre, Camus represented most vividly the aspirations of postwar literature at a shining moment when writers and intellectuals felt the world was theirs to remake. No other writer could have fit the bill for Sartre: Malraux was too much of an individualist; Guéhenno and Mauriac, much older men, had refused to publish above ground, and the Communists were indebted to their own masters. Camus had done exactly what needed to be done during the Occupation: he had marked time but he hadn't accepted the oppression; he had chosen struggle rather than silence. At thirty-two years old in 1945, he had reached the perfect age when youth meets maturity.

In January 1946, speaking to students at Yale about the French view of the American novel, Sartre singled out *The Stranger* as "the French novel which caused the greatest furor between 1940 and 1945." He placed his emphasis differently in this American context than he had in his *Cahiers du Sud* essay of 1943. Gone in his American lecture are references to Voltaire and the eighteenth-century morality tale. His focus now was on Camus's debt to Hemingway, the short disruptive sentences that in Hemingway were a feature of the writer's temperament but in Camus were rather a deliberate technique for expressing a philosophy of the absurd. Sartre entertained his audience with stories of the symbolic value of American literature when France was under German Occupation. He described the Café de Flore as the headquarters for a black market in American books. Not only did reading Faulkner and Hemingway novels became a symbol of resistance, he claimed, it was even the case—he couldn't resist a joke—that secretaries "believed they could demonstrate against the Germans by reading *Gone with the Wind* in the Metro." Sartre promised his audience, three months before the English-language publication of *The Stranger*, that French novels written during the Occupation would start to appear in translation. He was rolling out a thick red carpet for his friend.[14]

24

Consecration in New York

WHEN THE *OREGON* DOCKED in the New York harbor on March 25, 1946, Camus was the only passenger held for questioning by immigration officials.[1] He refused to answer any of their questions—which likely included what was then the standard for Cold War America: "Are you now or have you ever been a member of the Communist party?" He was silent for several hours until a staff member from French Cultural Services intervened and vouched for the writer. Word of the incident reached J. Edgar Hoover, always on the lookout for the Communist menace. Hoover ordered FBI surveillance, and a report.[2] The FBI's major source of information was a light-hearted article published by Hannah Arendt in the left-wing magazine the *Nation* a month before Camus's arrival in Manhattan. In "French Existentialism," Arendt claimed that France had become a place where "books so difficult as to require actual thinking sell like detective stories." The French existentialists were having more fun than any other intellectuals in the postwar world, and the two main representatives of this new existentialist movement were Sartre and Camus. After quoting Arendt at length, the report deescalated the threat, pointing out that with the Liberation, even the Communists in France had turned to nationalist concerns and the reconstruction of their country. In the end, the author of the report, special agent James E. Tierney, concluded there was really nothing to worry about: "Investigation fails to develop any subversive or political activity on subject's part. Informants state they believe subject is striving in his lectures to establish a closer relationship between the cultural views of the US and France and to explain his Philosophy of the Absurd. This philosophy recommends living lucidly with the absurd, enjoying life all the more fully because it had no meaning and taking advantage of the most complete liberty on earth once eternal liberty is suppressed."[3]

Waiting patiently at pier 88 to greet Camus that spring day was Nicola Chiaromonte, the Italian friend who'd sought refuge with Camus and his family in Algiers and Oran, who'd accompanied Camus on bike trips to Bouisseville beach, and had even lived for a time in the House Above the World. Chiaromonte had found safe passage to New York through Algeria, Morocco, and Portugal with Camus's help, and it was time to return his hospitality. The Italian refugee was now a prominent New York intellectual publishing in the best small magazines.

There would be no quiet walks on the beach for Camus and Chiaromonte, but instead many loud parties and evenings in honkytonk bars and fancy New York apartments. Blanche and Alfred Knopf threw a swank party to launch *The Stranger* on the rooftop garden of the Astor Hotel on Times Square, but Camus didn't mention it in his New York diary. Despite what the "existentialist ad" said, the novel he had conceived in 1939 and perfected in the depths of the Occupation no longer corresponded to his thinking or his mood.

The specialist in the flat first-person narrative, the creator of the alienated and solitary Meursault, had earned the right and privilege to step onto the lecture stage and speak as "we," representing the aspirations of liberated France. Four days after his arrival, Camus lectured at Columbia University.[4] The event was a panel on postwar France, organized by the Cultural Services of the French Embassy. Camus was joined by Vercors, the author of the underground novel *The Silence of the Sea,* and Thimerais, another writer published by the Éditions de Minuit, the legendary underground press.[5]

The event at Columbia was the talk of the town. Camus was hosted by Professor Justin O'Brien of Columbia's French department, a specialist in twentieth-century French literature who had only recently traded his military uniform for a professor's tweed jacket. The *Columbia Spectator* prepared the students for Camus's talk: "Camus . . . appears to live happily within this absurd, and not to sacrifice his lucidity and contentedness at the altar of metaphysical revelation."[6] It was a reassuring take on *The Myth of Sisyphus*: why be bogged down in the absurd when life is so much fun? O'Brien announced in the *New York Herald Tribune* that Camus was "the boldest writer in France today."

The day before the event, O'Brien called on Camus and the other speakers at the Embassy Hotel, a mothy establishment at 70th and Broadway: "The moment we were in his room and the athletic young man had stretched out on the bed with a few notes in front of him, he easily dominated the group."[7] Camus's charisma, composed of equal parts of physical presence, ease, and authority, worked its magic on men and women alike.[8]

The audience gathered in Columbia's McMillin Theater. Twelve hundred people were crowded into a space designed for six hundred, some of them carrying copies of *Combat*. O'Brien remembered, "Everyone was eager to hear French spoken again and to see in flesh and blood some survivors of the black years of the occupation."[9]

In his speech at Columbia, "The Human Crisis," Camus mentioned neither *The Stranger* nor *The Myth of Sisyphus*. Speaking in French, he described his generation, born during the World War I, reaching adolescence during the Depression, coming of age during the civil war in Spain and the rise of Hitler, and living through the defeat of France and four years of struggle against an enemy occupation.[10] He spoke, with no regret, of the fashion for "the absurd" that had captured writers such as himself before the war, and of a literature that was "in revolt against lucidity, narration, and even the sentence." This was no longer his world. Camus was preoccupied, as were the characters in his novel in progress, *The Plague*, with preventing the return of a deadly scourge. Like an epidemic brought under control, Hitler's death ended one cycle of evil, but it should not make them complacent. He called for the elimination of the death penalty, for dialogue across borders, for indulgence towards others and rigor towards oneself, and he praised the French people who had been willing to die for the truth. He likened them to so many modern-day Socrateses. After the losses from two world wars, France would doubtless see history being made by other nations—that was a fact. French writers and thinkers faced a daunting task: they needed to emerge from the Nazi era with pessimism about the world and optimism about mankind.

·

A writer for the *New Yorker* who visited Camus in his room at the Embassy Hotel found him studying the Knopf edition of his novel quizzically. Camus didn't read English very well, but he knew something was wrong: "There are too many quotation marks in it," he told his visitor. "I am sure that there weren't that many quotation marks in the original."[11] Any chance he got, Gilbert substituted a direct quotation for Camus's indirect speech. Even a passing remark like "I answered no" became, in Gilbert's version, "I answered: 'No.'"[12] There were consequences: while Camus had chosen to use indirect speech to distance the reader from Meursault—to deprive us of direct dialogue—Gilbert apparently preferred quotations, which create an entirely different mood.[13]

Like many talented translators faced with radical literary innovation, Gilbert wanted to make *The Stranger* sound good in idiomatic English. But he changed the style so drastically that anyone who knew the French and happened upon Gilbert's translation was appalled. Thirty years later, a French professor named John Gale who had been asked to lecture on the novel to a group of students reading it in English was so taken aback by his first contact with Gilbert's *The Stranger* that he wrote a manifesto, "Does America Know *The Stranger*?"[14] Gilbert translates "I'll arrive" ("j'arriverai") as "I should get there" and "It's not my fault" ("Ce n'est pas de ma faute") as "Sorry, sir, but it's not my fault, you know." "I don't know" in the French ("je ne sais pas") becomes "I can't be sure" in Gilbert's translation. Meursault isn't indifferent in this translation—he can't make up his mind. Gilbert substitutes complex sentence structures for Camus's stripped-down prose, and asserts causality that Camus worked so hard to avoid. Camus writes: "I'll take the bus and I'll arrive in the afternoon" ("Je prendrai l'autobus à deux heures et j'arriverai dans l'après-midi"); and Gilbert translates: "With the two o'clock bus I should get there well before nightfall." The sentences are no longer the "islands" that so fascinated Sartre. Gilbert's style also elevates the characters to a higher social class. Even Raymond Sintès sounds British. "You've knocked around the world a bit," Sintès says to Meursault in Gilbert's translation, where Camus reports the conversation indirectly: "he wanted to ask my advice . . . since I was a man, I knew life . . ." ("il voulait me demander un conseil . . . que moi, j'étais un homme, je connaissais la vie").

Camus landed in New York on March 25, 1946. On April 11, a more hesitant, classier, and vaguely more British Meursault stepped gingerly onto the pavements of American literature.

·

In reviews that appeared from April to July, there was a discrepancy between the political spokesman of 1946 and the solitary writer of *The Stranger*. Existentialism, from what American critics had read, appeared to be a practical and hopeful philosophy designed to pull France, and the rest of the world, out of the wartime morass.[15] But the man and his novel didn't match. Camus, preoccupied with political change, had moved beyond the absurd, but *The Stranger* couldn't—it would forever be the fruit of Camus's solitude in Oran and Paris, the book conceived before the fall of France. The American press would try to make sense of the novel as a reflection of its author, who in their minds represented the Resistance. Certain articles forced the connection.

View, the stylish New York surrealist magazine edited by a team of French avant-garde writers and artists in exile, published an excerpt from the new Knopf edition. It chose Meursault's scene with the chaplain, and the table of contents that surrounds that scene from *The Stranger* in *View*'s 1945–1946 issue is an impressive orchestration of midcentury French literature, gleaned in part from the various small magazines that had made their reputations during the Occupation: Jean Genet's *Pompes funèbres* (translated as "It's your funeral"); a Sartre essay on occupied Paris; Henri Michaux's poetry; and a selection of short anecdotes by the eccentric André de Richaud, author of *La Douleur*, the book that had inspired Camus to believe in his own future as a writer. Yet in the same issue, *View* published a disdainful review of *The Stranger* by the Greek surrealist poet Nicolas Calas (another Paris exile, and a friend of André Breton), who made fun of existential writing influenced by detective novels, and updated the historical resonance of *The Stranger* by claiming that "Camus's hero lives in a collaborationist world." According to Calas, Meursault is a pure collaborationist who "does not lose himself in action, but abandons hope and becomes a cynic."[16] It was to be expected, given the intense focus on France's wartime experience, that critics would begin to read a book conceived in 1939 through the lens of 1945. Camus's status as a hero didn't prevent Calas from knocking *The Stranger*'s protagonist as an enemy of the Resistance.

The Talk of the Town column in the *New Yorker* published a sketch entitled "The Absurdiste." The magazine cut the French literary star down to size by describing him as a cartoonish-looking character whose skinny frame showed the effects of the Occupation diet and whose suit was ten years out of date.[17] Camus, in his own journals, complained about American bad taste—the ugliest neckties he had ever seen![18] He wrote to Janine and Michel Gallimard in Paris that the girls at *Vogue* were calling him "the little Bogart," and he figured he could probably get a film contract whenever he wanted.[19] One young journalist at *Vogue* named Patricia Blake became his American companion, and she grew close enough to notice his sudden sweats and fevers without realizing that he suffered from tuberculosis. New York exposed the best and the worst features of life in the limelight.

Chiaromonte reviewed Gilbert's translation for the *New Republic*. He was the most adept of all the American critics at reconciling the Albert Camus of 1946 with the *The Stranger*. He began his review much as Camus began "The Human Crisis," speaking in the "we" about the shared experience of their generation. For him there was a deep connection between Meursault's refusal to lie and Camus's own honesty, which gave *The Stranger* an ethical force that differentiated it from any of the American novels to which it was compared.[20] John L. Brown, a former officer for the OSS, wrote from Paris for the Sunday *New York Times*. The mood in Paris dominated his review. Brown knew Camus's entire crowd and was especially close to Jacqueline Bernard, who survived Ravensbrück and joined the postwar team at *Combat*. For him, the 1942 novel evoked the fear, the hunger, the dimmed lights of the recovering city of 1946. He knew the Paris literary scene, and Camus's own history, in depth, and he described the young editor at Gallimard as a person to whom "the tormented, uncertain, often unbalanced but always courageous adolescents of post-Liberation France [come] to discuss their problems with someone who they feel understands them better than anyone else."[21] His Camus was an "apostle."

The Stranger didn't fare as well with Edmund Wilson in the *New Yorker*. He found the novel sociologically inconsistent; if what Meursault wants is to keep the Arabs in their place—and even that isn't sure—"he ought to be shown as himself being kicked or squeezed by some other social group." In other words, Wilson wanted a realist novel.[22]

Charles Poore also wrote about Algeria. A journeyman critic for the *New York Times* who had served with the Civil Affairs Division in North Africa and Italy, he had only just returned to civilian life. He was excited about the new French fiction, which he found so much livelier than the gaudy historical novels American novelists seemed to be writing with an eye to movie sales. Poore was the first US critic to address the men who had landed on the coast of Algeria in 1942, who were bound to have a unique understanding of *The Stranger*: "The scene of *The Stranger* is Algiers—not the Algiers full of Allied uniforms and beefs and armament and confusion and jeeps roaring up the Rue Michelet that so many Americans have known—but a purely French and Arab Algiers of some time before the war hit that steep town. The frying-wet heat of summer, however, is familiar."[23]

He didn't make the darker connection between Meursault's crime and the war — the fact that millions of Americans, whether they had fought in Normandy, in North Africa, or in the Pacific, were living with the memory of killing a nameless enemy. To them, *The Stranger* held out a dark and grimly satisfying mirror.[24] Just maybe, by some miracle of literary transmission, the many problems with the Gilbert translation did not stand in the way of English-speaking readers grasping what was essential about *The Stranger*, and the force of the original came through, allowing the novel to take hold.

Poore's review left in parentheses an issue he didn't quite know what to make of, as if he was putting it aside for some later discussion: "(Incidentally, the fate of the Arab's family is completely overlooked in the proceedings.)"

25

A Book for Everyone

IN REFUSING THE EXISTENTIALIST LABEL, Camus may have hoped to keep his distance from the close-knit Sartre clan, but his claim was also sincere. He and Sartre had a completely different sense of the absurd, and a different notion of human potential. Man, for Camus, was his own end, and men, as he put it in *The Myth of Sisyphus*, "secrete the inhuman." He considered that book "anti-existential." For Sartre what mattered was consciousness—people getting along, or not getting along with one another. Whereas for Camus what mattered was the insignificance of man against the world, the inanimate essence of things. This difference was clearest in the style and themes of their novels—*Nausea* with its dread of the other; the universe of *The Stranger* with its tender indifference to man. These basic distinctions between the work of Camus and Sartre were erased by the demands of publicity and by the excitement over the latest intellectual fashion.

During Camus's American journey, even the high school students at the Lycée Français de New York needed to know whether Camus was an existentialist. He joked with them that he had just been asked at Harvard how many members there were in his "existentialist party." He told them he had responded, "We're not a party; we're more like a climate." How many in your climate then, the Lycée students wanted to know? "Exactly 10,471," he said.[1] In his audience that day were many French teenagers who, by necessity, had spent the war years in the United States. They were starved for news of home, and thrilled to hear about this new "climate."

Camus could deny that he was an existentialist all he wanted, it didn't matter. Thousands of young people listening to jazz and swing-dancing in the basement clubs of Saint-Germain des Prés were there to prove him wrong, for they were all existentialists now. To them, Camus's trench coat was existentialist; his cigarettes were existentialist. Now that the war was over, he was smoking unfiltered Gauloises Disque Bleu.[2] Existentialism combined a rugged pessimism born of the war with the giddy exhilaration of the Liberation. The existential mood exuded a sense of the urgency of life and a need for action, drawing its inspiration from a mythology of the Resistance. Existentialism as a fashion was a quest for a way of life where freedom could coexist with responsibility; it was, like the philosophy it purported to represent, what people made of it. It had trickled down to mass culture from works like *The Myth of Sisyphus* and from Sartre's much-quoted "Existentialism is a Humanism."[3] But it drew its powers of persuasion from jazz and from fiction.

The existentialist label would stick to Camus for the rest of his life, even after he and Sartre split over Cold War politics and the Algerian War. Arendt said it clearly in the *Nation* in 1946, on the eve of Camus's trip to New York: existentialism could no longer be considered a school of philosophical thought; it was a literary, intellectual movement and *The Stranger* was an excellent example of the new existentialist creed. When he published *The Plague* in 1947, the merely respectable sales figures of *The Stranger* faded in the wake of a massive best seller: 96,000 copies of *The Plague* were sold in France in the first three months after publication, and the novel was considered a blueprint for political commitment in the postwar world.[4] Camus was never completely satisfied with his second novel, and he wrote to Michel Gallimard with his driest wit: "*The Plague* has more victims than I expected."[5]

In the United States, where "existentialism" became an intellectual commodity, *The Plague* and *The Stranger* were both popular, and in the first years following the translations, *The Plague* outsold *The*

Stranger.[6] But *The Stranger* soon surpassed *The Plague* because of one essential quality. Teachers realized that Camus's first novel was perfectly suited to teaching French, a perfect bridge from language study to literature. In the words of Camus's friend Germaine Brée, then a professor at New York University by way of Oran, the novel succeeded "because of its dramatic action, its direct style, and because also of its hero who incarnates one of the disturbing problems of our time."[7] Meursault was making his way, slowly but inexorably, from the beaches of Algiers to the classroom.

That Meursault spoke the language of students became unhappily apparent to Camus himself when, in 1948, a young murderer tried to enlist *The Stranger* as part of his defense. A high school student named Claude Panconi killed his classmate, Alain Guyader, with the encouragement of two of his friends. The crime story that emerged in the press involved fantasies of espionage and counter-espionage, love triangles, denunciations, and class warfare in a private high school in Melun, a town near Paris. Panconi claimed to the examining magistrate that he was inspired in his crime by several modernist novels, including Meursault's act of murder in *The Stranger*. Not "the sun made me do it," but "Meursault made me do it." Panconi did not think that the judges could understand his act if they didn't understand Meursault, who had murdered without hate.

Raoul Guyader, the victim's father, wrote to Camus during the long lead-up to the murder trial, pleading with the author of *The Stranger* to condemn Panconi's literary self-defense. If Camus himself denied any effect the book might have had on the murderer, Panconi would be forced to take full responsibility for his actions. Guyader was afraid that Panconi's literary defense would work, and that his son's violent death would go unpunished.

Camus refused. To be sure, it was pretty clear that *Thérèse Desqueyroux*, Mauriac's novel about a woman who poisons her husband, doesn't encourage people to poison their spouses, any more than *Oedipus Rex* encourages people to kill their fathers, but Camus couldn't swear that the murderer wasn't influenced by his book. Here Camus was sounding like an existentialist: he was going on record that writers bore responsibility for their words, the position Sartre had defended in "Existentialism is a Humanism" and *What Is Literature?* Camus argued that he could not be entirely sure that he wasn't in some secondhand way responsible for influencing Panconi's crime and therefore guilty himself. He wrote to Raoul Guyader, and his private letter was soon leaked to the press and reprinted in both the very serious daily *Le Monde* and the tabloid *Ici Paris*: "If I deny firmly, with no exceptions, that *The Stranger* can incite crime, this book, nevertheless, like all my other books, illustrates, in its own way, my horror of capital punishment and my anguished questions at any suspicion of guilt. My work, Monsieur—and for once I am saying this with sorrow—does not consist in accusing people. It consists in understanding them, in giving a voice to their shared unhappiness. This is why, no matter what I think, I cannot side with the accusation, even if it would spare my reputation as a writer."[8]

Because he might indeed be guilty of influencing a murderer, he could not let himself off the hook in order to accuse a murderer of a fully independent intention. In a trial that might lead to a terrible punishment, he could not risk serving the prosecution. This was why he signed the petition to save Brasillach, and it would be why he wrote private letters to French President Coty to save Algerian revolutionaries facing the guillotine in 1957 and 1958.[9] Panconi was blaming Meursault, and by refusing to shuck off that blame, Camus was taking responsibility for the harm that language can do, as well as the good.

For the French press, Panconi and his friends were symbols of a generation sacrificed to wartime: they were nine years old when the war began, and, in 1948, when the crime took place, they were seventeen. The Occupation had deprived them of a normal childhood. The trial came to be known as the J3 Murder—J3 after the category of wartime ration tickets that guaranteed extra food for growing children.[10] Françoise Dolto, a French child psychologist, was disturbed by the crime's utter senselessness; Joseph Kessel was fascinated by the part of fantasy and fiction in the crime.[11] The stories generated by the J3 trial were the start of a vigorous new subgenre with a life of its own: subsidiaries of *The Stranger*.

The J3 trial was a rare instance of literature crossing over into the law. In general Camus tried to insist that Meursault was not a real person, and could not be invoked to model behaviors, whether they were murderous or merely unconventional. While the J3 trial remained in the news—the murder occurred in 1948 and the trial wasn't held until 1951—Camus's publisher started thinking about issuing mass-market editions of its best-selling books, including *The Stranger*. Camus was reticent: "No, I have no real desire to see *The Stranger* leave the rather selective circle of readers of the 'Blanche' edition" (the cream-colored books that were the mark of the *NRF*). "Unlike *The Plague*, it is not a book for everyone. Maybe later."[12]

The J3 trial and resulting publicity around *The Stranger* made him uncomfortable, and while he didn't think that *The Plague*, his ode to resistance, could do any harm, he wasn't sure he wanted *The Stranger* to reach a popular audience. When he inscribed the book for friends, his comments were distant and sarcastic: "If you don't want to be condemned to death, be sure to cry at your mother's funeral."[13] When encouraged to hold forth about Meursault, Camus remained elusive. While the prosecutor in *The Stranger* called Meursault "Monsieur Antichrist,"[14] Camus referred to him, in a special introduction he prepared for a 1955 American school edition of *The Stranger* as "the only Christ we deserve." It wasn't a blasphemous thought, he insisted, only the sign of "the slightly ironic affection that an artist has the right to feel towards the characters he has created."[15] He liked to sign his letters to Emmanuel Roblès, his friend from Oran who shared his Spanish origins, "Camusso": if you say it out loud, it sounds a lot like Ca-meursault.[16] Camus was not Meursault, but he had found the man who didn't love his mother, who killed on a whim, somewhere inside him.

Camus wrote of Meursault: "I see something positive about him and that is his refusal, unto death, to lie. Lying is not only saying what isn't true, it is also accepting to say more than one knows, mostly to conform to society. Meursault is not on the side of the judges, the laws of society, conventional feelings. He exists, like a stone or the wind or the sea, under the sun—and those things never lie."[17] But Meursault was not just a stone or the wind or the sea—he was Camus's negative truth. In the existential climate of the postwar era, he was taking on a more positive sheen, his awkwardness giving way to heroic candor.

·

In the end, Camus didn't get his wish to keep *The Stranger* limited to a select circle of readers—and that is a colossal understatement! During his lifetime, he bowed, little by little, to the demands of success. In 1954, he recorded *The Stranger* for French national radio, reading in a formal manner, with barely a trace of his Algerian accent remaining.[18] He wrote a preface to the Appleton-Century-Crofts French-language edition in 1955, an edition that was designed for the American classroom and omitted four sexual allusions that the editors warned "might prove embarrassing" to students and their teachers. It sold in the millions.

It is difficult to imagine today a moral universe in which phrases like "what bothered him was that he 'still thought she was a good lay'" were considered unfit for students to read—difficult to measure the shock that a godless Meursault and his friend Raymond represented to Americans in the Eisenhower years.[19] One unfortunate teacher in Michigan's Upper Peninsula purchased copies of the Knopf edition, which included the "embarrassing" sentences, and he taught the opening of the book to five slow readers. He thought the simple style would be accessible, and that the story could help them. He was promptly arrested for teaching lewd material, fined $100, and sentenced to three months behind bars (the prosecutor's wife was hired to teach his classes). Finally a judge in a neighboring county took up his cause and discovered he had been indicted under an obscenity statute previously abolished by the State of Michigan. He was free, but unemployed. An absurd miscarriage of justice, happily more ridiculous and less tragic in the end than Meursault's trial.

If Panconi was the first person to use Meursault as an alibi for murder, Franklyn C. Olson, the teacher from Thompson, Michigan, was the novel's first legal martyr.[20] The Thompson case could have been a harbinger of trouble to come—Knopf took note. But oddly, *The Stranger* was a classroom success, in French and in English editions, all over the country. Whether they were learning French or getting their first glimpse of Continental thought, droves of American students read about Meursault, his friend the pimp, and his prostitute mistress.

In 1957 came an event that exposed Camus, and his writing, to even more relentless publicity. He was awarded the Nobel Prize in Literature. *The Stranger* was singled out specially by the secretary of the Swedish Academy: "... using an art with complete classic purity of style, he has embodied these [existential] problems in such fashion that characters and action make his ideas live before us, without commentary by the author. This is what makes *L'Étranger* (The Stranger), 1942, famous. The main character, an employee of a government department, kills an Arab following a chain of absurd events; then, indifferent to his fate, he hears himself condemned to death. At the last moment, however, he pulls himself together and emerges from a passivity bordering on torpor."[21]

This was the only Camus novel that the Swedish Academy characterized as "famous"—indeed it had become as famous as Camus himself. Several photos by Henri Cartier-Bresson captured Camus's aura in those years. In the first, from 1944, he faces the camera in three-quarters profile, the collar of his winter coat pushed up, his hair slicked back, and a cigarette dangling from his mouth—the writer who's come in from the cold. In a second series of Cartier-Bresson photos from 1956, he stands in his office at Gallimard against a wall of books and looks straight at the camera, a mischievous smile at the corners of his lips. He is sporting the Bogart-style trench coat that Blanche Knopf had made to order for him at Brooks Brothers.[22]

After his New York trip, Camus had written ruefully in his notebooks, "What is a famous man? It's a man whose first name doesn't matter. For everyone else, a first name has a meaning all of its own."[23]

It was as though Camus was now officially severed from Albert. Even Meursault had been upgraded by the Swedes: they had made him a government employee, working for a ministry.

In 1957, the year of the Nobel, Camus finally approved the first mass-market edition of *The Stranger* in France.[24] It was in a series called Le Livre de Poche (pocket book), published by Hachette, Gallimard's partner for paperback reprints until the 1970s. On the cover of the Livre de Poche edition of *L'Étranger* is a painting of Meursault on the beach. He looks like a young Rimbaud, or a Claude Panconi, with one hand in his pocket. On the back of the book is a photograph of a mature Camus who also has one hand in his suit pocket; his face is tilted, and he holds an existential cigarette to his lips. Next to his image are the words, "Nobel Prize in Literature 1957."

The second mass-market edition of *The Stranger* was introduced in 1972, when Gallimard launched its own pocket-book series, Folio. The Folio collection was inaugurated by André Malraux's *Man's Fate*; *The Stranger* was number two in the series. Camus would have enjoyed the fact that *The Stranger* came out in Folio right after Malraux. When he won the Nobel Prize, he said again and again, in private and in public, that the prize should have gone to Malraux rather than to him.[25] The author of *Man's Fate* had ushered him on to the stage of French literature in 1942, and Camus knew, better than anyone, the extent of his debt. Folio number two become the bestselling mass-market paperback in French publishing history. In 1972, the Folio edition of *The Stranger* was offered in exchange for bonus points by Total gas stations throughout France, one of a set of prizes that included plates, comic books, and small plastic busts of heroes of the French Republic such as Louis Pasteur, Gustave Eiffel, and, bizarrely, the Maréchal Pétain.

·

Camus didn't live to see the popular triumph of his first published novel, and it's impossible to say what exactly he would have made of it. In early January 1960, he was heading to Paris with Michel and Janine Gallimard in the passenger seat of a finicky Facel-Vega sports car. It's unclear whether bad brakes or worn tires were at fault. The car veered off the road, smashed into a plane tree, and wrapped itself around another. Camus was killed instantly. His body was taken to the city hall of the nearby town of Villeblevin before being transferred to his family home in Lourmarin. When Francine Camus arrived on the scene at the Villeblevin town hall, she couldn't help but think of the wake at Marengo in *The Stranger*.[26] *The Stranger* might seem like cold comfort, but the thought was also consoling, for the difficult birth of that novel had coincided with the beginning of her life with Camus. With his death, the power of its scenes lived on.

News of Albert Camus's death was reported on front pages around the world. In a sorrowful echo of *The Stranger*, several French newspapers chose the simple headline, "Albert Camus est mort." Many articles noted that a train ticket was found in Camus's pocket; he'd decided only at the last minute to travel with his friends by car. His own words were marshaled to describe his death. It was absurd. The car accident on National Route 6 that silenced his voice forever meant that he would be forever forty-six, a man in the prime of life, never any grayer or more wrinkled than the man-in-a-trench-coat staring from the Cartier-Bresson photo. Certainly if he had gotten to choose he would have preferred the indignities of old age. He would have preferred to struggle with resentment and self-satisfaction—the two dangers, so he had written after the Nobel, that threaten successful writers.[27] He never saw his two children grow up, never learned the outcome of the Algerian War or saw an end to the violence on both sides. He never had to face Algerian independence and what it might mean for his family. When he died he was working on a novel he called *The First Man*, an ode to his Belcourt childhood as tender and emotional as *The Stranger* was cool and disturbed. The manuscript was recovered from the wreck of the Facel-Vega; it was finally published thirty-four years after his death, to universal acclaim. There would be no bad books for Albert Camus, and he would never disappoint his readers. Nor would he ever have to say "Aujourd'hui, maman est morte." His mother died in Algiers, nine months after losing her son.

·

Camus was gone, but *The Stranger* remained, heading into its own uncertain future. In 1967, the novel saw new life as a film. Through the protracted negotiations of filmmaker Luchino Visconti with Francine Camus, the first adaptation of *The Stranger* illustrates the delicate situation where an author, deceased and unable to defend or represent his work, is represented by his literary executors, who cannot write or edit for him but who defend what he has created and represent, to their best ability, his intentions. French law considers this "the moral right" of all literary heirs.

Visconti had begun his film career in 1942 in fascist Italy with a neorealist masterpiece called *Ossessione* (Obsession), an Italian adaptation of *The Postman Always Rings Twice*—the same literary inspiration as Camus. He was drawn to *The Stranger* because he believed Camus had anticipated by a quarter century the youthful rebellion of the 1960s, by creating in Meursault a character who refuses to lie and thereby rejects society's hypocrisy.[28] In previous films he had shown that he was a master of fading civilizations, temperamentally suited to depict the twilight years of French Algeria. For these reasons, there were great expectations of what he would do with the novel.[29]

Visconti began work on the adaptation of *The Stranger* a year after Algeria won its independence from France. He wanted to bring Camus's story into a present-day history, where Meursault would represent "the terror of the pied noir," the Frenchman in Algeria about to lose the land that doesn't belong to him. His imagined *Stranger* would resonate with the spirit of Algerian revolution and the violence of the French "ultras," the Secret Army Organization that had resorted to terrorism in a desperate attempt to keep Algeria French.[30] But the last thing Francine Camus wanted was for recent history and most especially the demise of the French in Algeria to overwhelm the treatment of her late husband's novel. Nor could she accept Visconti's giving Meursault the first name "Albert"—combining *The Stranger*'s narrator with its author, as though they were one and the same. Visconti ended up naming his main character "Arthur Meursault."

Francine Camus rejected Visconti's first screenplay and he began a second treatment in 1966. Emmanuel Roblès, brought in as co-screenwriter, kept an eye out for the family's concerns.[31] He has a nonspeaking cameo in the film as foreman of the jury — a fitting role, given the circumstances.

Visconti obtained authorization to film on location in Algiers. The bus heading out of Belcourt, the changing cabins on the beach, the inside of the courtroom where Camus himself had followed so many trials in the 1930s, make *Lo Straniero* a precious record of Camus's lost world. But Visconti was unable to capture, with a conventional voiceover, the special quality of Meursault's voice, nor could he represent the island-like verbs or the strange jumps in tenses on the page.

In his first version of *Lo Straniero*, Visconti filmed the death scene, complete with guillotine. He was eager to capture the moment when Meursault is greeted at the scaffold with cries of hate. Both Roblès and Francine Camus objected: central to the meaning of *The Stranger* is the fact that the reader of the novel never learns whether Meursault actually goes to his death, or if he does, how he can tell his story. "This is true," Visconti replied, "but cinematographically, it's a good ending." Ultimately, attentive to the wishes of the family and despite pressure from his producer, Visconti cut the last scene.[32] Countless adaptations, illustrations, transformations of Camus's fiction into other languages and other media have followed. Of the sixty translations that are often cited, two into Arabic — one from Lebanon and another from Egypt — represent a particularly arduous passage from one culture to another, and deserve to be studied for the choices of language and style and especially for their reception.[33]

What would Camus have thought of *The Stranger* morphed into song? In 1979 Robert Smith, songwriter for the English punk rock group The Cure, condensed the entire novel into a lyrical snapshot of the beach scene. He had read *The Stranger* in college. Stripping the novel down to its essence was a form of fidelity to Camus's es-thetics that hit the mark, in its modest way, better than the elaborate realism of Visconti's film: "Standing on a beach with a gun in my hand. Staring at the sky, staring at the sand. . . . /Staring down the barrel at the Arab on the ground/ I can see his open mouth but I hear no sound/I'm alive/I'm dead/I'm the Stranger/Killing an Arab."

In the context of 1970s Britain, immigration politics, skinheads, "Killing an Arab" was a dangerous song, and the group, alarmed by a popular outcry, put a disclaimer sticker on their compilation album, *Standing on the Beach,* disavowing any racist connotation.[34] In the coming years, the group renamed their song "Kissing an Arab," "Kill-ing Another," "Killing an Ahab" (an homage to *Moby Dick*). Smith had managed to reproduce the flat tone of Camus's novel in a few well-chosen phrases, but he could not inoculate "Killing an Arab" against the possibility that someone would hear it as an invitation to kill Arabs. This problem, too, is perfectly in keeping with the life of Camus's novel, and with the contradictory energies that keep *The Stranger* on the center stage of world literature.

26

What's in a Name?

AFTER *THE STRANGER* had made its way around the globe, acquired millions of readers, and became the very example of the modern novel; after Algeria's bloody war of independence, resulting in nationhood and citizenship for the Muslim population; after all of that, a question continued to haunt Camus's 1942 novel. Why doesn't the Arab in the story have a name? Why doesn't he talk?

If there has been one consistent criticism of Camus's novel since its publication, it has turned around the nameless, voiceless Arab shot by Meursault on a beach in colonial Algeria. Edward Said remarked succinctly, in an essay that would become one of the founding texts of postcolonial studies: "The Arabs of *The Stranger* are nameless beings used as background for the portentous metaphysics explored by Camus."[1]

Said made a bold move by dismissing the reading of Camus as an "existentialist," and reading him instead through his political context — almost, as the American writer Edmund White later remarked with some regret, as though the murder on the beach could be reduced to a page from recent history.[2]

Neither the existential nor the political approaches have much connection to the creative instinct that drove Camus in 1940. To him, *The Stranger* was a black-and-white sketch. He was representing a harsh colonial world in which a man could go on trial for murdering an Arab without the court bothering to ask about the person he had killed. *The Stranger* is not a novel in the realist tradition, it is a

personal vision, a nightmare: Camus called it a "photographic negative," the underside of his humanism.

The political reading of *The Stranger* was welcomed in the 1980s
as a brand-new discovery, an ethical advance. What no one noticed
was that a political criticism of Camus had been in place from the
very beginning, in Cyril Connolly's five-page introduction to *The
Outsider*. Connolly took a tone both sympathetic and judgmental,
impressed and grumpy—a risky stance for an introduction. He situ-
ated the book in Algeria, not Europe—as though you could ignore
the fact that Camus was the product of a traditional French literary education. There are no Troubadours or Enlightenment philosophers getting in Camus's way, he claimed, only Romans and Turks
and Moors. In his mind, Meursault's trial was made absurd by a rigid
and pompous administration pretending that Algeria was part of
France. He maintained that Meursault, as a "neo-pagan," was closer
to a poor white living in Hemingway's Key West, or in Faulkner's or
Caldwell's Deep South, than to any French literary forefather. You
sense in Connolly's reading a view of the novel as growing from the
soil. Then, to this rather romantic picture, he added an indictment:
". . . the other sufferer in his story, the Moorish girl whose lover
beats her up and whose brother is killed when trying to avenge her,
is totally forgotten. She too may have been 'privileged' to love life
just as much, so may her murdered brother, for they too were 'foreigners' to the Colonial System, and a great deal besides."[3]

If you want novels to give equal opportunity to their characters,
Connolly is right. In two sentences, he anticipated seventy years of
debate around *The Stranger*: the analysis of gender, of sexuality, of
women caught in the violent relations between men, not to mention
an entire field, postcolonial studies. He was writing about a "Colonial System" in 1946, just as England's decolonization went into full
swing, a year before Indian independence. French critics of the Occupation years had been deaf to the colonial issues. Even Sartre,
who later came down so hard on Camus for not supporting Algerian independence, was indifferent to the Arab in his 1943 essay on
The Stranger, except to say that the whole book had the quality of an

Arabic chant. It wasn't until 1961, at the height of the Algerian War of Independence, that a young historian named Pierre Nora proposed "Another Explanation of *The Stranger*": Meursault, in killing the Arab, represented the unconscious wish of the French in Algeria—keep the land and destroy the enemy.[4] Nora's interpretation was perfectly attuned to a country on the verge of revolution. The war that ended with Algerian independence in 1962 began on May 8, 1945, at Sétif, in eastern Algeria. Colonial police murdered a demonstrator for holding an Algerian flag. A hundred Frenchmen died that day, in the ensuing chaos, and between 5,000 and 15,000 Muslims died in the bloody repression that followed. Judge Louis Vaillant, Camus's inspiration for the examining magistrate in *L'Étranger* who brandishes a crucifix at Meursault, was killed by a mob on the streets of Sétif. A socialist mayor and a Communist also died—moderates in a new world of struggle with no place for moderation. While Camus's judge and his silver crucifix remain frozen in the late 1930s, the real Judge Vaillant could not stop the motion of history.[5]

Identifying the sociological underpinnings of Camus's story and understanding the everyday life of Algerian Arabs in 1930 and 1940 are complex affairs. Reports on "natives" filed regularly with the French administration in Algeria during World War II jolt us with a vision of the situations Camus was reversing, and abstracting. Zéralda, a beach outside Algiers, was the site of one of the worst tragedies of the war years. The event was reported, but only in brief, in the first week of August 1942, when most Europeans in Algeria, including Camus, were vacationing far from the cities.[6]

The Zéralda round-up combines the murderous dehumanizing hatred of Vichy and colonialism. The mayor of the town, a wounded World War I veteran and retired postal worker, put a sign on the local beach in the summer of 1942: "Arabs and Jews are not allowed." Next to it was the sign that had always been there: "Horses and Dogs are not allowed." The beach at Zéralda became a painful symbol. Muslim youth invaded the forbidden territory, damaging property and robbing some of the "cabanons"—the little wooden changing cabins that figure in *The Stranger*. The mayor organized a round-up of all the Arabs he could find on the beach and throughout the sur-rounding countryside, using police, civilians armed with hunting rifles, and the "gardes-champêtres"—the equivalent of local sheriffs. Forty Muslim men were thrown into a cell so small they couldn't breathe and were left there overnight. By morning twenty-five of them were dead; the other fifteen barely survived. They had never been asked their names.

In Orléansville, at dawn on July 8, 1942, a European chased after an Arab he had spotted near his house; he assumed the Arab was try-ing to rob him, so he fired several shots and killed him. The police released the European pending an investigation, and the Muslim population of the city was outraged. This real Meursault got away with murder.[7]

·

There is such a thing as a zeitgeist, a spirit of the times. Maybe our current zeitgeist amounts to impatience with talk of the "absent" Arab, and a wish to describe his reality and tell his story. An Alge-rian novelist named Kamel Daoud has given a name and a life to that Arab, to his brother and his mother, in a novel called *The Meursault Investigation*.[8]

The unlikely hero of Daoud's *The Meursault Investigation* is Harun, who tells his bitter tale in the Titanic Bar in downtown Oran. He is the brother of an Arab who was murdered in a well-known book, a masterpiece of modern literature that never bothers to give the vic-tim a name. Harun is furious that his brother was murdered, and just as furious that he was denied his own story. In the French-language editions of the novel, (published in 2013 in Algeria and 2014 in France) the Arab killed by Meursault is named Moussa, a name that delicately echoes Meursault. The English translator of *The Meursault Investigation*, John Cullen, has followed English rather than French rules for transliteration from the Arabic, and changed the spelling of "Moussa" to "Musa," which is closer to Ca*mus* than to "Meursault."[9] There is a lot in a name! And this is not the first name change that

The Meursault Investigation has undergone in its travels from Algeria, to France, to the United States.

In the first, Algerian, edition of the novel (2013), Harun calls the man who killed his brother "Albert Meursault." Daoud did this for a reason in Algeria. He wanted to mock a literary climate where people have always confused Meursault, who killed an Arab in a book, with the author of that book, Albert Camus, considered guilty because he did not support the Algerian Front de Libération Nationale in the 1950s. What better way than this absurd moniker, "Albert Meursault," to make the point that Camus is still on trial in Algeria for his intentions—hostage to a fatal confusion of author and character?

When *The Meursault Investigation* was reissued by a publisher in France in 2014, "Albert Meursault" was changed simply to "Meursault." Camus's heirs had the same discomfort over the invention of an "Albert Meursault" that Francine Camus had had in the 1960s in her negotiations with Visconti. They did not want author and work conflated. French law gives Daoud the right to represent Camus the real person, but he cannot appropriate a literary character as his own. What he has done instead is ingenious: he has shuffled the cards, combining the character and the function of the writer, without ever mentioning Camus by name.[10] By changing the name of Meursault's victim from *Moussa* to *Musa*, Cullen has put Meursault's victim's name inside Camus's name (Ca*mus*/*Mus*a)—a critical intervention that distinguishes this translation from the original, yet seems endemic to the nature of this book, where names and identities are so slippery.

"An overwhelming book, like a sun in a box," Harun's girlfriend, a researcher, calls the novel that recounts Musa's murder at the hands of Meursault.[11] It doesn't take Daoud many adjustments to transpose the Belcourt setting of the 1930s to Algeria after independence: Meursault gets bored on Sunday; the narrator Harun gets bored on Friday; Meursault's neighbor Salamano won't stop yelling at his dog; Harun's neighbor drives him crazy with his night-long recitations of the Koran. The Algerians in *The Stranger* watch the Europeans silently; in *The Meursault Investigation*, the *Roumi* (Europeans) return to Algeria and wander in silence "trying to find a street, or a house, or a tree with initials carved in its trunk."[12]

Harun hates both Meursault, the man who killed his brother, and the man who left his brother's name out of the story—character and murderer are one and the same. He suspects that Meursault is still alive, as though, at the end of *The Stranger*, the narrator had managed to avoid the guillotine, and wrote a book instead.

Daoud has rejected some aspects of *The Stranger* and embraced others. There is no flat narrative voice. Daoud writes in the first person, but his Harun is much closer to Clamence, the angry narrator of Camus's novel *The Fall*, than to Meursault. *The Meursault Investigation* is the same length as Camus's *The Stranger* (33,000 words), and in the perfect middle of the story, Daoud places a murder, just as Camus did before him. Harun, urged on by his bereaved mother, kills a European named Joseph Larquais, who had gone into hiding in a European farmhouse during the battle for the liberation of Algieria. "Larquais," a typical French name with the faintest echos of "laquais" (a lackey), and "largué" (dumped or abandoned), is a good name for a victim. After the murder Harun is arrested and confronted with a ridiculous state bureaucracy—just as Meursault was before him. A colonel scolds him because he killed Larquais after July 4, 1962, the day of Algerian national independence. He could have been a triumphant revolutionary hero if he had killed the *Roumi* only a few days earlier, during the war. Instead he is a banal murderer.

Kamel Daoud, an editorialist for an Oran daily newspaper, is an analyst of Algerian society and is familiar with its contradictions and its hypocrisies. He has been a constant critic of a country trapped in a time warp, unable to move beyond worship of past revolutionary glory and a religious conformism that refuses difference. But *The Meursault Investigation* is a literary text, not a political pamphlet. Harun might sometimes sound like Clamence in *The Fall*, but he shares plenty of verbal tics with Meursault that are signs of weary nihilism ("That meant nothing to me"; "I didn't see what difference that made").[13] Lyrical anger and searing social analysis make for the particular alchemy of *The Meursault Investigation*. Daoud's novel is entirely different from Camus's and yet always aware of that difference.

By the end of the novel, Harun's rage against Meursault has transformed itself into empathy and a near-brotherly identification. After all, they are both murderers, both victims of the absurd. One has killed an Arab, the other a European, and both were indicted by foolish authorities. Harun turns his rage to the city of Algiers, which he despises as much as Camus despised Oran, and to the mosques and the imams and the broken ideals of the Algerian Revolution. Now an old man, Harun cries out: "There have certainly been moments when I had a terrible urge to shout out to the world that I was Musa's brother and that we, Mama and I, were the only genuine heroes of that famous story, but who would believe us? Who? What evidence could we offer? Two initials and a novel where no given name appears?"[14]

Musa's name appears a hundred times in the novel. But naming him doesn't help Harun picture him, beyond his blue overalls and espadrilles. He was only seven when his brother died, and he doesn't remember much. So in the end, Harun starts to call everyone Musa—the bartender, the guy in the back of the bar, and the thousands of Musas strolling along the beaches.

Epilogue

L'Écho d'Oran

If, in his fiction, Daoud has recovered Musa and Meursault from the ruins of history, what is left for nonfiction to do? I was still looking for an Arab. He wasn't a symbol or an example of anything. He was an individual—a man who got in trouble on the beach in the summer of 1939. I was looking for him with the tools I had, as a researcher, a traveler, an outsider.

On my first trip to Oran in the summer of 2014 I met briefly with Kamel Daoud. *The Meursault Investigation* had been on the syllabus of the seminar I offered at Yale on Camus and the Algerian question the previous spring, before the novel was published in France. It took us months to locate a few copies of the Algerian edition from a French bookstore. Since then, *The Meursault Investigation* had made its way from Algeria to France, with a French edition and a US translation under way, and Daoud was on the verge of international fame. His novel had challenged me to think about the missing person at the heart of Camus's novel, and as we spoke, he made a remark in passing I haven't stopped thinking about since: "We don't read *The Stranger* the same way as Americans, French, Algerians," he said. Or as students, teachers, writers, critics, historians, he might have added. "We each have our 'lecture fantasmée,'" our reading fantasy.[1]

.

In the art of fiction, a source is only the beginning, the spark of invention. But it is worth returning to the story the Bensoussan brothers recounted to Olivier Todd for a simple reason: the Arab in the story about Bouisseville beach has come down to us as a cipher, as nameless and faceless as Camus's Arab in *The Stranger*.[2]

For two years, I had traveled to the places in France and Algeria connected to *The Stranger*: I had walked down the former rue de Lyon in Algiers, past Camus's childhood home. With photographer Kays Djilali, I climbed the steep Chemin Sidi Brahim, knocking on doors until we found the House Above the World, now the home of three generations of Kabyle women who speak neither French nor Arabic. With Father Guillaume Michel from the Glycines Study Center in Algiers, I drove out to gold and blue vistas of Tipasa. In Paris, I stood in the dreary spot on the hill of Montmartre where Camus wrote in solitude.

Oran was my last stop. I toured the city thanks to Abdeslem Abdelhak, one of the founders of Bel Horizon, an independent association working to promote an understanding of every phase, and every ethnicity, involved in Oran's long history. Abdel knew Camus's habits and movements and writing about Oran inside out, and he could show me every street, café, and restaurant Camus had frequented, and quote him from memory. We walked past the restaurant that had once been an art gallery run by Camus's friends, and through the old Jewish neighborhood past the synagogue. We stopped to look at a few of the buildings where Camus tutored Jewish students who had been expelled from their public schools. We stopped for a drink at the Titanic Bar, the setting for *The Meursault Investigation*. In a tiny shop across from the Faure apartment where Camus put the finishing touches on his novel, Abdel introduced me to *calentica*, the baked chickpea pie sprinkled with cumin seeds that has been a favorite snack in Oran since the Spanish conquest—it's a great protein boost for a walker in the city that Camus dubbed "The Chicago of our Absurd Europe."[3] As we ate, he told me about the Abbé Lambert, the defrocked priest turned fascist populist mayor who had promised to make water flow in the streets of Oran and who, in the 1930s, veered in a matter of months from philo- to anti-Semitism. Camus hated living in Lambert's city. On a side street,

Abdel showed me the offices of *El Djoumhouria* (The Republic), the Arab language paper that had once housed the right-wing daily *L'Écho d'Oran*. He arranged with the front desk for me to return the next day to work in their archives.

I was thinking about them all—Raoul and Edgar Bensoussan, Raymond Sintès, Meursault, the unnamed Arab—on my last morning in Oran, as I walked three flights up intricately tiled steps to a room where the bound pages of the 1930s issues of *L'Écho d'Oran* were spread on wide tables, far easier to read than microfilm would have been. I began to read from 1939, Camus's last summer working at *Alger-Républican*, when he traveled regularly to Oran to visit Francine Faure. In the July 31 issue, a title jumped out at me. "A Brawl on the Beach in Bouisseville." The article was short, but full of detail, and to my astonishment, it mentioned both Raoul Bensoussan and the "native" in the fight. Raoul Bensoussan, an auto mechanic, had come out from the city on a motorboat with his wife, his brother Edgar, and a friend:

> The young people were having fun when two natives, doubtless in a state of intoxication, picked a fight with Monsieur Bensoussan and his companions. First insults, then blows rained down, with fists and then a knife. Monsieur Bensoussan was rather badly injured, stabbed twice with a fixed blade knife that wounded his left bicep and his right cheek. The attack was carried out by a certain Kaddour Betouil, age 19, living in Aïn-el-Turck, with his parents. He was restrained and arrested by the Republican Guard Dubois and the gendarme Berger who were keeping watch on the road and came quickly as soon as they learned of the fight. The second aggressor fled but an alert is out and he will soon be arrested. In the altercation, Kaddour Betouil received various blows to his eyebrow and his head.

On August 3, a follow-up snippet reported that Kaddour Betouil had been placed in detention.[4]

So there it was, the name of the man who had scuffled with

Camus's friends—Kaddour Betouil, nineteen years old, from Aïn-el-Turck. If the Bensoussans hadn't learned the name from the police, they would have seen it in the newspaper. Yet the name was not part of the Bensoussans' story to Todd, and was therefore absent in Todd's biography of Camus.

The attitude conveyed in the article was typical for colonial Algeria. Raoul Bensoussan enjoyed the benefits of French nationality—he was "Monsieur." The "native" was "a certain Kaddour Betouil," assumed to be intoxicated. There were enough of these incidents that the Oran newspaper had a regular column in its back pages called "Attacks."

It was easier than I expected to take the next step. I was in luck, because Abdeslem Abdelhak, my guide, happened to live in Aïn-el-Turck. He recognized the name immediately and explained to me that the young man mentioned in the article came from a leading local family. A few weeks after my departure, he made contact with them. Kaddour had died in 2002, but his brother and sister were still living in Aïn-el-Turck.[5] The family name was actually Touil, not Betouil, as *L'Écho d'Oran* had written. The French would add a "Ben" or a "Be" to Arab and Jewish names arbitrarily, since Hebrew and Arabic share the prefix meaning "the son of"—it was a way both of marking and disregarding the names of the "others." Through his wife's colleague at a local school, Abdel Abdelhak reached out to the Touils. At Bel Horizon he is in the business of finding missing people, reconnecting French pied noirs with lost Algerian friends and places, and his gesture on my behalf was not unlike the reunions and visits he organizes every week, as more and more French Algerians return to a once-familiar place after thirty, forty, fifty years' absence.

I returned to Algeria in October. Abdel Abdelhak and I drove out from Oran above the coast road, along a gash in the thick cliffs, then down into the village of Aïn-el-Turck.[6] We stopped at a place where you could see all the way to Bouisseville beach. A spout of fresh water emerged from the rock, a gift from the natural springs that gave the town its name—Aïn-el-Turck, or Fountain of the Turks—

and we waited as a villager filled his plastic bottle. Then we drank from the cool, clean source.

That fountain was my introduction to an Algerian beach town of the 1930s, to the sun and sand in which Camus grew his novel. By 1939, Aïn-el-Turck was still the year-round residence of a few native families and had become a popular weekend resort town for Europeans like Camus, who enjoyed the nearby beaches. The rituals of its European society weren't much different from those of Deauville or Arcachon. In its smaller native society were two prominent families, the Touils and the Boukhatems. The Touils had settled in Aïn-el-Turck back in 1805, during Turkish rule. The Boukhatems traced their ancestry back to men who helped the French vanquish the Turks in 1830. From 1918 through his death in 1942, Bahari Boukhatem had been the village caïd, the local official appointed by the French to keep the natives in line. (The French had reinstituted this old tribal functionary for their own administrative purposes.)[7] Bahari Boukhatem collected taxes, watched over the morality of the villagers, and settled disputes. And his disapproving gaze fell often upon the Touils, who owned the land next to his. Tension between the two families was constant, and in 1935, the caïd filed a complaint with the mayor, who reported to the prefect, who reported to the state prosecutor, that Kaddour Touil's father was threatening to kill him.

·

Kaddour's surviving brother, Djilali Touil, and his wife, daughter, and sister were surprised that an American wanted to see them for her research on Albert Camus, but they had accepted my request with good humor and welcomed me into their home with mint tea and a tray of the sweet, delicate cakes, home-baked, that I had only seen in bakeries.

The Touils' apartment complex is built on the site of the former Villa Emerat, the old Spanish farm where an ailing Camus had vacationed with his friends in August 1942 as he waited for permission to travel to mainland France for tuberculosis treatments.

Kaddour Touil had no qualms about venturing onto a European

beach at Bouisseville that hot July day in 1939. He was perfectly at home there, and always had been. His father was a well-to-do man by village standards, the father of twelve children, eight daughters and four sons. Kaddour, who had earned the certificate marking the end of primary school, helped with his father's business and spoke four languages: French, dialectical Arabic, Spanish (Spaniards were the leading European ethnicity of the Oran region), and Berber, useful with the recent group of Moroccan immigrants who lived in little more than shacks down the road from the Touils' brick villa. There were very few native families in Aïn-el-Turck, and, as Kaddour's sister put it "Kaddour only liked to step out with the Europeans," who flocked to the beach town on Saturdays. Kaddour Touil had a French girlfriend named Suzy, but Suzy's parents wouldn't let her marry him. He was devilishly handsome and, as his brother and sister remember him, "hot-blooded." Kaddour's surviving sister Kheïra, radiant in a white silk gown at ninety-five years old and addressing me in formal, elegant French, remembered that Kaddour spoke in a bark that made people think he was coming after them. He drank, and he was always getting into fights. But he was a good brother, loyal to a fault. She didn't remember that day on the beach, but clearly what happened was nothing special.

Raoul and Edgar Bensoussan, Jews from Oran whose father owned a furniture store, Palace Meubles, were sporting types — Raoul was known for driving a run-down Bugatti sports car to high school. Like most youths in Oran, the Bensoussan boys were wild about boxing and not adverse to a good fight, or "castagne," as the locals liked to say. Abdeslem Abdelhak, imagining the confrontation of Raoul Bensoussan and Kaddour Touil, summed it up pretty well: "Two young roosters on the beach."

·

If Camus was in fact inspired by the brawl between Bensoussan and Touil, what he did with that fight on the beach changed it into a mythical scene that would endure in literary history as one of the great esthetic achievements of the twentieth-century novel — a sense of heat and sweat so elemental that when Meursault tells an examining magistrate that the sun made him kill, the reader understands exactly what he means.

As he was contemplating the novel in the summer of 1939, Camus registered a powerful image: "On the beach: the man, his arms in a cross, crucified in the sun."[8] That man on the beach could be the Arab who is killed in the sun, or he could be the European who kills him and is sentenced to die in turn. But in his preface to the 1955 French edition of the novel designed for American students, Camus came down clearly on one side: he wanted to portray *Meursault* as "the only Christ we deserve." As he was writing, the Arab died, fell away, and disappeared.

·

After that July day in 1939, the forces of history propelled Albert Camus, the Bensoussan brothers, and Kaddour Touil in various directions, but strangely, Kaddour Touil and Albert Camus took parallel paths.

Kaddour Touil, like Camus, was ineligible for military service because of illness.[9] Soon after the brawl at Bouisseville, he was imprisoned for the rape of a young Moroccan immigrant girl who lived not far from the Touil villa. Djilali Touil and his sister don't know whether the rape charge meant use of force or whether he had taken her virginity in a consensual affair, which also counted as a crime. The Touil parents tried to save the situation by arranging a marriage, but Caïd Boukhatem would not give his approval, and he reported Kaddour to the French authorities. Kaddour was in the middle of serving his prison sentence when the longstanding feud with the Boukhatems came to a head. A younger Touil brother assassinated Caïd Boukhatem over a land dispute—knifed him in the back on the streets of Aïn-el-Turck. Their father tried to take the blame to save his son, to no avail. Kaddour's brother spent a few months languishing in prison, awaiting trial, then died behind bars. The official cause of death given to his family was typhus, the disease that inspired *The Plague*.[10] Unlike his brother, Kaddour Touil survived his prison sentence, but he contracted tuberculosis during his detention. After serving several years of his sentence, he was able to travel to Aix-les-Bains in the Haute Savoie (Alps) for treatment.

Camus, too, left Algeria in 1942 for his treatments in the Massif Central. Before the advent of antibiotics, a combination of mountain air and artificially collapsed lungs was the medical protocol that he and Kaddour Touil would have shared. Kaddour Touil married his French nurse and the couple returned to Aïn-el-Turck in 1954. He became a prominent businessman and shopkeeper with his own bar, the Copa Cabana.

That no one in Aïn-el-Turck remembers the day that the Bensoussan brothers fought with Kaddour Touil at Bouisseville is not in the least surprising. The dramatic assassination of the caïd by a Touil brother and, to a lesser extent, Kaddour Touil's long imprisonment on charges of rape, overshadowed what was in fact an ordinary event in those years, a few young men fighting on the sand on a sunny day. It could have ended in murder, but it didn't. The brawl is memorable only because of the way Camus drew upon it in fiction.

Still, there is something very satisfying about recovering this real man, Kaddour Touil, from the symbolic weight of Camus's novel The Arab on the beach in 1939 had a name. He spoke four languages and he had a French girlfriend.[11] He carried a knife and used it. Like Camus he was tubercular and exempt from military service. The two men didn't cross paths in a hospital ward in France; they were separated by the Rhone River and their dates don't quite align. But they might have. My search for *The Stranger* ends with this fantasy of reconciliation—Kaddour Touil and Albert Camus in their respective mountain clinics, healing.

Cassis, December 1, 2014

Acknowledgments

I LOOKED FOR *THE STRANGER* in libraries, in archives, in neighborhoods on three continents, and I had a lot of expert help at every stop. At Yale's Sterling Library, Benjamin Mappin-Kasirer did superb work on Algerian murder trials in the *Alger-Républicain* microfilms. Peter Leonard, director of Yale's Digital Humanities Lab, introduced me to new tools for exploring Camus's style and influences. Michael Printy found treasures in the Sterling Library stacks. At Yale's Beinecke Rare Book and Manuscript Library, Timothy Young shared knowledge of the library's extraordinary Camus collections and taught me to read the distinctive markings of a first edition. Kevin Repp introduced me to a typescript, heretofore unknown to Camus scholars, of the 1946 lecture "Crise de l'homme." He spoke to my classes with wit and erudition about the Beinecke manuscript of *Le Mythe de Sisyphe*. Laura Claridge, the biographer of Blanche Knopf, generously responded to queries. Anne Quinney, a brilliant Camus scholar, corresponded with me while she was working at the Harry Ransom Center at the University of Texas on the Knopf-Camus correspondence. I am grateful to Elizabeth Garver, who made available to me the Harry Ransom Center's rich and varied collection of material related to *The Stranger* from the Knopf and Bradley Agency collections. My thanks go to Karla Nielson at the Columbia University Rare Book and Manuscript Library, which houses the archive of Pantheon Books. Angela Waarala at the University of Illinois enabled me to scan a rare copy of Pierre Vrillon's beautiful 1940s map of Algiers. Yvonne Boyer from Vanderbilt provided scans of the books Camus dedicated to Pascal Pia, which are part of the Pascal Pia collection at Vanderbilt's W. T. Bandy Center. Isabelle Richefort, director of the archives of the French Ministry for Foreign Affairs, and archivist Elodie Monserand made available the files on Camus's 1946 French government–sponsored trip to the United States. I'm grateful to Laurence Marie, head of the book department at the Cultural Services of the French Embassy in New York, for her support in obtaining access to these archives, in preparation for our commemorative roundtable on Camus's 1946 visit to new York. The lecture course on the Modern French Novel, which gave me the chance to speak about *The Stranger* and *The Plague* and benefit from the insights of my co-teacher Maurice Samuels, has been one of the highlights of scholarly life at Yale. In the French Department front office, I am grateful for the tremendous support of Agnes Bolton, from the grant-writing to the proofreading phases of production.

In Lourmarin, France, Catherine Camus and her assistants Alexandre Alajbegovic and Béatrice Vaillant were endlessly patient with my stream of questions about *The Stranger*. It was a pleasure and a privilege to work with them. At the Centre de Documentation Camus at the Bibliothèque Méjanes in Aix-en-Provence, Marcelle Mahasella guided me expertly as I learned to read the Camus manuscripts; I benefited from the depth of her knowledge at every phase. I learned a great deal about Camus and Malraux from Sophie Doudet, editor of their correspondence. Conversations about Camus with Joël Calmettes, writer of three documentary films about Camus, and with David Oelhoffen, writer and director of *Far from Men*, were inspiring, as was my work on Camus with John Palatella, book editor at the *Nation*, and John Kulka, the editor at Harvard University Press who guided my edition of *Algerian Chronicles* in Arthur Goldhammer's beautiful translation.

At the Camargo Foundation in Cassis, France, in the fall of 2014, I worked day and night on the manuscript for two months, benefiting from the support and intellectual camaraderie of Natalka Bilocerkivec, Lia Brozgal, Felix de la Concha, John Gibson, Lauren du Graf (title brainstorming in the library), Naomi Jackson, and Camargo's director, Julie Chenot.

At the Archives d'Outre Mer in nearby Aix-en-Provence, Daniel Hick enabled me to navigate an exceedingly complex set of documents on colonial Algeria.

In Paris, André Abbou, a leading specialist in *L'Étranger* manuscripts, answered my many questions with patience and generosity. Philippe Vaney, Camus scholar and an expert on the history of Camus's lecture on "The Human Crisis," generously shared his scholarship.

In Algeria, Père Guillaume Michel, the director of the Centre d'Études "Les Glycines," gave me the best possible introduction to intellectual life in the city through the vibrant community for study and exchange he creates. I am grateful for the opportunity to discuss work in progress with an interdisciplinary community of scholars and artists including Andrew Bellisari, Delia Dunlap, Jill Jarvis, Elisabeth Leuvrey, Elisabeth Perego, and Corbin Treacy. In Oran, Robert Parks, whose Algerian branch of the American Institute for Maghrib Studies (AIMS) has assisted the research of close to five hundred international scholars, was helpful on many fronts.

Photographer Kays Djilali accompanied me on photographic treks in Algiers and Oran, taking beautiful pictures of the traces of Camus's life and work and advancing my research in countless ways. In Oran, Abdeslem Abdelhak of Bel Horizon was a master teacher as well as a guide. Malika Rahal, historian of colonial and postcolonial Algerian history at the Institut d'histoire du temps présent, was a specially valued interlocutor. Inspiration came as well from Kamel Daoud, author of *The Meursault Investigation*, from writers Boualem Sansaal and Salim Bachi, discerning readers of Camus, and from Sofiane Hadjaj and Selma Hallal, editors at the Éditions Barzakh, who are transforming literary publishing in Algeria.

I was fortunate to have the opportunity to present work in progress from *Looking for the Stranger* at Yale's Whitney Humanities Center; at the Camargo Foundation; at the Carolina Seminars; at the National Humanities Center (with special thanks to my friends Don Reid and Lloyd Kramer); at Case Western Reserve, where I was honored to speak in memory of Walter Strauss; at the Winthrop King Institute for French Studies at Florida State University; at the Division of Literatures, Cultures, and Languages, Stanford University; at the University of New Mexico, at a conference on "Centennial Filiations" organized by Rajeshwari Vallury in memory of Philip Watts; and at a work-in-progress colloquium with Alice Conklin and Leonard Smith at the Glycines in Algiers.

I am grateful to the graduate and undergraduate students in my spring 2014 seminar on Camus and the Algerian Question: Jennifer Carr, Catherine Chiabaut, Jessica Kasje, Katherine Kinnaird, Indrani Krishnan-Lukomski, Benjamin Mappin-Kasirer, Jake Nelson, Robyn Pront, Sean Strader, and John Sununu, and to the students, too numerous to name, in my undergraduate courses on "Camus and the Postwar Era" in Spring 2010 and Spring 2012. I benefited greatly from advising Andrew Giambrone, Henry Grabar, and Chris Merriman, whose brilliant senior essays touched on Algerian history and on Camus's early education. I am grateful to Julie Elsky for sharing her research on the Triolet–Camus correspondence, and to Mary Anne Lewis, teaching fellow in my 2012 Camus undergraduate course. Historians Bruno Cabanes, Henry Rousso, and Patrick Weil, lent their expert knowledge of France at war.

Support for my research in France and Algeria was provided by the Camargo Foundation in Cassis France, by the Griswold Fund of the Whitney Humanities Center, and by the MacMillan Faculty research grant at Yale and additional funds for research generously administered by the MacMillan Center for International and Area Studies. The Florence Gould Foundation has granted a generous translation subvention for the French edition in preparation at the Éditions Gallimard. I am grateful to the Yale University Provost and Dean's Office for providing me with a semester of leave from teaching that enabled me to complete the research for my book. Special thanks go as always to Deputy Provost and Dean of Faculty Affairs Emily Bakemeier for her support.

At the Rusoff Agency, Marly Rusoff and Michael Radulescu have accompanied me in this project since the very first draft of a proposal.

Laurel Goldman and her Tuesday-night writing workshop— Chrys Bullard, Ken Calhoun, Alex Charns, Linda Finigan, Danny Johnson, David Halperin, Kathleen O'Keeffe, and Martha Pentecost—listened to the very first chapters and then to the very last, giving me, each time, a sense of what was working and what wasn't yet. I benefited greatly from Evelyne Bloch-Dano's keen understanding of biography and narrative structure. Stéphan Alamowitch, my editor at *Contreligne* in Paris, annotated the entire manuscript. I am grateful to him for so many insights and wise suggestions, and for his keen sense of history. Poet and translator Laura Marris, my research assistant, improved every page of this book with her fine sense of the language. She gave the notes and bibliography their proper form, and accompanied me through countless edits. Four readers vetted a first full draft of the book for the University of Chicago Press: Raymond Gay-Crosier, the editor of Camus's complete works, one of the foremost Camus scholars in the world; Michael Gorra, esteemed critic and "biographer" of Henry James's *Portrait of a Lady*; David Carroll, whose book *Camus the Algerian* has had such a huge impact on Camus studies; and a fourth anonymous reader who I hope will discover my debt to his or her suggestions in these pages. Lia Brozgal and Maurice Samuels provided valuable comments on the penultimate draft.

At Gallimard, Alban Cerisier, an expert on the publishing history of *The Stranger*, archivist Eric Legendre, Françoise d'Avout and Blandine Chaumeil, Géraldine Blanc, and Blanche Cerquiglini were trusted interlocutors. Eric Vigne, my French editor, brings his discernment and wit to the French edition. I feel very lucky to be working once again with Patrick Hersant, a superb translator.

At the University of Chicago Press, Levi Stahl, promotions director, made crucial suggestions on an early manuscript; I am grateful for his literary acumen. It is a pleasure to work once again with Anita Samen, whose kindness and high standards make the copy-editing process rewarding. Randy Petilos was my guide for all issues of rights and illustrations. My deepest thanks go once again to Alan Thomas, my editor since 1993, for giving me the tough and generous criticism, page by page, that makes me want to reach higher.

I am grateful to the close friends and family, whose support sustained me: they are in Minnesota, in Manhattan and Brooklyn, in Durham, North Carolina, in Guilford, Connecticut, in Tréguier, and in Paris.

Finally, I thank Roger Grenier, my literary advisor and mentor for twenty years. He read every chapter, answered hundreds of questions, and opened his archives, sharing his mastery of Camus's thought and his knowledge of the man. He gave me the magical impression of traveling with him in Camus's world.

For permission to consult and quote unpublished material, I am grateful to Jean-Claude Barat, Catherine Camus, Michel Dorget, Françoise Mutin de Fréminville, Alice L. Knopf, Florence Malraux, the Harry Ransom Center at the University of Texas at Austin, and Éditions Gallimard.

I have incurred a significant debt to the Camus scholars who have preceded me, and to the many insightful students and colleagues who challenge and delight me. Any errors that remain are entirely of my own making.

Notes

Prologue

1   Critics have found many meanings inside the name Meursault: *meur* (death), *mer* (sea), *mère* (mother), and *sol* (sun).

2   On the colonial question, see Edward Said, "Representing the Colonized: Anthropology's Interlocutors," *Critical Inquiry* 15, no. 2 (Winter 1989):223, and the differently nuanced *Culture and Imperialism* (New York: Knopf, 1993), 185; and later, David Carroll, *Camus the Algerian: Colonialism, Terrorism, Justice* (New York: Columbia University Press, 2007). On *The Stranger* as a primer of existentialism, there is a vast literature. See, for example, Frantz Favre, "*L'Étranger* and Metaphysical Anxiety," in *Camus's L'Étranger: Fifty Years On*, ed. Adele King (London: Palgrave Macmillan, 1992). On Camus as a moralist rather than an existentialist, and on "a Hemingway rewrite of Kafka" see Jean-Paul Sartre's "Explication de *L'Étranger*," discussed in chapter 20.

3   Yosei Matsumoto, "Le Processus d'élaboration de *L'Étranger*," *Études camusiennes: Société japonaise des Études camusiennes* 12 (2015): 72–86, which I discovered to my delight as this book was going to press, contains an excellent summary of Camus's writings—correspondence, notebooks, manuscripts— that allows Matsumoto to track Camus's writing process.

4   Roland Barthes credits *The Stranger* with initiating a new "transparent form of speech": *Writing Degree Zero*, trans. Annette Lavers and Colin Smith (New York: Hill & Wang, 1968), 82. Franco Moretti's writing about literary evolution is wonderfully suggestive: *Graphs, Maps, Trees: Abstract Models for Literary History* (London: Verso, 2005): forms "change by always *diverging* from one another" (69); "a new species . . . arising when a population migrates into a new homeland, and must quickly change in order to survive" (90).

5   Michael Gorra, *Portrait of a Novel: Henry James and the Making of an American Masterpiece* (New York: Liveright), 2013.

6   Much later, when I had finished the first draft of this book, the critic Ann Jefferson directed me to a fascinating antique. In 1924, a French writer named Pierre Audiat published *La Biographie de l'œuvre littéraire* (the biog-

raphy of the literary work). Ninety years ago, Audiat was already weary of conventional biography, which considers the work simply as a "mirror" of the writer's life. He also wanted to get beyond the kind of criticism interested only in passing judgment. He argued that the task of a biographer of a work is to seek out privileged moments and artistic impulses during the process of the creation and see what those moments produce. What experiences, what teachers, what other books, what forces of history make a book what it is? And after it was born, how do its first readers understand it? See Pierre Audiat, *La Biographie de l'œuvre littéraire: esquisse d'une méthode critique* (Paris: Champion, 1924). For a discussion of Audiat and his influence on phenomenological criticism, see Ann Jefferson, *Biography and the Question of Literature* (Oxford: Oxford University Press, 2007).

7   Lloyd Kramer, professor of French history at the University of North Carolina, Chapel Hill, commenting on a discussion of my work in progress, French History and Culture Carolina Seminar, National Humanities Center, Research Triangle Park, North Carolina, April 26, 2015.

8   The figure 10.3 million copies represents the French editions (*Les Échos*, March 4, 2011, 8). In recent years, sales of *L'Étranger* have been running neck and neck with *Le Petit Prince*. Figures including paperback sales from 2010, quoted in *Gallimard: un siècle d'édition 1911–2011*, ed. Alban Cerisier and Pascal Fouché (Paris: Éditions Gallimard/Bibliothèque nationale de France, 2011) give *Le Petit Prince*, at 13,096,000 copies, the edge over *L'Étranger*, at 10,035,000 copies. In-house sales figures for the paperback (Folio) edition of L'Étranger in November 2011 came to 6,900,000, beating out Saint-Exupéry's *Le Petit Prince* at 5,987,650. The third all-time bestseller for 2010 was Camus's *La Peste*, with 6,813,000, including paperback . (2011 figures courtesy of Roger Grenier, Éditions Gallimard). The figure of sixty translations is from Alban Cerisier, *Brève histoire illustrée de la publication de L'Étranger d'Albert Camus* (Paris: Gallimard, 2013), 12.

Chapter One

1   Albert Camus, *Carnets 1935–1948, Œuvres complètes*, ed. Jacqueline Lévi-Valensi, vol. 2, 1944–1948 (Paris: Gallimard, Bibliothèque de la Pléiade, 2006), 850; in English, *Notebooks 1935–1942*, trans. Philip Thody (New York: Knopf 1963, rpt. New York: Roman & Littlefield, 2010), 86. A photocopy of the notebook is housed in the Centre de Documentation Albert Camus, Cité du livre, Bibliothèque Méjanes, Aix-en-Provence.

2   Albert Camus to Francine Faure, October 30, 1939, quoted in Olivier Todd, *Albert Camus: Une vie* (Paris: Gallimard, 1999), 283. All subsequent page numbers refer to the French edition unless otherwise noted. Here I quote the translation by Benjamin Ivry of the substantially abridged version of Todd's book, *Albert Camus: A Life* (New York: Knopf, 1997), 88.

3   For one of the best introductions to Camus's notion of the Absurd, see the chapter entitled "Absurdity" in Robert Zaretsky's *A Life Worth Living: Albert*

Camus and the Quest for Meaning (Cambridge, MA: Harvard University Press, 2013), 11–58.

4   Jacqueline Lévi-Valensi has traced Camus's beginnings as a writer step by step in her *Albert Camus ou La Naissance d'un romancier, 1930–1942* (Paris: Gallimard, 2006). She is interested in Camus's hesitations as a fiction writer, contrasted with his precocious, authoritative voice in critical essays.

5   "Not even in the flow of prayers offered for her during the sacrifice of our redemption, with the body placed by the grave (according to local custom) before its burial—not even during those prayers did I weep." Saint Augustine, *Confessions*, trans. Garry Wills (New York: Penguin, 2012), 204.

6   See Albert Camus, "Nietzsche and Music," in *Sud*, June 1932, reprinted in *The First Camus*, ed. Paul Viallaneix, trans. Ellen Conroy Kennedy (New York: Paragon House, 1990), 138–46.

7   Camus, *Carnets 1935–1948*, *Œuvres complètes*, 2:800; in English, *Notebooks*, trans. Thody, 10, edited. Wherever I quote a previously published translation with alterations for accuracy or style, I have qualified it as "edited."

8   The speech is described in the Algerian Communist Party magazine *La lutte sociale*, July 31, 1935. See Jacqueline Lévi-Valensi, "La Condition Sociale en Algérie," in *Journalisme et politique—l'entrée dans l'Histoire, 1938–1940*, ed. André Abbou and Jacqueline Lévi-Valensi, *La Revue des Lettres Modernes: Albert Camus 5* (Paris: Lettres Modernes/Minard, 1973), 11–33.

9   See the scene in his unfinished autobiographical novel, *Le premier homme*, *Œuvres complètes*, ed. Raymond Gay-Crosier, vol. 4, 1957–1959 (Paris: Gallimard, Bibliothèque de la Pléiade, 2008), 798. In English, *The First Man*, trans. David Hapgood, (New York: Vintage, 1996), 94–95.

10 Todd, *Une vie*, 231; *A Life*, trans. Ivry, 73. He was informed of his ineligibility in October 1938, the month he joined the staff of *Alger-Républicain*

11 Todd, *Une vie*, 283, quoting letters from Camus to Francine Faure, October 29 and 30, 1939.

12 Report quoted and reproduced by Todd, ibid., 204, n.d.

13 "La mort dans l'âme," *L'envers et l'endroit*, *Œuvres complètes*, ed. Jacqueline Lévi-Valensi, vol. 1, 1931–1944 (Paris: Gallimard, Bibliothèque de la Pléiade, 2006), 57; in English, "Death in the Soul," *Lyrical and Critical Essays*, trans. Ellen Conroy Kennedy (New York: Vintage, 1970), 43.

14 Camus to Faure, October 29 and 30, 1939, quoted in Todd, *Une vie*, 293; *A Life*, trans., Ivry, 103.

15 *The Wrong Side and the Right Side* (1937) and *Nuptials* (1939), published by the Éditions Charlot in Algiers. *L'envers et l'endroit* and *Noces, Œuvres complètes*, ed. Jacqueline Lévi-Valensi, vol. 1, 1931–1944 (Paris: Gallimard, Bibliothèque de la Pléiade, 2006). Both books were reissued after World War II at Gallimard.

16 Henry de Montherlant to Camus, June 29, 1939, Centre de Documentation Albert Camus. Cité du livre. Bibliothèque Méjanes, Aix-en-Provence. In November 1938, Camus describes Montherlant as "one of the most astonishing prose writers of the century" in his "Salon de Lecture" column in *Alger-Républican, Œuvres complètes*, vol. 1, 802, and on November 22, 1938, praises

his *Images d'Alger* (ibid., 804); on February 5, 1939, he writes a positive review of Montherlant's *The September Equinox* (ibid., 817–19).

17 He described the novel to his fellow journalist Emmanuel Roblès as "L'indifferént." See Roblès's memoir, *Camus, frère de soleil* (Paris: Le Seuil, 1995), 22. On the cycles of his work, see Roger Grenier, *Albert Camus: Soleil et ombre* (Paris: Gallimard, 1987), as well as Camus's own notebooks. Other titles Camus considered were *A Free Man; A Happy Man; A Man like Others*. Albert Camus, *Théâtre, récits, nouvelles*, ed. Roger Quilliot (Paris: Gallimard, 1962), quoted in Raymond Gay-Crosier, *Literary Masterpieces*, vol. 8: *The Stranger* (Detroit: The Gale Group, 2002), 57. Quilliot describes two manuscripts: one with drawings of a sun, scaffold, etc., which sounds very much like the "fake" that Camus himself produced in 1944 (see chapter 21); and a second manuscript, part handwritten and part typed, which sounds like the manuscript now available to scholars at the Centre de Documentation Albert Camus. The second team of scholars who produced a new Pléiade edition in the 1990s under the direction of Jacqueline Lévi-Valensi, worked from this second manuscript.

Chapter Two

1 Olivier Todd, *Albert Camus: Une vie* (Paris: Gallimard, 1999), 89. In English, Olivier Todd, *Albert Camus: A Life*, trans. Benjamin Ivry (New York: Knopf, 1997), 28.

2 Yves Bourgeois, "Été 1936: le voyage en Europe centrale," *Cahier de l'Herne Camus*, ed. Raymond Gay-Crosier and Agnès Spiquel-Courdille (Paris: Éditions de l'Herne, 2013), 106.

3 According to Alain Vircondelet's vivid portrait of Simone Hié, in a section of his biography subtitled "Surrealist Muse," her nickname was Nadja. Alain Vircondelet, *Albert Camus: fils d'Alger* (Paris: Fayard, 2010), 103.

4 In 1930 Grenier returned to Algiers from mainland France. He lived in a small moorish-style villa in El Biar, with a view of the sea. In 1932 he purchased a larger villa on rue no. 9 in the same housing development where Camus lived with Simone Hié on rue no. 12. Toby Garfitt, *Jean Grenier: un écrivain et un maître* (Rennes: Éditions La Part Commune), 196, 219, 226.

5 Grenier describes his visit to young Camus in *Albert Camus: souvenirs* (Paris: Gallimard, 1968), 9–11.

6 Albert Camus, "L'Été à Alger," in *Noces, Œuvres complètes*, ed. Jacqueline Lévi-Valensi, vol. 1, 1931–1944 (Paris: Gallimard, Bibliothèque de la Pléiade, 2006), 117; translated by Ellen Conroy Kennedy as "Summer in Algiers," in *Lyrical and Critical Essays*, ed. Philip Thody (New York: Vintage, 1970), 80: "What one can fall in love with in Algiers is what everybody lives with: the sea, visible from every corner, a certain heaviness of the sunlight, the beauty of the people." The essay was written in the summer of 1937 and the following summer, after his separation.

7 Bourgeois, "Été 1936," 106.

8 According to Vircondelet, *Albert Camus: fils d'Alger*, 134.

9   Jacqueline Lévi-Valensi, *Albert Camus ou la Naissance d'un romancier* (Paris: Gallimard, 2006), 547–48, my translation.

10   "Les Voix du quartier pauvre," *Œuvres complètes* 1:77, translated by Ellen Conroy Kennedy as "Voices from the Poor Quarter," in *Youthful Writings by Albert Camus* (New York: Paragon, 1990), 245.

11   Grenier encouraged Camus to join just as he was marking his own distance from the communists. On the dangers of joining the party, see Grenier's 1935 essay "l'Intellectuel dans la société," reprinted in *Essai sur l'esprit d'orthodoxie* (Paris: Gallimard/Idées: 1967) 115–28. An artist who joins the party to escape his self-absorption, Grenier argues, is like a young girl who makes a quick marriage to escape from her family—these are unhappy unions. In Grenier's retrospective *Albert Camus: Souvenirs* (Paris: Gallimard, 1968), 37–44, he comments at length on his advice to Camus. He also quotes an August 2, 1934, letter from Camus that is not included in the published Grenier-Camus correspondence where Camus reflects on his desire to join. See also a September 15, 1951, letter from Camus to Grenier in which Camus comes close to open criticism of his mentor: "I did not understand how you could advise me to become a Communist and then yourself take a position against Communism." *Albert Camus-Jean Grenier, Correspondance 1932–1960*, ed. Marguerite Dobrenn (Paris: Gallimard, 1981), 179–80; in English, *Albert Camus and Jean Grenier Correspondence, 1932–1960*, trans. Jan F. Rigaud (Lincoln: University of Nebraska Press, 2003), 152. The best study of Jean Grenier's intellectual history is Toby Garfitt, *Jean Grenier: un écrivain et un maître* (Rennes: La Part Commune, 2010).

12   Two police reports on Camus's speeches from meetings of the Amsterdam Pleyel Committee on April 1 and April 2, 1936, are preserved in a dossier on the Communist Party in the archives of the General Government of Algeria, series GGA 7 G30, Archives Nationales d'Outre-Mer, Aix-en-Provence.

13   "La culture indigène: la nouvelle culture méditerranéenne," lecture given at the Maison de la Culture, Algiers, February 8, 1937, *Œuvres completes* 1:565–72; in English, "The New Mediterranean Culture," *Lyrical and Critical Essays*, trans. Kennedy, 189–98. On Camus's activism, see Jacqueline Lévi-Valensi, "L'engagement culturel," in *Journalisme et politique—l'entrée dans l'Histoire, 1938–1940*, ed. André Abbou and Jacqueline Lévi-Valensi, La Revue des Lettres Modernes: Albert Camus 5 (Paris: Lettres Modernes/Minard, 1972), 82–106.

14   Camus, *Carnets 1935–1948, Œuvres complètes*, ed. Jacqueline Lévi-Valensi, vol. 2, 1944–1948 (Paris: Gallimard, Bibliothèque de la Pléiade, 2006), 795; in English, *Notebooks 1935–1942*, trans. Philip Thody (New York: Knopf, 1963, rpt. New York: Rowman & Littlefield, 2010), 3, edited.

15   Camus to Grenier, August 4, 1935, *Correspondance*, 21; *Correspondence*, trans. Rigaud, 9.

16   Camus to Grenier, dated first semester, 1936, *Correspondance*, 24; *Correspondence*, trans. Rigaud, 12.

Chapter Three

1   The Parc Saint-Saens in Camus's day; now the Parc Beyrouth. Donated to the city in 1936 by Madame Janon according to some accounts; Madame Dela-noé according to others. Fichu, who owned the House Above the World, is said to have been her chauffeur, or gardener, and she gave him the house. He lived on the ground floor, Camus's friends on the second floor. On the history of the park, see *Alger: Paysage urbain et architectures 1800–2000*, ed. Jean-Louis Cohen, Nabila Oulebsin, and Youcef Kanoun (Besançon: Les Éditions de l'imprimeur, 2003), 302.

2   *La mort heureuse, Œuvres* complètes, ed. Jacqueline Lévi-Valensi, vol. 1, 1931–1944 (Paris: Gallimard, Bibliothèque de la Pléiade, 2006), 1155. Translated by Richard Howard as *A Happy Death* (New York: Knopf, 1972), 85.

3   Camus, *Carnets 1935-48, Œuvres complètes*, ed. Jacqueline Lévi-Valensi, vol. 2, 1944-1948 (Paris: Gallimard, Bibliothèque de la Pléiade, 2006). 813. Translated by Philip Thody as *Notebooks, 1935-1942* (New York: Knopf, 1963, rpt. New York: Rowman & Littlefield, 2010), 31.

4   There's a good description of the neighborhood of the House Above the World, and of a typical villa, in Jean-Jacques Delux's architectural memoir, *Alger: chronique urbaine* (Paris: Éditions Bouchène, 2001), 115.

5   *La mort heureuse, Œuvres completes* 1:1155; *A Happy Death*, trans. Howard, 84. I've used Richard Howard's translaton of "Maison devant le monde" as "house *above* the world." The other more literal translations—"the house before the world;" "the house in front of the world"—are not as resonant. From *A Happy Death*, trans. Howard, 85: "The house perched on a hilltop with a view of the bay. It was known in the neighborhood as the House of the Three Students. A steep path led up to it, beginning in olive trees and ending in olive trees. Between, a kind of landing followed by a grey wall covered with obscene figures and political slogans to encourage the winded visitor. . . . After a great deal of sweating and panting, the visitor pushed open a little blue gate, avoiding the bougainvillea tendrils, and then climbed a stairway as steep as a ladder, but drenched in a blue shade that already slaked his thirst. Rose, Claire, Catherine and the Boy called the place The House Above the World."

6   *Carnets, Œuvres complètes* 2:815, *Notebooks*, trans. Thody, 33, edited.

7   Emmanuel Roblès, "Camus, un homme nécessaire," *Cahier de l'Herne Camus*, ed. Raymond Gay-Crosier and Agnès Spiquel-Courdille (Paris: Éditions de l'Herne, 2013), 363.

8   Malraux's literary influence on Camus dates back to 1936, when Camus adapted *Days of Wrath* for his Théâtre du Travail. Todd recounts that Mal-raux sent a telegram with one word: "Joue!" (play!) to give the troupe his blessing. Olivier Todd, *Albert Camus: Une vie* (Paris: Gallimard, 1999), 164. An undated letter from Camus to his friend Claude de Fréminville suggests that the telegram may be a legend, or at least that the request to adapt went through the Société des Auteurs et Compositeurs Dramatiques rather than the timid young playwright; "I wrote a play based on *Days of Wrath*. I just have to get Malraux's permission. The SOI (SACD?) will ask him. I'd be too

timid even to have my name mentioned." Centre de Documentation Albert Camus, Cité du livre, Bibliothèque Méjanes, Aix-en-Provence.

9   *La Mort Heureuse, Œuvres complètes* 1:1196; *A Happy Death*, trans. Howard, 151.

10   Albert Camus to Jean Grenier, June 18, 1938, *Albert Camus–Jean Grenier, Correspondance 1932–1960*, ed. Marguerite Dobrenn (Paris: Gallimard, 1981), 28–32. In English, *Albert Camus and Jean Grenier Correspondence, 1932–1960*, trans. Jan F. Rigaud (Lincoln: University of Nebraska Press, 2003), 16–17, edited.

Chapter Four

1   Albert Camus, *Carnets 1935–48, Œuvres complètes*, ed. Jacqueline Lévi-Valensi, vol. 2, 1944–1948 (Paris: Gallimard, Bibliothèque de la Pléiade, 2006), 816, my translation. In English this is available as *Notebooks 1935–1942*, trans. Philip Thody (New York: Knopf, 1963, rpt. New York: Rowman & Littlefield, 2010).

2   There is no surviving letter from Grenier in response to Camus's heartfelt question about whether he should continue to write, but there is a response from Camus to Grenier's response: "Thank you for your letter. It indicates a certain number of paths to take. I will try to follow them as best I can." That letter is dated July 1938—the month when Grenier left Algiers to take a new teaching position at the Lycée Michelet in Vanves. *Albert Camus–Jean Grenier Correspondance 1932–1960*, ed. Marguerite Dobrenn (Paris: Gallimard, 1981), 32. In English, *Albert Camus and Jean Grenier Correspondence, 1932–1960*, trans. Jan F. Rigaud (Lincoln: University of Nebraska Press, 2003), 15, edited.

3   Camus, *Carnets, Œuvres complètes* 2:814; in English, *Notebooks*, trans. Thody, 33 (although he translates "La mort dans l'âme" as "Iron in the Soul").

4   Catherine Lépront's phrase about "les locataires du dessus" (the neighbors upstairs) is often cited. "Je ne distingue pas l'art de la vie: rencontre avec Catherine Lépront," (I don't distinguish art from life: a conversation with Catherine Lépront), René de Ceccaty, *Le Cercle Points: créateurs de lecteurs*, lecerclepoints.com/entretien—je-ne-distingue-pas-art-vie-rencontre-avec-catherine-3.htm, n.d.

5   Camus, *Carnets, Œuvres complètes* 2:810–11. This passage is missing in the Thody *Notebooks* translation.

6   Ibid., 814; *Notebooks*, trans. Thody, 32, edited.

7   Ibid., 816; *Notebooks*, trans. Thody, 35, edited.

8   José-Henry Lasri, *Oran Républicain*, May 23, 1937, quoted in Olivier Todd, *Albert Camus: Une vie* (Paris: Gallimard, 1999), 45; in English, *Albert Camus: A Life*, trans. Benjamin Ivry (New York: Knopf, 1997), 63.

9   Camus, *Carnets, Œuvres complètes* 2:824; *Notebooks*, trans. Thody, 45, edited.

10   Ibid., 823; *Notesbooks*, trans. Thody, 44, edited.

11   Letter to Jacques Heurgon, friend and professor of Latin at the University of Algiers. Quoted in Todd, *Une vie*, 217; *A Life*, trans. Ivry, 66. The letter is re-

produced in full in *Cahier de l'Herne Camus*, ed. Raymond Gay-Crosier and Agnès Spiquel-Courdille (Paris: Éditions de l'Herne, 2013), 162.

12 Pierre-Georges Castex, *Albert Camus et "L'Étranger"* (Paris: Corti, 1965), 19.

13 Camus, *Carnets, Œuvres complètes* 2:852, 860. *Notebooks*, trans. Thody, 89–101.

14 Ibid., 853; *Notebooks*, trans. Thody, 90.

15 Ibid., 859; *Notebooks*, trans. Thody, 99–100, edited. The original French, "Il a encore 'un sentiment pour son coït,'" resists translation. Ward translates the nearly identical line in the novel as "he 'still had sexual feelings for her.'" *The Stranger*, trans. Matthew Ward (New York: Knopf, 1988), 31.

16 Ibid., 859; *Notebooks*, trans. Thody, 100. Page 41 of the original notebook consulted at the Centre de documentation Albert Camus, Cité du Livre, Bibliothèque Méjanes, Aix-en-Provence.

17 Camus, Carnets, *Œuvres complètes* 2:862; *Notebooks*, trans. Thody, 103, edited.

18 Ibid., 856; *Notebooks*, trans. Thody, 95, edited.

19 Ibid., 863; *Notebooks*, trans. Thody, 105.

20 Ibid., 863. Since these are the same words in French as in the published novel, I use a modified version of the 1988 Matthew Ward translation of the novel (New York: Knopf, 1988) rather than the Thody translation.

21 Camus, *Carnets, Œuvres complètes* 2:877 (April 1939, written in Oran); *Notebooks*, trans. Thody, 124, edited.

22 Camus would use his hellish dissatisfaction with *A Happy Death* ten years later to create one of his most beloved characters, Joseph Grand, the municipal employee in *The Plague* who has so much trouble finding his words but vows to become an author, writing and rewriting the same first paragraph over and over. At the end of *The Plague*, Grand, who has miraculously survived the epidemic, is finally satisfied with his first paragraph: he has simply removed all the adjectives. It's tempting to conclude that Camus was winking at himself as he remembered his agony, his overblown style, and how he finally made it right. *A Happy Death* was published posthumously, in 1971.

Chapter Five

1 Olivier Todd, *Albert Camus: Une vie* (Paris: Gallimard, 1999), 219; in English, *Albert Camus: A Life*, trans. Benjamin Ivry (New York: Knopf, 1997), 81.

2 Victor Malan in *The First Man* is inspired in part by Jean Grenier. Albert Camus, *Le premier homme, Œuvres complètes*, ed. Raymond Gay-Crosier, vol. 4, 1957–1959 (Paris: Gallimard, Bibliothèque de la Pléiade, 2008), 756–57; in English, *The First Man*, trans. David Hapgood (New York: Knopf, 1995), 31–32.

3 Pia had significant experience as a journalist in Paris, in addition to his extensive literary connections to leading artists and publishers—all of which would play a role in Camus's success. See Roger Grenier, *Pascal Pia ou le droit au néant* (Paris: Galllimard, 1989).

4 Pascal Pia to André Abbou, December 1970, *Œuvres complètes*, ed. Jacque-

line Lévi-Valensi, vol. 1, 1931–1944 (Paris: Gallimard, Bibliothèque de la Pléiade, 2006), 864.

5   Albert Camus to Jean Grenier, dated end of 1938, *Albert Camus–Jean Grenier, Correspondance 1932–1960*, ed. Marguerite Dobrenn (Paris: Gallimard, 1981) 32–33; in English, *Albert Camus and Jean Grenier Correspondence*, trans. Jan F. Rigaud, (Lincoln: University of Nebraska Press, 2003), 19, edited.

6   *La mort heureuse, Œuvres complètes* 1:1157; in English, *A Happy Death*, trans. Howard, 89: "The boy was conscientiously lounging on a couch in the terrace room, a detective story in his hands."

7   *Guide Bleu* (Paris: Éditions Hachette, 1938).

8   Of those Europeans, 11 percent were Jews, French citizens by virtue of the Crémieux Decree of 1870. See Robert Tinthoin, "La démographie algérienne," *Annales de Géographie* 47 (1938): 543–46. On the construction of colonial statistics, see Kamel Kateb, *Européens, "indigènes" et Juifs en Algérie, 1830–1962* (Paris: Presses Universitaires de France, 2001). For example, the number of Europeans was exaggerated, not only because it was easier to count Europeans in the city than Muslim "natives" in sparsely populated areas, but because a story of European growth reinforced the idea that Algeria was becoming more and more French.

9   Camus supported the failed Blum Viollette legal initiative that was intended to give political rights to some 200,000 Muslim voters, a small elite. At the Communist Party cultural center, which he directed, he offered evenings of Arab culture, though few people attended. See "Manifeste des intellectuels d'Algérie en faveur du project Violette," *Œuvres complètes* 1:572–74, and Todd, *Une vie*, 190, trans. Ivry, *A Life*, 74.

10 See Joshua Schreier, *Arabs of the Jewish Faith: The Civilizing Mission in Colonial Algeria* (New Brunswick, NJ: Rutgers University Press, 2010); and on the paradoxes of Jewish citizenship in Algeria, Maurice Samuels, *The Right to Difference: French Universalism and the Jews* (Chicago: University of Chicago Press, 2016), chapter 3.

11 Subsequent references to *Alger-Républicain* and *Le Soir Républicain* are from the microfilmed collection of those newspapers, MICR D-12 and MICR D-242, Bibliothèque nationale de France (BNF); translations are my own. Many articles from the two newspapers attributed to Camus are reprinted in *Œuvres complètes* 1:575–864, and in *Cahiers Albert Camus 3: Fragments d'un combat 1938–1940, Alger-Républicain, Le Soir Républicain*, ed. Jacqueline Lévi-Valensi and André Abbou (Paris: Gallimard, 1978). Seeing the pages of the newspaper is helpful for understanding the context, the articles by Camus's colleagues, and the severity of censorship after 1939.

12 "L'Affaire Hodent: Devant le tribunal correctionnel de Tiaret," *Alger-Républicain*, 21 March 1939; for the quips by Navarro (403) and the judge (402) see *Cahiers Albert Camus 3*, 396–404. (Other articles on the Hodent trial can be found in *Œuvres complètes* 1:603.)

13 "L'innocence de Hodent," *Alger-Républicain, Œuvres complètes* 1:629.

14 Camus to Grenier, July 19, 1939, *Correspondance*, 35; *Correspondence*, trans. Rigaud, 21. Camus's last article on the trial was dated June 29.

15   21 June 1939, *Œuvres complètes* 1:672–73. Akacha then claimed to have been operating under instructions from the police.

16   "Le Christ devant les juges," in the series "L'assassinat du Muphti," *Alger-Républican*, June 24, 1939, *Œuvres complètes* 1:701–2. Camus is amused when, later in the deliberations, a clever defense lawyer refers back to that crucifix, reminding the jurors that Christ was the first victim of a judicial error.

17   "La cour criminelle reconnaissant l'innocence de Cheikh El-Okbi et d'Abbas Turqui les a acquittés," (the court, recognizing the innocence of Cheikh El-Okbi and Abbas Turqui, aquits them), *Alger-Républican*, June 29, 1939; *Œuvres complètes* 1:724.

18   *Alger-Républicain*, July 26, 1939, in *Œuvres complètes* 1:738 (quoting from the headline: The Affair of the "Arsonists" of Auribeau: Innocent men sentenced to forced labor, and their families condemned to misery "in the name of the French people").

19   "Aux Assises d'Alger: Malgré les dépositions favorables de ses employeurs et de ses camarades de travail le docker Cozzolino a été sévèrement condamné," *Alger-Républicain*, March 4, 1939.

20   "Billota knows that France is a republic, but the president's name escapes him. He has heard of Italy, but knows nothing of its form of government. Hitler, as far as he's concerned, is the emperor of Germany, etc. A more impoverished, less inquisitive mind would be hard to find, which does not prevent Billota from enjoying voting rights, but strips him of any exact notion of social obligations," *Alger-Républicain*, July 7, 1939.

Chapter Six

1   "Réflexions sur la guillotine," *Œuvres complètes*, ed. Raymond Gay-Crosier, vol. 4, 1957–1959 (Paris: Gallimard, Bibliothèque de la Pléiade, 2008), 127; in English, "Reflections on the Guillotine," in *Resistance, Rebellion, and Death*, trans. Justin O'Brien (New York, Knopf, 1960), 171.

2   The shrapnel fragment is mentioned in "Les Voix du quartier pauvre," *Œuvres complètes*, ed. Jacqueline Lévi-Valensi, vol. 1, 1931–1944 (Paris: Gallimard, Bibliothèque de la Pléiade, 2006), 77; in English, "Voices from the Poor Quarter," *Camus' Youthful Writings*, trans. Ellen Conroy Kennedy (New York: Paragon, 1990), 244, and in *Le premier homme*, *Œuvres complètes* 1:783; in English, *The First Man*, trans. David Hapgood (New York: Knopf, 1995), 72.

3   Patrice tells his story of the man condemned to death: "I see that man. He is inside me . . . He is living and breathing with me. He is afraid with me," my translation, Camus, Cahier I, *Carnets 1935–48*, *Œuvres complètes*, ed. Jacqueline Lévi-Valensi, vol. 2, 1944–1948 (Paris: Gallimard, Bibliothèque de la Pléiade, 2006), 810–11. The passage is not included in the Thody translation.

4   Justin O'Brien, a professor of French at Columbia University who would become one of Camus's primary American translators, wrote from his sabbatical in Paris just before the outbreak of war: "The Americans in Paris last summer could not fail to notice how difficult it was becoming to discuss contemporary French literature with enlightened Frenchmen, since all the

young and enthusiastic intellectuals would much prefer to talk of American literature." Justin O'Brien, "American Books and French Readers," *College English* 1 (March, 1940): 480-87. The French, he wrote, "wonder why they have not heard from James M. Cain since *Le Facteur sonne toujours deux fois* appeared."

5   James M. Cain, "The Art of Fiction," interview with David Zinsser, *The Paris Review* 73 (Spring/Summer, 1978): 117-38.

6   Harold Strauss, the *New York Times Book Review*, February 18, 1934, 8.

7   James M. Cain, *The Postman Always Rings Twice* (New York: Random House, 1934), 116; in French, James Cain, *Le Facteur sonne toujours deux fois*, trans. Sabine Berritz with a preface by Irène Némirovsky (Paris: Gallimard, 1936). There's a mistake in the French translation of the last line: "Les voilà. Le Père O'Connell dit ses prières pour m'aider"—in other words "Father O'Connell says his prayers to help me."

8   Camus's response to Jean Desternes's survey on American literature "Que pensez-vous de la littérature américaine?" *Combat*, January 17, 1947. Reprinted in *Camus à Combat*, ed. Jacqueline Lévi-Valensi (Paris: Gallimard, 2002), 645-49; in English, *Camus at Combat: Writing 1944-1947*, trans. Arthur Goldhammer (Princeton: Princeton University Press, 2006), 277-80.

9   On the two novels, see Richard Lehan, "Camus's *L'Étranger* and American Neo-Realism," *Twentieth Century Literature* 38 (1964), referring to a conversation with Frohock, and Bernard Pingaud, *L'Étranger d'Albert Camus* (Paris: Gallimad/Foliothèque, 1992), 61-63. Pia, interviewed by Pingaud, recalled that Camus read the Cain novel in 1939; Frohock told Lehan that Camus had credited Cain's novel as an influence in a private conversation. Among the earliest American reviewers to compare Cain and Camus, see Edmund Wilson, *New Yorker*, April 13, 1946, 113-14; W. M. Frohock, "Camus: Image, Influence, and Sensibility," *Yale French Studies* 4 (1949): 91-99, Germaine Brée, *Camus* (New Brunswick, NJ: Rutgers University Press, 1959), 101.

10 As argued brilliantly by Philip Watts in "Camus and Film," *Romanic Review* 105 (January–March 2014): 133-42.

11 *Le Schpountz* (illustrated screenplay), *L'Avant-scène du cinéma, spécial Pagnol* 105-6 (July–September 1970): 7-77.

12 Olivier Todd, *Albert Camus: Une vie* (Paris: Gallimard, 1999), 843; in English, *Albert Camus: A Life*, trans. Benjamin Ivry (New York: Knopf, 1997), 359— no date given for the remark. The French-Tunisian writer Albert Memmi draws the same comparison: "He [Camus] had a lot of charm, though I was a bit disappointed when I saw him: people said he was extremely handsome . . . I thought his face was too long, his mouth too big, his teeth too prominent . . . A successful Fernandel, only his eyes, witty and intelligent, made up for the rest." Albert Memmi and Victor Malka, *La terre intérieure: entretiens avec Victor Malka* (Paris: Gallimard, 1976), 159, my translation.

13 See especially the conclusion to Camus's "Misère de la Kabylie," and "l'Algérie nouvelle," in *Chroniques algériennes, Œuvres complètes* 4; in English, Camus, "Misery of Kabylia," and "The New Algeria" in *Algerian Chronicles*, ed. Alice Kaplan, trans. Arthur Goldhammer (Cambridge, MA: Harvard University Press, 2013).

14 "Misère de la Kabylie," *Œuvres complètes* 4:330; in English,"The Misery of Kabylia," trans. Goldhammer, 75. The 400 billion francs, an exaggerated figure, refers to France's huge war loans to its European allies in World War I, its loans to Tsarist Russia, repudiated by the Bolsheviks and never reimbursed, and its aid for famine relief in parts of the former Russian Empire. If you add the costs of the war itself, the figure is massively disproportionate to spending for the colonies. See Jennifer Siegel, *For Peace and Money: French and British Finance in the Service of Tsars and Commissars* (New York: Oxford University Press, 2014).

15 "Weidmann a été exécuté hier matin à Versailles," *Alger-Républicain*, June 18, 1939, includes a wire service photo of a guillotine with Weidmann's face in the upper left corner and an account of the execution; they quote Moro-Giafferi in part, but the full and more sensational quotation given here is from "Weidmann a été décapité," *L'Écho d'Alger*, June 18, 1939, 3. In his "Reflections on the Guillotine" (1957), Camus evokes a full-page illustration of the "appetizing event" published in *Paris-Soir* a few hours after the execution. "Reflexions sur la Guillotine," *Œuvres complètes* 4:131; in English, "Reflections on the Guillotine," trans. Justin O'Brien, 177.

Chapter Seven

1 Albert Camus to Jean Grenier, August 1939, *Albert Camus–Jean Grenier, Correspondance 1932–1960*, ed. Marguerite Dobrenn (Paris: Gallimard, 1981), 37; in English, *Albert Camus and Jean Grenier Correspondence*, trans. Jan F. Rigaud, (Lincoln: University of Nebraska Press, 2003), 23, edited.

2 Albert Camus, *Carnets 1935–1948*, *Œuvres complètes*, ed. Jacqueline Lévi-Valensi, vol. 2, 1944–1948 (Paris: Gallimard, Bibliothèque de la Pléiade, 2006), 883; in English, *Notebooks 1935–1942*, trans. Philip Thody (New York: Knopf, 1963, rpt. New York: Rowman & Littlefield, 2010), 136.

3 A defrocked abbot, Gabriel Lambert, was elected on the promise of bringing water to the city. From his populist origins, he veered towards the anti-Semitic right. He was replaced by a Vichy-appointed mayor in 1940. On the politics of *L'Écho d'Oran* in the 1930s, see Francis Koerner, "L'extrême droite en Oranie, 1936–1940," *Revue d'histoire moderne et contemporaine* 20:4 (October–December 1973): 568–94: "*L'Écho d'Oran* fait une propagande forcenée par l'image en faveur de l'Allemagne hitlerienne." (Through its images, *L'Écho d'Oran* published fanatic propaganda in support of Hiter's Germany.)

4 Herbert Lottman interviewed Christiane Galindo Davila and Pierre Galindo as he was preparing his 1979 biography, *Albert Camus* (Corte Madera, California: Gingko Press, 1997), 207. Olivier Todd interviewed Raoul and Loulou Bensoussan separately in 1992 as he was preparing *Albert Camus: Une vie* (Paris: Gallimard, 1999), 313–15; in English, *Albert Camus: A Life*, trans. Benjamin Ivry (New York: Knopf, 1997), 113–14.

5 Abdeslem Abdelhak, conversation with the author, Oran, December 2014.

6 Roland Dorgelès, "C'est une drôle de guerre" (it's a funny kind of war), in

Gringoire, Octobre 26, 1939, quoted by Jean-Pierre Azéma and François Bédarida, "Huit mois d'attente et d'illusion: la drôle de guerre," in *La France des années noires*, I:38 (Paris: Le Seuil/Points), 46.

7   Albert Camus to Francine Faure, October 29–30, 1939, quoted in Todd, *Une vie*, 281; *A Life*, trans. Ivry, 103.

8   "Pétrone et les ciseaux," *Le Soir-Républicain*, December 18, 1939, *Cahiers Albert Camus 3: Fragments d'un combat 1938–1940, Alger-Républicain, Le Soir Républicain*, ed. Jacqueline Lévi-Valensi and André Abbou (Paris: Gallimard, 1978), 708–10.

9   *Carnets, Œuvres complètes* 2:885–86; *Notebooks*, trans. Thody, 139, edited.

10   *Le Soir-Républicain*, October 6, 1939, in the series called "Sous les éclairages de guerre," see on Huxley, "Contre les Dictateurs Belliqueux" (against bellicose dictators), November 22 and 23, 1939; "La doctrine du national-socialisme" (National-Socialist doctrine), signed "Zaks" but attributed to Camus; October 11, 1939, "Sous les éclairages de guerre: Croisade?" (under the streetlights of war: National-Socialist doctrine: crusade?), also signed Zaks; November 20, 1939, "Contre les Dictateurs Belliqueux: Relisons Voltaire" (against bellicose dictators: let us reread Voltaire).

11   Simone Weil offers a particularly nuanced case in point: after the fall of France, she regretted her pacifism of the 1930s but maintained a commitment to nonviolent resistance. Camus felt a great affinity with Weil's thought, and published her *L'Enracinement* (the need for roots) in 1949 in a series of books he edited at Gallimard entitled "Espoir" (hope). There is disagreement among scholars as to when exactly Weil abandoned her pacifism.

12   Eclairages de guerre: "Allô! L'écrivain Jean Giraudoux vous parle: *La guerre de Troie n'aura pas lieu*" (Streetlights of war: Hello! Writer Jean Giraudoux here, saying, *the Trojan War will not take place*). Le *Soir Républicain*, November 26, 1939, 2.

13   "Napoléon et la Censure" (Napoléon and censorship), *Le Soir Républicain*, November 26, 1939.

14   "Sous les éclairages de la guerre: Comment aller vers un ordre nouveau" (Under the streetlights of war: How to move towards a new order), *Le Soir Républicain*, November 16, 1939. Signed Irénée and attributed to Camus.

15   Julian Jackson, "The Phoney War Blues," in *The Fall of France: The Nazi Invasion of 1940* (Oxford: Oxford University Press, 2003). Jackson's book is a lucid guide to a very complicated event and its historiography.

16   The Irish song was taken up by French soldiers in 1939 and popularized in France by Ray Ventura.

17   Camus on *La Nausée, Œuvres complètes*, ed. Jacqueline Lévi-Valensi, vol. 1, 1931–1944 (Paris: Gallimard, Bibliothèque de la Pléiade, 2006), 794–96; English version in *Lyrical and Critical Essays*, trans. Ellen Conroy Kennedy (New York: Vintage, 1970), 199.

18   *Carnets, Œuvres complètes* 2:885; *Notebooks*, trans. Thody, 139.

19   *Le Mythe de Sisyphe, Œuvres complètes* 1:229; in English, *The Myth of Sisyphus and Other Essays*, trans. Justin O'Brien (New York: Vintage, 1991), 14. Julia Kristeva's *Strangers to Ourselves*, trans. Leon Roudiez et al., takes as its title a line from *The Myth of Sisyphus*—"I will always be a stranger to myself"—in

order to explore the condition of foreigners and outsiders in literature and philosophy, including Meursault.

20 Letters to Francine Faure quoted in Todd, *Une vie*, 292-93.

21 *Carnets, Œuvres complètes* 2:800; In English, *Notebooks*, trans. Thody, 10, edited.

22 Note beginning with the heading "Roman" (novel) in *Carnets, Œuvres complètes* 2:902; *Notebooks*, trans. Thody, 164, edited.

23 "Questionnaire de Carl A. Viggiani (janvier–juin 1958)," *Œuvres complètes* 4:647. See also Roger Grenier, *Albert Camus: Soleil et ombre* (Paris: Gallimard, 1987), 96-97, and Macha Séry, *Albert Camus à 20 ans*, 140 (Paris: Au Diable Vauvert, 2011), 140.

24 *Carnets, Œuvres complètes* 2:907; *Notebooks*, trans. Thody, 170.

Chapter Eight

1 Yosei Matsumoto addresses this issue in detail in "Le Processus d'élaboration de L'Étranger" (the process of creating L'Étranger), *Études camusiennes: Société japonaise des Études camusiennes* 12 (2015): 72-86.

2 "Le Minotaure ou la Halte d'Oran," *Œuvres complètes*, ed. Raymond Gay-Crosier, vol. 3, 1949-1956 (Paris: Gallimard, Bibliothèque de la Pléiade, 2008), 582-83; in English, "The Minotaur, or Stopping in Oran," *Lyrical and Critical Essays*, trans. Ellen Conroy Kennedy (New York: Vintage, 1970), 129, edited.

3 The European or non-Muslim figure included, along with the French, Jews— French citizens as of 1870—and many people of Spanish heritage. Kamel Kateb, *Européens, "indigènes" et juifs en Algérie, 1830-1962* (Paris: Presses Universitaires de France, 2001), 286. See David Carroll's brilliant analysis of René Lespès colonialist demographics in *Camus the Algerian: Colonialism, Terrorism, Justice,* (New York: Columbia University Press, 2007), 45-50.

4 Olivier Todd, *Albert Camus: Une vie* (Paris: Gallimard, 1999), 305.

5 "Le Minotaure ou la Halte d'Oran," *Œuvres complètes* 3:567-85; *Lyrical and Critical Essays*, trans. Kennedy, 109-33: "The streets of Oran are reserved for dust, pebbles and heat" and "All the bad taste of Europe and the Orient meets in Oran."

6 Albert Camus, *Carnets 1935-1948, Œuvres complètes*, ed. Jacqueline Lévi-Valensi, vol. 2, 1944-1948 (Paris: Gallimard, Bibliothèque de la Pléiade, 2006), 905; in English, *Notebooks: 1935-1942*, trans. Philip Thody (New York: Knopf, 1963, rpt. New York: Rowman & Littlefield, 2010), 168, edited.

7 *L'Étranger, Œuvres complètes*, ed. Jacqueline Lévi-Valensi, vol. 1, 1931-1944 (Paris: Gallimard, Bibliothèque de la Pléiade, 2006), 141. *The Stranger*, trans. Matthew Ward (New York: Knopf, 1988), 3, edited.

8 Ryan Bloom argues convincingly that the best translation of the first line of *The Stranger* should begin with the word "today"—as does the French sentence, which emphasizes the fact that Meursault lives in the present. Matthew Ward, whose excellent translation I use in all other instances, begins with "Maman died today."See "Lost in Translation: What the First Line of 'The

Stranger' Should Be," *New Yorker*, May 11, 2011; http://www.newyorker.com /books/page-turner/lost-in-translation-what-the-first-line-of-the-stranger -should-be (accessed September 1, 2015).

9   Jean Dagron, a physician specializing in deaf culture, describes the connection between Camus's object-oriented writing and the verbal style of his deaf mother and uncle. Dagron compares the wall between Meursault and the rest of the world to the perceptions of the nonhearing. See Jean Dagron, *Albert Camus, l'empreinte du silence* (Marseille: Éditions du Crilence, 2013).

10   Camus, Carnets, *Œuvres complètes* 2:862; in English, *Notebooks*, trans. Thody, 103.

11   Alfred Noyer-Weidner, referring to a 1959 conversation with Camus, in his article "Structure et Sens de 'L'Étranger," *Albert Camus 1980*, ed. Raymond Gay-Crosier (Gainesville: University Press of Florida), 72.

Chapter Nine

1   Susan Suleiman offers a succinct analysis of the overlapping but not synonymous aspects of "foreigness" and "strangeness" in the French word *étranger* in "Choosing French: Language, Foreignness, and the Canon (Beckett/ Némirovsky)," *French Global: A New Approach to Literary History*, ed. Christie McDonald and Susan Rubin Sulciman (New York: Columbia University Press, 2011), 473–74.

2   Albert Camus, *Carnets 1935–1948*, *Œuvres complètes*, ed. Jacqueline Lévi-Valensi, vol. 2, 1944–1948 (Paris: Gallimard, Bibliothèque de la Pléiade, 2006). 906; in English, *Notebooks 1935–1942*, trans. Philip Thody (New York: Knopf, 1963, rpt. New York: Rowman & Littlefield, 2010), 170, edited.

3   *Carnets 1935–1948*, *Œuvres complètes* 2:913; in English, *Notebooks 1935–1942*, trans. Thody, 179.

4   Albert Camus to Jean Grenier, spring 1940, *Albert Camus–Jean Grenier, Correspondance 1932–1960*, ed. Marguerite Dobrenn (Paris: Gallimard, 1981) 39; in English, *Albert Camus and Jean Grenier Correspondence*, trans. Jan F. Rigaud, (Lincoln: University of Nebraska Press, 2003), 25, edited.

5   Albert Camus, *Noces, Œuvres complètes*, ed. Jacqueline Lévi Valensi, vol. 1, 1931–1944 (Paris: Gallimard, Bibliothèque de la Pléiade, 2006), 108; in English, "Nuptials," *Lyrical and Critical Essays*, trans. Ellen Conroy Kennedy (New York: Vintage, 1970), 69.

6   Camus reused a similar scene in *The Plague*, with Tarrou in Oran. The languid gaze from a balcony, a Sunday where nothing happens: this was as essential a scene, in its own way, as the scene at the guillotine (*La Peste, Œuvres complètes* 2:51–52).

7   Albert Camus to Francine Faure, February 10, 1938, quoted in Olivier Todd, *Albert Camus: Une vie* (Paris: Gallimard, 1999), 226.

8   Ibid., 335, referring to letters from Camus to Francine Faure, April 13 and April 18, 1940.

9   Albert Camus to Yvonne Ducailar, 19 April 1940, ibid., 327–28.

Chapter Ten

1   Albert Camus, *Carnets 1935–1948*, *Œuvres complètes*, ed. Jacqueline Lévi-Valensi, vol. 2, 1944–1948 (Paris: Gallimard, Bibliothèque de la Pléiade, 2006), 909; in English, *Notebooks 1935–1942*, trans. Philip Thody (New York: Knopf, 1963, rpt. New York: Rowman & Littlefield, 2010), 174, edited.

2   He describes the suicide in his notebook for March 1940 (*Carnets, Œuvres complètes* 2:910).

3   "La mort dans l'âme," *L'envers et l'endroit, Œuvres complètes*, ed. Jacqueline Lévi-Valensi, vol. 1, 1931–1944 (Paris: Gallimard, Bibliothèque de la Pléiade, 2006), 55–63; in English, "Death in the Soul," *Lyrical and Critical Essays*, trans. Ellen Conroy Kennedy (New York: Vintage, 1970) 40–51. In *A Happy Death*, there is an episode in Prague where Mersault discovers a dead, bloody body on the street (*La mort heureuse, Œuvres complètes* 1:1145–47); in English, *A Happy Death*, trans. Richard Howard (New York: Knopf, 1972), 69.

4   *Carnets, Œuvres complètes* 2:910 (March 1940).

5   For example, Camus's comment on Léger, matter, and color in his notebooks reappears, slightly altered, in a footnote to the chapter on absurd creation in *The Myth of Sisyphus*: "It is curious to note that the most intellectual kind of painting, the one that tries to reduce reality to its essential elements, is ultimately but a visual delight. All it has kept of the world is its color." *Œuvres complètes* 2:910; in English, *Notebooks 1935–1942*, trans. Philip Thody (New York: Knopf, 1963, rpt. New York: Rowman & Littlefield, 2010), 176; and "Création absurde," *Œuvres complètes* 1:287; in English "Absurd Creation," *The Myth of Sisyphus and Other Essays*, trans. Justin O'Brien (New York: Vintage, 1991), 99.

6   Albert Camus to Francine Faure, April 30, 1940, quoted in Bernard Pingaud, *L'Étranger d'Albert Camus* (Paris: Gallimard/Foliothèque, 1992), 147–48.

7   "When he told me the woman's name I realized she was Moorish." *The Stranger*, trans. Matthew Ward (New York: Knopf, 1988), 32.

8   On straight line narrative, see Camus's essay on the novel, "L'intelligence et l'échafaud" (intelligence and the scaffold), discussed in chapter 20.

9   *La mort heureuse, Œuvres complètes* 1:1123; *A Happy Death*, trans. Howard, 31.

10 In a December 1959 interview—his last—Camus suggests that critics, too eager to pin philosophical labels on his fiction, never took into account the instinctive quality of his work. *Œuvres complètes*, ed. Raymond Gay-Crosier, vol. 4, 1957–1959 (Paris: Gallimard, Bibliothèque de la Pléiade, 2008), 661.

11 Cyril Connolly, *The Unquiet Grave* (New York: Persea Books, 1981), 21.

12 "Le Minotaure ou la Halte d'Oran," *Œuvres complètes*, ed. Raymond Gay-Crosier, vol. 3, 1949–1956 (Paris: Gallimard, Bibliothèque de la Pléiade, 2008), 567–89. In English, "The Minotaur, or Stopping in Oran," *Lyrical and Critical Essays*, trans. Ellen Conroy Kennedy (New York: Vintage, 1970) 114–15: "In every detail they attempt to imitate the style, the brashness, the superiority of Mr. Clark Gable. This is why, thanks to their rather careless pronunciation, the town's more critical citizens have nicknamed these young men 'The Clarques.'"

13 Albert Camus to Jean Grenier, May 1940, *Albert Camus–Jean Grenier, Cor-*

respondance 1932–1960, ed. Marguerite Dobrenn (Paris: Gallimard, 1981), 40–41; in English, *Albert Camus and Jean Grenier Correspondence, 1932–1960*, trans. Jan F. Rigaud (Lincoln: University of Nebraska Press), 25–27.

Chapter Eleven

1   In a letter to his friend Jacques Heurgon, who thought the scene of the judge waving a crucifix wasn't quite believable, Camus insisted that the details were true: "That examining magistrate is living in Algiers. I heard him tell the story of the crucifix in a criminal court and I saw him crying in the middle of a trial as he rehearsed the failure of his efforts. I needn't add that he has since retired on account of nervous strain." (Albert Camus to Jacques Heurgon, July 31, 1942, *Camus: Cahier de l'Herne*, ed. Raymond Gay-Crosier and Agnès Spiquel-Courdille [Paris: Éditions de l'Herne, 2013], 164). In fact, Vaillant became a judge in Sétif (see chapter 26).

2   "Le Christ devant les juges," in the series "L'assassinat du Muphti," *Alger-Républican*, June 24, 1939, *Œuvres complètes*, ed. Jacqueline Lévi-Valensi, vol. 1, 1931–1944 (Paris: Gallimard, Bibliothèque de la Pléiade, 2006), 701.

3   *L'Étranger*, *Œuvres completes* 1:181; in English, *The Stranger*, trans. Matthew Ward (New York: Knopf, 1988), 69.

4   *Le Mythe de Sisyphe, Œuvres completes* 1:229; in English, *The Myth of Sisyphus and Other Essays*, trans. Justin O'Brien (New York: Vintage, 1991), 14–15.

5   Albert Camus to Francine Faure, April 30, 1940, quoted in Bernard Pingaud, *L'Étranger d'Albert Camus* (Paris: Gallimard/Foliothèque, 1992), 151.

6   The actual story, which appeared in *L'Écho d'Alger* on January 6, 1935, was about a man in Yugoslavia to whom this had happened. Reprinted in Raymond Gay-Crosier, *The Stranger, Gale Study Guides to Great Literature: Literary Masterpieces*, vol. 8 (Detroit, MI: The Gale Group, 2002), 44.

7   *L'Étranger*, *Œuvres completes* 1:190; *The Stranger*, trans. Ward, 85.

8   *L'Étranger*, *Œuvres complètes* 1:206; *The Stranger*, trans. Ward, 112. See note 15 in chapter 6 on the Weidmann execution in "Reflections on the Guillotine."

9   *L'Étranger*, *Œuvres completes* 1:212–13; *The Stranger*, trans. Ward, 122–23, edited.

10 Naomi Jackson, whose first novel, *The Star Side of Bird Hill* (New York: Penguin, 2015), was in press when we were fellows together at the Camargo Foundation in Cassis, France, helped me explore the kinds of feelings writers have when they finish a novel. Imagining your head cut off would not be an unusual reaction.

11 Albert Camus to Claude de Fréminville, 1935 (n.d.). Centre de Documentation Albert Camus. Cité du livre. Bibliothèque Méjanes, Aix-en-Provence.

12 Albert Camus to Francine Faure, April 30, 1940, reproduced in Pingaud, *L'Étranger d'Albert Camus*, 147–51, translated by Raymond Gay-Crosier in *The Stranger*, Gale Study Guides vol. 8, 55 and 57, edited. The letter gives a rare insight into Camus's combination of nervousness and pride at this key moment in his career. The date of the letter, April 30, doesn't match the date on the manuscript: Camus may have begun writing Francine before midnight, but he finished the letter in the wee hours of morning, technically May 1. Camus's

correspondence with Yvonne Ducailar from the same period, housed in the Raymond Gay-Crosier Albert Camus collection, Smathers Libraries, the University of Florida at Gainesville, includes an April 1940 letter from Camus to Ducailar about finishing *The Stranger*. In other letters, Camus teases Ducailar for calling him a stranger and calls her a stranger (une étrangère) in return. Whether their flirtatious letters played a role in the naming of novel, they are one more indication that the word was very much on his mind. See Raymond Gay-Crosier, "Encore une correspondance inédite: Albert Camus–Yvonne Ducailar 1939–1946," in *Textes, Intertextes, Contextes. Autour de la Chute. Albert Camus* 15, ed. Raymond Gay-Crosier (Paris: Lettres Modernes/Minard, 1993), 183–96. I'm grateful to Professor Gay-Crosier for sharing with me his sense of the correspondence and its representation of Camus's state of mind in Paris.

13 Marcel Proust, *Finding Time Again*, trans. Ian Patterson (London: Penguin Books, 2002), 188–89. Proust develops the idea of a work within in the scene at the Princesse de Guermantes's afternoon party: "So I had already come to the conclusion that we have no freedom at all in the face of the work of art, that we cannot shape it according to our wishes, but that as it pre-exists us, and both because it is necessary and hidden, and because it is, as it were, a law of nature, we have to discover it."

14 Pingaud, *L'Étranger d'Albert Camus*, 151, quoting Camus to Faure, April 30, 1940; my translation.

15 Camus reviewed *The September Equinox* favorably in his "Salon de Lecture" (reading room) column in *Alger-Républican*, February 5, 1939. *Œuvres complètes* 1:817–19.

16 Camus to Faure, May 1, 1940, quoted in Olivier Todd, *Albert Camus: Une vie* (Paris: Gallimard, 1999), 338; in English, *Albert Camus: A Life*, trans. Benjamin Ivry (New York: Knopf, 1997), 110.

Chapter Twelve

1 Albert Camus, *Carnets 1935–1948, Œuvres complètes*, ed. Jacqueline Lévi-Valensi, vol. 2, 1944–1948 (Paris: Gallimard, Bibliothèque de la Pléiade, 2006), 914. In English, *Notebooks 1935–1942*, trans. Philip Thody (New York: Knopf, 1963, rpt. New York: Rowman & Littlefield, 2010), 181.

2 Irène Némirovsky, "Storm in June," *Suite Française*, trans. Sandra Smith (New York: Knopf, 2006). Némirovsky's fictional account of the exodus is exceptional for having been written nearly simultaneously with the events. After her deportation and murder at Auschwitz, her manuscript remained unpublished until 2004. Scholar Susan Suleiman points out how astonishing it is that Némirovsky is able to write an historical novel as the history it recounted was unfolding—to write about the present as if it were history. See Susan Suleiman, "Irène Némirovsky and the 'Jewish Question' in Interwar France," *Yale French Studies* 121 (2012): 8–33.

3 His correspondence with Francine Camus indicates that he moved on June 4 (confirmed by Catherine Camus at the request of the author).

4   Albert Camus to Pascal Pia, n.d., *Correspondance, 1939–1947*, ed. Yves-Marc Ajchenbaum (Paris: Fayard/Gallimard, 2000), 21. All subsequent translations from the Pia–Camus correspondence are my own.

5   Albert Camus to Jean Grenier, September 3, 1940, *Albert Camus-Jean Grenier, Correspondance 1932–1960*, ed. Marguerite Dobrenn (Paris: Gallimard, 1981), 42. In English, *Albert Camus and Jean Grenier Correspondence*, trans. Jan F. Rigaud (Lincoln: University of Nebraska Press, 2003), 27, edited.

6   *Paris-Soir* had close ties with the new government of unoccupied France: in its new Clermont-Ferrand headquarters, the newspaper rented printing presses that belonged to Vichy's Prime Minister Pierre Laval, the wily citizen of the Auvergne whose policies and personality came to define the darkest collaboration with the Nazis.

7   Daniel Lanief et al., *À Albert Camus, ses amis du livre* (Paris: Gallimard, 1962), 31–32.

8   Rirette Maîtrejean was the former companion of the great Russian anarchist Victor Serge. Traditionally, proofreaders in the newspaper business tended to come from anarchist milieux.

9   *À Albert Camus*, 32.

10 Georges Altschuler, "Albert Camus journaliste," in *L'École et la Vie* (February 6, 1960). Quoted in Herbert Lottman, *Albert Camus* (Corte Madera, California: Gingko Press, 1997), 226.

11 *Carnets, Œuvres complètes* 2:915 (September 1940). In English, *Notebooks 1935–1942*, trans. Philip Thody (New York: Knopf, 1963, rpt. New York: Rowman & Littlefield, 2010), 182, edited.

12 The *Paris-Soir* letterhead is visible in the manuscript of *Le Mythe de Sisyphe*, Beineke Rare Book and Manuscript Library, Yale University.

13 *Le Mythe de Sisyphe, Œuvres complètes*, ed. Jacqueline Lévi Valensi, vol. 1, 1931–1944 (Paris: Gallimard, Bibliothèque de la Pléiade, 2006), 254. In English, *The Myth of Sisyphus and Other Essays*, trans. Justin O'Brien (New York: Vintage, 1991), 51.

14 Ibid., 256; English ibid., 54.

15 *Carnets, Œuvres complètes* 2:915.

16 Ibid., 915; English ibid., 182. Camus's notebook doesn't specify, but in fact the Bank of France moved to Chamalières, a suburb of Clermont-Ferrand.

17 Albert Camus to Francine Faure, 8 July 1940, quoted in Olivier Todd, *Albert Camus: Une vie* (Paris: Gallimard, 1999), 350–51. In English, *Albert Camus: A Life*, trans. Benjamin Ivry (New York: Knopf, 1997), 115.

Chapter Thirteen

1   André Abbou, telephone interview with the author, October, 2014. Abbou is the editor of the scholarly edition of *L'Étranger* in *Œuvres complètes*, ed Jacqueline Lévi-Valensi, vol. 1, 1931–1944 (Paris: Gallimard, Bibliothèque de la Pléiade, 2006). Camus finally obtained a pass to travel to Paris in January 1943.

2   Sarah Stein has studied a fascinating exception, the Jews of the Mzab, in the

southern Saharan region, who were never given French citizenship in the first place. See *Saharan Jews and the Fate of French Algeria* (Chicago: University of Chicago Press, 2014).

3   Quoted by Pierre-Jean Le Foll-Luciani, *Les juifs algériens dans la lutte anticoloniale: Trajectoires dissidentes, 1931-1965* (Rennes: Presses Universitaires de Rennes, 2015), 101.

4   Raoul Bensoussan, dossier de résistant, series GR16P, Service Historique de la Défense, Vincennes.

5   The Crémieux decree wasn't reinstated until October 6, 1943.

6   Hélène Cixous, "Pieds nus," *Une enfance algérienne* (Paris: Gallimard, 1997), 53-64; also Catherine Malabou and Jacques Derrida, "De l'Algérie," *La Contre-allée* (Paris: La Quinzaine Littéraire, 1999), 78-94; and Jacques Derrida, *Monolingualism of the Other; or, The Prosthesis of Origin*, trans. Patrick Mensah (Stanford, CA: Stanford University Press, 1998).

7   Paul Benaïm, "Quand Albert Camus enseignait le français à Oran," http://www.judaicalgeria.com/pages/quand-albert-camus-enseignait-le-francais-a-oran.htm (accessed September 15, 2015).

8   *Le Mythe de Sisphe, Œuvres complètes* 1:285; in English, *The Myth of Sisyphus and Other Essays*, trans. Justin O'Brien (New York, Vintage, 1991), 96.

9   Albert Camus, *Carnets 1935-1948, Œuvres complètes*, ed. Jacqueline Lévi-Valensi, vol. 2, *1944-1948* (Paris: Gallimard, Bibliothèque de la Pléiade, 2006), 920; in English, *Notebooks: 1935-1942*, trans. Philip Thody (New York: Knopf, 1963, rpt. New York: Rowman & Littlefield, 2010), 189, edited.

10   Camus's letter has not survived, but Pia's response is dated March 16, 1941: "what little you tell me about your health worries me. That you hesitate to spend eleven hours on the train to get from Oran to Algiers seems alarming: you are ordinarily more intrepid." Albert Camus and Pascal Pia, *Correspondance, 1939-1947*, ed. Yves-Marc Ajchenbaum (Paris: Fayard/Gallimard, 2000), 33.

Chapter Fourteen

1   Pascal Pia to Albert Camus, March 9, 1941, *Correspondance 1939-1947*, ed. Yves-Marc Ajchenbaum (Paris: Fayard/Gallimard, 2000), 29.

2   Jean Grenier to Albert Camus, April 19, 1941, *Albert Camus-Jean Grenier, Correspondance 1932-1960*, ed. Marguerite Dobrenn (Paris: Gallimard, 1981), 50-51. In English, *Correspondence*, trans. Jan Rigaud (Lincoln: University of Nebraska Press, 2003), 34-35, edited.

3   Marie in the water: "I brushed against her breasts" (19); Marie at the movies: "I was fondling her breasts" (20); Marie coming to visit Meursault: "You could make out the shape of her firm breasts" (34); and Marie on the witness stand: "I could just make out the slight fullness of her breasts" (93). *The Stranger*, trans. Matthew Ward, (New York: Knopf, 1988).

4   Grenier to Camus, April 19, 1941, *Correspondance*, 50-51. In English, *Correspondence*, trans. Rigaud, 34-35, edited.

5   Grenier to Camus, ibid., 32; English ibid., 16. See also chapter 4, note 2.

6   Description of Pérez, *L'Étranger, Œuvres complètes*, ed. Jacqueline Lévi-

Valensi, vol. 1, 1931–1944 (Paris: Gallimard, Bibliothèque de la Pléiade, 2006), 150; in English, *The Stranger*, trans. Matthew Ward (New York: Knopf, 1988), 18.

7   Pia to Camus, April 25, 1941, *Correspondance*, 58.

Chapter Fifteen

1   Albert Camus to Jean Grenier, May 5, 1941, *Albert Camus–Jean Grenier, Correspondance 1932–1960*, ed. Marguerite Dobrenn (Paris: Gallimard, 1981), 53. In English, *Albert Camus and Jean Grenier Correspondence*, trans. Jan F. Rigaud, (Lincoln: University of Nebraska Press, 2003), 36, edited.

2   For Roger Grenier (no relation to Jean), Camus's strong response to Jean Grenier was a milestone in Camus's becoming a writer. See Roger Grenier, *Albert Camus: Soleil et ombre* (Paris: Gallimard, 1987), 118.

3   Gabriel Audisio, *Cagayous, ses meilleures histoires* (Paris: Gallimard, 1931). Camus reviewed Brua's *Les Fables Bônoises*, in the same genre, in *Alger-Républicain*, November 22, 1938.

4   Camus-Grenier, *Correspondance*, May–June 1941, 56; in English, *Correspondence*, 39, edited.

5   Quoted in a letter from Pia to Camus dated May 1941, *Correspondance 1939–1947*, ed. Yves-Marc Ajchenbaum (Paris: Fayard/Gallimard, 2000), 61. Pia only says that Paulhan wrote to him on the 5th and the 15th but doesn't say which month. It can't have been May, since he was in prison.

6   Nicola Chiaromonte, "Albert Camus," *Dissent* (Summer 1960): 266–70. http://www.dissentmagazine.org/wp-content/files_mf/1410902856Albert _Camus_1960_Summer.pdf (accessed July 1, 2015).

7   Pia to Camus, 31 May 1931, *Correspondance*, 71–72.

Chapter Sixteen

1   Pia to Camus, *Correspondance, 1939–1947*, ed. Yves-Marc Ajchenbaum (Paris: Fayard/Gallimard, 2000), 67–69.

2   Malraux's letter to Pia has not surfaced. Yves-Marc Ajchenbaum, the editor of the Camus-Pia correspondence, explains that Pia destroyed much of his correspondence in 1943–1944 when he was on the run from the Gestapo. Letter to the author, July 8, 2015.

3   A photocopy of the manuscript can be consulted at the Centre de Documentation Albert Camus, Bibliothèque Méjanes, Aix-en-Provence.

4   *The Stranger*, trans. Matthew Ward (New York: Knopf, 1988), 59; *L'Étranger*, *Œuvres completes*, ed. Jacqueline Lévi-Valensi, vol. 1, 1931–1944 (Paris: Gallimard, Bibliothèque de la Pléiade, 2006), 175–76.

5   Pia to Camus (quoting Malraux), *Correspondance*, 67–69.

6   According to Pia, ibid.

7   Ibid. "If G.G. proves *a priori* reticent for all three books—which would be normal—Malraux and Martin du Gard, once they've read it, could certainly intervene."

8   Malraux to Camus, October 30, 1941. Quoted in *Camus: Cahiers de l'Herne*, ed. Raymond Gay-Crosier and Agnès Spiquel-Courdille (Paris: Éditions de l'Herne, 2013), 229. All subsequent translations from the Malraux–Camus correspondence are my own.

9   André Malraux to Gaston Gallimard, November 8, 1941. The letter is quoted in Alban Cerisier, *Brève histoire illustrée de la publication de L'Étranger d'Albert Camus* (Paris: Gallimard, 2013). The pages are unnumbered, and the letter is reproduced among illustrations.

Chapter Seventeen

1   Albert Camus and Pascal Pia, *Correspondance 1939-1947*, ed. Yves-Marc Ajchenbaum (Paris: Fayard/Gallimard, 2000), 74. In a letter to Camus dated December 1, 1941, Pia quotes Paulhan's November 10, 1941, praise of *The Stranger*.

2   The reader's report is reproduced in full in the catalog of the 2011 exhibit, *Gallimard 1911-2011: un siècle d'édition*, ed. Alban Cerisier and Pascal Fouché (Paris: Bibliothèque nationale de France/Gallimard, 2011), 270.

3   On the literary prize, see the notes for *L'Étranger, Œuvres complètes*, ed. Jacqueline Lévi-Valensi, vol. 1, 1931-1944 (Paris: Gallimard, Bibliothèque de la Pléiade, 2006), 1264. The prize announcement was a news-service dispatch, dateline Dijon, Burgundy. Camus could have spotted a similar announcement in any newspaper on any subsequent November, including November 1940 or November 1941(as he was putting finishing touches on his novel).

4   Photocopies of the original are available for consultation by scholars at the Centre de Documentation Albert Camus, Bibliothèque Méjanes, Aix-en-Provence.

5   André Abbou, in his note on the manuscripts of *L'Étranger, Œuvres complètes* 1:1261-62, describes three distinct documents: the Camus manuscript at the Centre de Documentation Albert Camus, Bibliothèque Méjanes; the Millot manuscript—a reconstruction created by Camus under circumstances described in chapter 21, and a half-page fragment of text, which appears to be the only surviving piece of an early draft of the novel, where the Raymond character is called "Raoul"—presumably a trace of the Raoul Bensoussan story. I was unable to locate this fragment in the Fonds Albert Camus at the Bibliothèque Méjanes (see epilogue).

Chapter Eighteen

1   Pia wrote to Camus on December 1: "For the contract that G.G. might propose, don't hurry—unless he makes you a marvelous offer. He is so tight fisted that you shouldn't go along with his conditions without making an effort to improve them. Albert Camus and Pascal Pia, *Correspondance 1939-1947*, ed. Yves-Marc Ajchenbaum (Paris: Fayard/Gallimard, 2000), 75.

2   Alban Cerisier, *Brève histoire illustrée de la publication de L'Étranger de Camus* (Paris: Gallimard, 2013).

3   Alban Cerisier, *Une histoire de "La NRF"* (Paris: Gallimard, 2009), 419.

4   Alban Cerisier, in his history of the *NRF*, makes an important distinction between what the Propaganda-Staffel said about Drieu's functions and power at Gallimard and the role Drieu actually played at the publishing house from 1940 until his resignation as editor of the *NRF* in 1943. Drieu, Cerisier argues, was the window dressing that allowed Gallimard to retain its own capital and continue to publish.

5   His "Solstice de juin" was published in the *NRF* in November 1941.

6   Camus to Grenier about Montherlant, September 27, 1940, *Correspondance*, 43; in English, *Correspondence*, 29.

7   Roger Grenier, interview with the author, February 15, 2015.

8   Albert Camus to André Malraux, January 6, 1942, Fonds Malraux, Bibliothèque Jacques Doucet, Paris.

9   Camus to Malraux, May 4, 1942, Bibliothèque Doucet.

10   Bernard Grasset, ed., *À La Recherche de la France: notes à leur date* (Paris: Grasset, 1940), 20–22. The title means "In Search of France." Grasset followed up in 1941 with Drieu la Rochelle's *Ne plus attendre* (1941), which had the same drawing on its cover: a map of France shaded in white with a dotted line of demarcation and "Paris" in large letters, the only city indicated. See Gisèle Sapiro, *La Guerre des écrivains, 1940–1953* (Paris: Fayard, 1999); in English, *The French Writers' War 1940–1953*, trans. Vanessa Doriott (Durham, NC: Duke University Press, 2014), for a detailed history of publishers' choices during the occupation.

11   Olivier Corpet and Claire Paulhan, *Collaboration and Resistance: French Literary Life under the Nazi Occupation*, trans. Jeffrey Mehlman, preface by Robert O. Paxton (New York: Five Ties Publishing, 2009) reproduce Gaston Gallimard's terse letter to Schiffrin in November 1940, as well as an affectionate letter from Raymond Gallimard to Schiffrin in New York in 1945, assuring him that his royalties were accounted for and sent to his in-laws, and that Gallimard awaited his return to Paris.

12   Pia to Camus, December 1, 1941, *Correspondance*, 75.

13   Ibid., March 16, 1942, 83.

14   Jean Guéhenno has gone down in French literary history as an exemplary figure of resistance for refusing to publish a word as long as his country was under foreign control. It's easier to refuse publication when you're a seasoned writer with a reputation, and in Guéhenno's case, when you have another source of income as a civil servant in the teaching corps.

15   Gaston Gallimard to Albert Camus, February 5, 1942, reproduced in Cerisier, *Brève histoire illustrée*, 34. Raymond Queneau sent Gallimard an interzone postcard the same day in the laconic style that was a sign of the time, saying only that there were "local difficulties" with publishing *The Myth of Sisyphus*. Raymond Queneau to Albert Camus, February 5, 1942, quoted in Olivier Todd, *Camus: Une vie* (Paris: Gallimard, 1999), 390.

16   Camus, "L'espoir et l'absurde dans l'œuvre de Franz Kafka," *L'Arbalète* 7 (Summer 1943): unnumbered pages. By 1943, Nazi censorship of content had

given way to the monitoring of paper supplies as a means of control; it's likely that Camus's essay on a Jewish writer, subversive as it was, went entirely unnoticed by the Propaganda-Staffel. See Pascal Fouché, *L'Edition française sous l'occupation 1940–1944* (Paris: Bibliothèque de littérature française contemporaine de l'université de Paris VII, 1987).

17   Queneau to Pia, February 25, 1942, reproduced in Cerisier, *Brève histoire illustrée*, 28. Camus to Queneau, March 10, 1942, in *Albert Camus de Tipasa à Lourmarin: une exposition pour le centenaire*, ed. Hervé Valentin and Eva Valentin (Orleans: Sisyphe, 2013), 37.

19   Postcard from Camus to Queneau, February 12, 1942, *Albert Camus de Tipasa à Lourmarin*, 37.

Chapter Nineteen

1   For estimating today's value for the 1942-era French franc, see http://www .insee.fr/en/themes/indicateur.asp?id=29&type=1&page=achatfranc .htm (accessed February 12, 2016). Camus would get royalties on the first 4,000 copies if they sold, and the printers produced the standard 10 percent "pass"—400 additional books for which no royalties would be paid, to cover damage, loss, and theft as the books made their way to readers.

2   In the strange ideological mishmash that was typical of the era, two Gallimard authors who were neighbors and friends but had opposite political views—the collaborator Ramon Fernandez and Marguerite Duras, future member of the Resistance—worked together on that board.

3   Albert Camus to Gaston Gallimard, May 28, 1942, *Camus: Cahier de l'Herne*, ed. Raymond Gay-Crosier and Agnès Spiquel-Courdille (Paris: Éditions de l'Herne, 2013), 233.

4   Camus to Malraux, May 25, 1942. Ibid.

5   Malraux finally wrote to Camus on July 26, 1942, that he had read the novel and approved of the revisions: "vous en avez tiré le meilleur" (you've made the best of it). Ibid., 234.

6   Stendhal, *Aux âmes sensibles*, ed. Emmanuel Boudot-Lamotte (Paris: Gallimard, 1924). Publishers in France refer to a "program" or list of books scheduled to be published in the same month; the publishing house operated according to a set schedule of programs. *The Stranger* was on Gallimard's program for April 1942, along with twelve new books and nineteen reprints. A list is reproduced in Alban Cerisier, *Brève histoire illustrée de la publication de* L'Étranger *d'Albert Camus* (Paris: Gallimard, 2013).

7   On the literary relations and literary institutions, from the German Occupation to the Liberation, see Gisèle Sapiro's essential study, *La Guerre des écrivains 1940–1953* (Paris: Fayard, 1999); in English, *The French Writers' War 1940–1953*, trans. Vanessa Doriott Anderson and Dorrit Cohn (Durham, NC: Duke University Press, 2014).

8   José-Henri Lasry, *Oran républicain*, May 23, 1937, cited by Olivier Todd, *Albert Camus: Une vie* (Paris: Gallimard, 1999), 1073, note 45. Lasry had acted in Camus's Théâtre de l'Équipe; later, under the pen name Henri Hell, he reviewed *The Stranger* for *Fontaine*. See chapter 20, note 13.

9   "Note sur le texte," *Noces, Œuvres complètes*, ed. Jacqueline Lévi-Valensi, vol. 1, 1931–1944 (Paris: Gallimard, Bibliothèque de la Pléiade, 2006), 1233.

10   Adrienne Monnier, "Bataille à l'Exposition Henri Michaux," *Le Figaro*, June 30, 1942, 3. Adrienne Monnier described the guests at an exhibit of paintings by Henri Michaux at the Galerie de l'Abbaye in Paris on June 12, 1942. The opening amused Monnier both because so many big names from French publishing were there, but also because a young man made a scene, denouncing the paintings, and had to be carted off by the police. On Monnier and La Maison des Amis du Livre, see Laure Murat, *Passage de l'Odéon: Sylvia Beach, Adrienne Monnier et la vie littéraire dans l'entre-deux guerres* (Paris: Gallimard, 2005).

11   André Malraux to Albert Camus, July 3, 1942, Cité du livre, Bibliothèque Méjanes, Aix-en-Provence; Camus to Malraux, July 12, 1942, Fonds Malraux, Bibliothèque Doucet, Paris.

12   Marcel Arland, "Un écrivain qui vient . . ." *Comœdia*, July 11, 1942, 1–2; all subsequent translations from the first reviews of *The Stranger* are my own.

13   He does the same thing for the courtroom scene, inventing quoted speech where Camus had preferred indirect discourse. Arland: "They insist: 'You are a monster: you didn't cry over your mother's cadavre, you smoked, drank coffee; you didn't even know the age of that poor woman.'" Camus quoted the prosecutor indirectly: "He reminded the court of my insensitivity; of my ignorance when asked Maman's age; of my swim the next day . . ." *L'Étranger, Œuvres complètes* 1:199; in English, *The Stranger*, trans. Ward (New York: Knopf, 1988), 99.

14   By September 3, Camus was already in France, but *Comœdia* would have been forwarded to him from Oran to Le Panelier. Jean Grenier to Albert Camus, September 3, 1942, *Albert Camus–Jean Grenier, Correspondance 1932–1960*, ed. Marguerite Dobrenn (Paris: Gallimard, 1981), 74. In English, *Albert Camus and Jean Grenier Correspondence*, trans. Jan F. Rigaud, (Lincoln: University of Nebraska Press, 2003), 53.

15   Camus to Grenier, July 25, 1942, *Correspondance*, 71; in English, *Correspondence*, 50; Grenier responded to Camus on August 19 by commenting on Rousseaux's article, which appeared that very weekend: "A. Rousseaux judges all books from a moral and religious point of view, if not a patriotic one. What he says isn't wrong, but finally his criterion seems infinitely too narrow. What might he have written about [Gide's] *Immoralist* and so many other books? He could not taste the mixture of despair and ardor that underlies the cynicism of *The Stranger*." *Correspondence*, trans. Rigaud, 51, edited.

16   *Le Figaro*, May 28, 1938, 6.

17   *The Stranger*, trans. Ward, 65; *Œuvres complètes* 1:178.

18   The letter survives as an entry in his notebook, *Carnets 1935–1948, Œuvres complètes*, ed. Jacqueline Lévi-Valensi, vol. 2, 1944–1948 (Paris: Gallimard, Bibliothèque de la Pléiade, 2006), 952–953; in English, *Notebooks 1942–1951*, trans. Justin O'Brien (New York: Knopf, 1965), 20–22.

19   *Carnets, Œuvres complètes* 2:952, "je n'en ai donné qu'un cliché négatif"; in English, *Notebooks*, trans. O'Brien, 21.

20   He added, "There was a good article by Arland in *Comœdia* and another, equally favorable in the *NRF*." Postcard, August 10, 1942. He was referring to

Arland's, "Un écrivain qui vient," and Fieschi, "Chroniques des romans," *Nouvelle Revue Française*, September 1942, 364–70, both published in occupied Paris.

21 Maurice Blanchot, "Chronique de la vie intellectuelle: le roman de L'Étranger," *Le Journal des débats*, August 19, 1942, 3. Albert Camus, quoted by Roger Quilliot in *Théâtre, récits, nouvelles* (Paris: Gallimard, Bibliothèque de la Pléiade, 1962), 1940, my translation: "The first person narrative, usually confessional, is used in *The Stranger* in service of detachment." Quilliot's source is a red notebook used by Camus as he worked on *The Plague*.

22 Pascal Pia to Albert Camus, September 2, 1942, *Correspondance, 1939–1947*, ed. Yves-Marc Ajchenbaum (Paris: Fayard/Gallimard, 2000), 101.

23 Albert Camus to Claude de Fréminville, September 6, 1942, quoted in Raymond Gay-Crosier, *The Stranger*, Gale Study Guides to Great Literature: Literary Masterpieces, vol. 8 (Detroit, MI: The Gale Group, 2002), 106.

24 Camus to Malraux, September 2, 1942, quoted in *Camus: Cahier de l'Herne*, 235.

25 Pia to Camus, 4 November 1942, *Correspondance*, 108.

Chapter Twenty

1 Pascal Pia to Albert Camus, May 20, 1942, *Correspondance, 1939–1947*, ed. Yves-Marc Ajchenbaum (Paris: Fayard/Gallimard, 2000), 95.

2 Emmanuel Roblès, *Camus, frère de Soleil* (Paris: Le Seuil, 1995), 38–41.

3 Albert Camus, *The Plague*, trans. Stuart Gilbert (New York: Knopf, 1946). *La Peste, Œuvres completes*, ed. Jacqueline Lévi-Valensi, vol. 2, 1944–1948 (Paris: Gallimard, Bibliothèque de la Pléiade, 2006), 35.

4 For those in the know, and doubtless for his own amusement, Camus includes a wink at *The Stranger* in *The Plague*: Joseph Grand overhears a conversation in a tobacco shop about the recent arrest in Algiers of a young company employee who killed an Arab on a beach. *La Peste, Œuvres complètes* 2:71.

5 Roblès, *Camus, frère de soleil*, 54, and Albert Camus to Jean Grenier, October 15, 1942, *Albert Camus–Jean Grenier, Correspondance 1932–1960*, ed. Marguerite Dobrenn (Paris: Gallimard, 1981).

6 On Operation Torch, see Rick Atkinson, *An Army at Dawn: The War in North Africa, 1942–1943* (New York: Henry Holt, 2002).

7 *Carnets, Œuvres complètes* 2:966.

8 Camus to Pia, December 11, 1942, *Correspondance*, 120. In May he sent mushroom powder to Jean Grenier, May 19, 1943, *Correspondance*, 94.

9 Camus to Pia, December 26, 1942, *Correpondance*, 125, in a postscript.

10 "Les séparés" (those who have been separated). See *Carnets, Œuvres complètes* 2:979; in English, *Notebooks*, trans. O'Brien, 52: "notes on 'Les Séparés,' second part," edited.

11 Henri Hell, "Deux récits," *Fontaine* 4: 23, July–September, 1942, 352–55. *Fontaine* was published by Edmond Charlot, publisher and editor of Camus's first two books. The magazine was edited by Max-Pol Fouchet, another of

Jean Grenier's former students; Fouchet had been Camus's rival for Simone Hié.

12   Hell, "Deux recits," Fontaine 4:23, 355.

13   Ibid. The first novel discussed is Marc Bernard, *Pareils à des enfants*, which won the Goncourt Prize in November 1942.

14   Grenier to Camus, October 18, 1942, *Correspondance*, 80–81; in English, *Correspondence*, trans. Rigaud, 59.

15   Jean Paul Sartre, "Explication de *l'Étranger*," *Cahiers du Sud* 30 (February 1943): 189–206. In English, "*The Stranger* Explained," trans. Chris Turner, reprinted in We *Have Only This Life to Live: The Selected Essays of Jean-Paul Sartre 1939-1975*, ed. Ronald Aronson and Adrian Van Den Hoen (New York: New York Review Books, 2013), 43.

16   Sartre, "*The Stranger* Explained," trans. Turner.

17   *L'Étranger*, *Œuvres complètes*, ed. Jacqueline Lévi-Valensi, vol. 1, 1931-1944 (Paris: Gallimard, Bibliothèque de la Pléiade, 2006), 161; *The Stranger*, trans. Matthew Ward (New York: Knopf, 1988), 35; and Sartre, "*The Stranger* Explained," 41. Sartre's italics.

18   For example, he changes "Il y a toujours eu des choses dont je n'aimais parler" (there have always been things I didn't like to talk about) to "Il y a des choses dont je n'ai jamais aimé parler (there are things which I've never liked to talk about). He adds *alors* in ink to "J'ai pensé que je n'aurais pas dû lui dire cela" (I thought I shouldn't have told him this): "J'ai pensé *alors* que je n'aurais pas dû lui dire cela" (I thought then that I shouldn't have told him this). He changes "à ce moment, tout a vacillé" (at this moment, everything began to reel) to "C'est alors que tout a vacillé" (that's when everything began to reel).

19   Sartre, "*The Stranger* Explained," trans. Turner, 42.

20   Ibid, 43.

21   Grenier to Camus, March 31, 1943, *Correspondance*, 90; in English, *Correspondence*, trans. Rigaud, 67, edited.

22   François Mauriac and Jean Paulhan, April 8, 1943, *Correspondance 1925-1967* (Paris: Éditions Claire Paulhan, 2001), 203.

23   René Tavernier, introduction to the issue, "Problèmes du roman," *Confluences* 21–24 (July 1943): 13. My translation: "Clearly Kafka's *Castle* or Camus's *The Stranger* are incompatible with Mlle de Scudéry's *Grand Cyrus* or Apuleius's *Golden Donkey*, but do we think that *Poésie et vérité 1942* (*Poetry and Truth 1942: a collection of underground resistance poetry*) resembles Virgil?"

24   Alain Borne, "Sur Julien Green," in ibid., 160–65.

25   Camus, "L'intelligence et l'échafaud," *Confluences* 21–24 (July, 1943): 218–23, rpt. *Œuvres complètes* 1:894–900; in English, "Intelligence and the Scaffold," in *Lyrical and Critical Essays*, ed. Philip Thody (New York: Vintage, 1970), 210–18.

26   Grenier to Camus, May 11, 1941, *Correspondance*, 54–55; in English, *Correspondence*, trans. Rigaud, 38.

27   Jean Grenier, "Une œuvre, un homme," *Cahiers du Sud* (February 1943): 224–28.

28   Jean Grenier to Albert Camus, September 19, 1942, *Correspondance*, 77; in English, *Correspondence*, trans. Rigaud, 55–56. Camus's reply of September

22 is equally affectionate: "Yes, I remember your visit to Belcourt. Still today, I can remember every detail. Perhaps, speaking in absolutes, you represented Society. But you came, and I felt, that day, that I wasn't as poor as I thought" 57, edited.

Chapter Twenty-One

1   Elsa Triolet, "Quel est cet étranger qui n'est pas d'ici?" *Poésie 43*:14 (May–June 1943): 11–26, my translations.

2   Ibid., 26.

3   Triolet to Camus, January 6, 1944, courtesy of Julia Elsky's, work-in-progress on the Camus-Triolet correspondence, Centre de Documentation Albert Camus. Cité du livre. Bibliothèque Méjanes, Aix-en-Provence.

4   Albert Camus to Francine Camus, September 17, 1943. His letter reached her via Melilla, a Spanish-controlled city in Morocco. Courtesy of Catherine Camus.

5   Nicole Giannière to Catherine Camus, July 26, 2010; courtesy of Catherine Camus. On Triolet, see Julia Elsky, "French and Foreign: Émigré Writers in Occupied France" (Ph.D. dissertation, Yale University, May 2014).

6   Emmanuel Roblès, *Camus, frère de soleil* (Paris: Le Seuil, 1995), 72.

7   Ronald Aronson, *Camus and Sartre: The Story of a Friendship and the Quarrel That Ended It* (Chicago: University of Chicago Press, 2005), 9–10.

8   When Grasset published Friedrich Sieburg, a central personage among Nazi cultural figures in occupied Paris, Lemarchand interviewed him for in *La Gerbe*. See Olivier Corpet and Claire Paulhan, *Collaboration and Resistance: French Literary Life under the Nazi Occupation*, trans. Jeffrey Mehlman (New York: Five Ties Publishing, 2009), 136, quoting Lemarchand's diary entry on the interview.

9   The Brassaï photo is easily found online and is reproduced in Alan Riding, *And the Show Went On: Cultural Life in Nazi-Occupied Paris* (New York: Vintage, 2011).

10 From an interview with Françoise Seligman, surviving member of the *Combat* group, in Joël Calmettes's film, *Albert Camus journaliste*, Chiloé Productions, 2012.

11 Pia was responding to Malraux's advice that the chaplain scene needed to be further developed. And in fact Camus did continue to work on that scene. See chapter 16.

12 *Lettres à un ami allemand*, second letter, *Œuvres complètes*, ed. Jacqueline Lévi-Valensi, vol. 2, 1944–1948 (Paris: Gallimard, Bibliothèque de la Pléiade, 2006); in English, Albert Camus, "Letters to a German Friend," *Resistance, Rebellion, and Death*, trans., Justin O'Brien (New York: Knopf, 1960), 17–18.

13 *Combat* 57 (underground), May 1944, *Œuvres complètes*, ed. Jacqueline Lévi-Valensi, vol. 1, 1931–1944 (Paris: Gallimard, Bibliothèque de la Pléiade, 2006), 916, *Camus at Combat: Writing 1944–1947*, trans. Arthur Goldhammer (Princeton, NJ: Princeton University Press, 2006), 6. The passage is read aloud in Joël Calmettes's documentary, *Albert Camus journaliste*.

14   The detail of the papers on the floor was provided by Catherine Camus dur-
      ing an interview with the author in Lourmarin, November 14, 2014. On the
      counterfeit manuscript, see André Abbou's helpful note on what is called the
      Millot Manuscript of *L'Étranger*, *Œuvres complètes* 1:1262.

15   Albert Camus to Jean Grenier, March 9, 1943, *Albert Camus-Jean Grenier,
      Correspondance 1932–1960*, ed. Marguerite Dobrenn (Paris: Gallimard, 1981),
      89; in English, *Albert Camus and Jean Grenier Correspondence*, trans. Jan F.
      Rigaud, (Lincoln: University of Nebraska Press, 2003), 67, edited.

Chapter Twenty-Two

1   Albert Camus, "From Resistance to Revolution," *Combat*, August 21, 1944,
      collected in *Camus at Combat: Writing 1944–1947*, trans. Arthur Goldham-
      mer, (Princeton, NJ: Princeton University Press, 2006), 12–13.

2   A reel-to-reel tape of Camus's radio editorial, "Albert Camus speaks over
      Free French Radio on the Day of the Liberation of Paris," is available in the
      Michigan State University Library collection, Lansing, MI.

3   Mauriac charged Camus with arrogance, saying he was speaking "from the
      great heights of your *œuvre* to come." Quoted in Alice Kaplan, *The Collabora-
      tor: The Trial and Execution of Robert Brasillach* (Chicago: University of Chi-
      cago Press, 2000), 193.

4   See "Outlaws," an unsigned article in the underground *Combat* 56, April
      1944, rpt. in *Camus at Combat*, ed. Jacqueline Lévi-Valensi, trans. Arthur
      Goldhammer (Princeton, NJ: Princeton University Press, 2006), 4.

5   On the petition, see Kaplan, *The Collaborator,* 189–201.

6   Alban Cerisier, *Une histoire de "La NRF"* (Paris: Gallimard, 2009), 457–58.

7   Simone de Beauvoir, *La cérémonie des adieux suivi d'Entretiens avec Jean-
      Paul Sartre* (Paris: Gallimard, 1974), 380.

8   Roger Grenier recounts the anecdote in "À 'Combat' avec Albert Camus," *In-
      stantanés* (Paris: Gallimard, 2007), 55.

9   Camus on the three models for Meursault, quoted by Roger Grenier, *Albert
      Camus: Soleil et ombre* (Paris: Gallimard, 1987), 104. Yet another model for
      Meursault is often cited: Camus supposedly told his friend Sauveur Galliero,
      a painter in Algiers, that "he owed him a lot," quoted in Olivier Todd, *Albert
      Camus: Une vie* (Paris: Gallimard, 1999), 267; in English, *Albert Camus: A
      Life*, trans. Benjamin Ivry (New York: Knopf, 1997), 152.

10   Roger Grenier, *Paris ma grand'ville* (Paris: Gallimard, 2015), 30.

11   Roger Grenier, "Nazis sans le savoir," *Libertés*, October 26, 1944, 4. On
      Grenier's beginnings at *Combat*, see "À 'Combat' avec Albert Camus," 37–57,
      and *Paris ma grand'ville*, 57–58. On Grenier's experience with Pia and Camus
      at *Combat*, see also his *Pascal Pia: le droit au néant* (Paris: Gallimard, 1989).

12   Jacques Lemarchand, who shared an editor's office with Camus at Gallimard,
      soon took over the theater reviews and Grenier became a full-time reporter-
      at-large. During the Occupation Lemarchand had published book reviews in
      the collaborationist newspaper *La Gerbe*, but his fast friendship with Camus
      gave him a choice spot in the press of the Resistance.

13   Roger Grenier's *Le rôle d'accusé* (Paris: Gallimard, 1949) was based on his experiences covering the purge trials for *Combat*. It was published in a series edited by Camus at Gallimard entitled "Espoir."

14   Roger Grenier, "À 'Combat' avec Albert Camus," 44.

15   Albert Camus, *Carnets 1935–1948, Œuvres complètes*, ed. Jacqueline Lévi-Valensi, vol. 2, 1944–1948 (Paris: Gallimard, Bibliothèque de la Pléiade, 2006), 1033.

16   Elizabeth Hawes, *Camus, a Romance* (New York; Grove Press, 2009). Her chapter on New York in 1946 is the essential source on Camus's American travel. For the complete diplomatic history of the visit, see Fernande Bartfeld, "Le Voyage de Camus en Amérique du nord," in *L'homme révolté cinquante ans après*, Les Lettres Modernes: Albert Camus 19, ed. Raymond Gay-Crosier (Paris: Lettres Modernes/Minard, 2001), 203–27, as well as original documents in the archives of the French Ministère des Affaires Etrangères in La Corneuve, France (Relations Culturelles 1945–1959, sous-série 1945–1947). The ministry of foreign affairs paid Camus a stipend of $400 per month during a two-month tour, or "mission," which took him to Columbia, Harvard, Vassar, Bryn Mawr, and Brooklyn College.

Chapter Twenty-Three

1   Blanche Knopf to Jenny Bradley, February 23, 1945, in *Dictionary of Literary Biography* 355: *The House of Knopf 1915–1960, A Documentary Volume*, ed. Lanae H. Isaacson (Detroit, MI: Gale/Cengage Learning, 2010), 125. *The Dictionary of Literary Biography* has reproduced a small selection of the correspondence between Blanche and Alfred Knopf, Albert Camus, and Jenny Bradley held in the Knopf Collection at the Harry Ransom Center, University of Texas at Austin (UTA). On Blanche Knopf and Camus, see also Laura Claridge's biography, *The Lady with the Borzoi* (New York: Farrar, Straus and Giroux, 2016).

2   On the Hamilton contract, see Gaston Gallimard to Mrs. W. A. Bradley, September 10, 1945, Box 150.6, Bradley Collection, Harry Ransom Center, University of Texas at Austin (UTA). For the Knopf contract, see Mrs. William Bradley, Bradley Agency to Dionys Mascolo, Gallimard, June 1, 1945, Box 150.6, Bradley Collection, Harry Ransom Center, UTA. On the shared translation costs and Hamilton's suggestion of Gilbert as translator, see "Gallimard Contracts Pending," May 24, 1945, Box 89.7, Bradley Collection, Harry Ransom Center, UTA.

3   Roger Grenier, "15, place Vendôme," *Paris ma grand'ville* (Paris: Gallimard, 2015), 91.

4   Blanche Knopf, "Albert Camus in the Sun," *The Atlantic*, February 1961, 207, 77–84.

5   Blanche Knopf wrote the Bradley agency on September 11, 1945, that the translation for *L'Étranger* was on the way from England. Box 89.7, Bradley Collection, Harry Ransom Center, UTA.

6   Jamie Hamilton to Mrs. Alfred A. Knopf, 10 January 1946, Knopf Collection, Box 4.7, Harry Ransom Center, UTA.

7   Blanche Knopf to Jamie Hamilton, January 29, 1949, Box 4.7, Knopf Collection, Harry Ransom Center, UTA.

8   Jamie Hamilton to Mrs. Alfred Knopf, February 4, 1946, Box 4.7, Knopf Collection, Harry Ransom Center, UTA.

9   Herbert Weinstock, "Report on *The Stranger* by Albert Camus—English translation by Stuart Gilbert," *House of Knopf*, 126. At the Bradley agency, where the French manuscript was read as early as December 1944, one reader called *L'Étranger* "too slight to be worth translating"; the same reader filed a report with Knopf in January 1945: "the actual moment of the shooting is not altogether convincing"; "the turning point in the story isn't credible . . . the book is 'limited.'" *The Stranger* clippings file, Box 1318.5, Knopf Collection, Harry Ransom Center, UTA.

10   *Publishers Weekly*, 149:14, April 6, 1946. Jamie Hamilton writes Alfred Knopf on April 26, 1946, to "congratulate Blanche on her 'existentialist' ad" and ask for one of the photographs of Camus. Box 4.7, Knopf Collection, Harry Ransom Center, UTA.

11   "Books Sold to US" (January–June 1946), Box 89.8, Bradley Collection, Harry Ransom Center, U. "The Stranger by Albert Camus—published April 11, 1946. Sales through May 31st: 2,455" (figure crossed out but visible). Blanche Knopf to Jamie Hamilton, May 13, 1946: "*The Stranger* has received a fantastic press but sales are not too good." Box 4.7, Knopf Collection, Harry Ransom Center, UTA.

12   Albert Camus, "Non, je ne suis pas existentialiste," interview with Jeanine Delpech, *Les Nouvelles littéraires* 954 (November 15, 1945). *Œuvres complètes*, ed. Jacqueline Lévi-Valensi, vol. 2, 1944–1948 (Paris: Gallimard, Bibliothèque de la Pléiade, 2006), 655–58.

13   Sartre, "The New Writing in France," *Vogue*, July 1945, 84–85, http://www .vogue.com/archive/ (accessed September 15, 2015), and translated into French for the first time as "Nouvelle Littérature en France," in Jean-Paul Sartre, *Œuvres romanesques*, ed. Michel Contat and Michel Rybalka (Paris: Gallimard, Bibliothèque de la Pléiade, 1981), 1917–21.

14   The text of Sartre's lecture at Yale on January 24, 1946, was published in *The Atlantic* in August 1946, 114–18, five months after Camus's visit to the United States for the launch of the Knopf edition of *The Stranger*. Sartre's lecture was announced on January 18, 1946, in an article in *The Yale Daily News*.

Chapter Twenty-Four

1   Albert Camus, *Carnets 1935–1948*, *Œuvres complètes*, ed. Jacqueline Lévi-Valensi, vol. 2, 1944–1948 (Paris: Gallimard, Bibliothèque de la Pléiade, 2006), 1052; in English, *American Journals*, trans. Hugh Levick (New York: Paragon House, 1987), 31.

2   The report by special agent James E. Tierney, dated August 1946, concludes that Camus has no close connection to the Communists and is not a threat to American security. See Raymond Gay-Crosier, "Camus Fiché: le rapport officiel," in *Camus: Cahier de l'Herne*, ed. Raymond Gay-Crosier and Agnès

Spiquel-Courdille (Paris: Éditions de l'Herne, 2013), 109–14, which reproduces the report in full.

3   Camus FBI report, ordered through Freedom of Information Act.

4   Elizabeth Hawes, *Camus, a Romance* (New York; Grove Press, 2009). For a complete history of Camus's travel to New York, see materials listed above in note 16, chapter 22.

5   Camus first proposed as possible American lectures "The Free Press after a Year" and "A Plea for Europe," but the ministry found these topics too political (Camus to the Ministry of Foreign Affairs, December 11, 1945; with handwritten annotation: "requested exclusively literary topics," in Archives du Ministère des Affaires Etrangères, La Corneuve). He finally settled on "The Human Crisis" (the original French title was "La Crise de l'homme"). It was a more philosophical title for what remained in large part a plea for Europe. "La Crise de l'homme" became the title for the entire Columbia program, a panel discussion among three Resistance intellectuals. Vercors was the pen name of Jean Bruller (1902–1991), an artist-engraver whose 1942 novella about a "good" German officer billeted with a French family became a classic of Resistance literature. Thimerais (Léon Motchane), a physicist and mathematician, also published with the underground Éditions de Minuit (*La Pensée patiente*, 1943). Claude Lévi-Strauss took great pride in the event, in which he saw a dynamic new model for bringing French intellectual life to the United States. On March 30, he telegraphed his colleagues in Paris to report that the Columbia lecture had attracted an audience of 1,500.

6   "A note on the Resistance, The Absurd, and M. Camus," *Columbia Spectator*, March 26, 1946.

7   Justin O'Brien, "Albert Camus: Militant," in *Camus: A Collection of Critical Essays*, ed. Germaine Brée (New York: Prentice-Hall, Inc., 1962), 22. O'Brien's impression of Camus as "athletic" may have been fanciful and certainly belied Camus's tenuous health.

8   Camus had yet another mission in New York, unrelated to *The Stranger*. Two weeks after his arrival, he was joined by Raymond Gallimard, Gaston Gallimard's brother and the financial director of the firm, who came to New York to protect the firm's interests. The Éditions Gallimard had filed a law suit against the New York company Raynal & Hitchcock for publishing unlicensed English-language editions of Saint-Exupéry's *Wind, Sand and Stars, Flight to Arras*, and *The Little Prince*. Raynal & Hitchcock claimed that Saint-Exupéry had represented himself as sole possessor of his literary rights, and that Gallimard had never informed them otherwise. (Saint-Exupéry had lived in New York from 1941 to 1943, before returning to his squadron in North Africa. His plane was shot down in a reconnaissance mission in July 1944.) With Raymond Gallimard, Camus negotiated the rights situation with Saint-Exupéry's widow and Raynal & Hitchcock. On his entry papers, Gallimard gave as his official address in New York his friend Jacques Schiffrin's apartment at 101 East 75th Street. (New York Passenger Lists, 1820–1957, Transcontinental and Western Air, April 5, 1946, accessed via Ancestry.com library edition.) Pantheon's French edition of *L'Étranger*, duly licensed by Gallimard, rolled off the New York presses on May 25, 1946, during Raymond

Gallimard's visit. On the Gallimard lawsuit, see *Publishers Weekly*, April 13, 1946, 2094–95.

9   O'Brien, "Albert Camus: Militant," 21.

10 A typescript of the French text with Camus's handwritten corrections is in the Dorothy Norman papers, Beinecke Rare Book and Manuscript Library, Yale University. The lecture, delivered in French, was published in an awkward English translation by Lionel Abel in *Twice A Year* 1, no. 16-17 (1946–1947): 19-33, and was excerpted in *Vogue*, July 1, 1946, 86. See also Philippe Vanney's highly informative "'La Crise de l'homme' a-t-elle trouvé son texte," *Études camusiennes: société japonaise des Etudes camusiennes* 6 (May 2004): 76-96.

11 Lewis Thompson, "The Absurdiste," *New Yorker*, April 20, 1946, 22. It is possible that Camus never saw the translation in manuscript. Blanche Knopf was opposed on principle, though the Hamish Hamilton company, not Knopf, was shepherding the translation. See Blanche Knopf to Jenny Bradley, July 9, 1945: "A little knowledge is dangerous, and a lot of knowledge even more so in matters of this kind. I am sure that Stuart Gilbert can be counted on to do a good job. However what I have written is probably, in this particular instance, academic because if you are going to get hold of this translation for submission to Camus you will have to get it from Hamish Hamilton, and not from us." Box 89.7, Bradley Collection, Harry Ransom Center, University of Texas at Austin (UTA).

12 Gilbert trans, *The Stranger*, trans. Stuart Gilbert (New York: Knopf, 1946), 19; Camus, *L'Étranger*, *Œuvres complètes*, ed. Jacqueline Lévi-Valensi, vol. 1, 1931-1944 (Paris: Gallimard, Bibliothèque de la Pléiade, 2006), 156 (". . . j'ai répondu que non.").

13 Matthew Ward's 1988 retranslation, quoted here, addressed just these issues, while Sandra Smith's 2013 translation, published in England by Viking, makes further inroads in the direction of authenticity, such as restoring "tender" to the phrase "tender indifference of the world," which Gilbert rendered as "the benign indifference of the universe" and Ward as "the gentle indifference of the world."

14 John E. Gale, "Does America Know *The Stranger*?: A Reappraisal of a Translation" in *Modern Fiction Studies* 2.2 (1974): 139-47. Among the first reviewers, Eleanor Clark, a poet, was keenly aware that the translation distorts Camus's style. See "Existentialist Fiction: *The Stranger*," *The Kenyon Review* 84 (Autumn 1946): 674-78.

15 In 1947, a French chargé d'affaires in Washington described the American understanding of existentialism this way: "The undisputed fad for 'Existentialism' in this country can be explained by the idea that with this school of thought, France has become the only country in the world possessing what a representative of the Rockefeller Foundation described to our cultural attaché as 'an operative philosophy.' In all domains—political, economic, philosophical, literary, artistic and religious—America wants to know if France has something to say that can help other countries, and America itself, overcome their own problems." Francis Lacoste, Chargé d'affaires de France aux Etats-Unis to Georges Bidault, Ministre des Affaires Etrangères, March 20,

1947, Relations Culturelles 1945–1947, Archives du ministère des Affaires étrangères et du Développement international, La Courneuve, France, my translation.

16   *View* (special issue on Paris, entitled *View: Paris*), March–April 1946, "Books by Camus and Blanchot reviewed by Nicolas Calas," 31; "The Stranger: An Excerpt," 23.

17   Thompson, "The Absurdiste," 22–23.

18   *Carnets*, *Œuvres complètes* 2:1053; in English, *American Journals*, trans. Levick, 33.

19   The letter itself is lost, but is described in Roger Grenier's file on Michel Gallimard. Roger Grenier, personal collection.

20   Nicola Chiaromonte, *New Republic*, April 26, 1946, https://newrepublic.com /article/115492/albert-camus-stranger (accessed January 9, 2016).

21   John L. Brown, "Albert Camus, Apostle of Post-Liberation France," *New York Times Sunday Book Review*, April 7, 1946, http://timesmachine.nytimes.com /timesmachine/1946/04/07/93081787.html?pageNumber=128 (accessed January 9, 2016).

22   Edmund Wilson, *New Yorker*, April 13, 1946, 113–14.

23   Charles Poore, "Books of The Times," *New York Times*, April 11, 1946, https:// www.nytimes.com/books/97/12/14/home/camus-stranger.html (accessed January 9, 2016).

24   Neil Oxenhandler, *Looking for Heroes in Postwar France: Albert Camus, Max Jacob, Simone Weil* (Hanover, NH: University Press of New England, 1996) makes the connection between his experience in combat and his discovery of *The Stranger*.

Chapter Twenty-Five

1   Pierre Brodin, "Quand Camus parlait aux élèves du Lycée Français de New York," (April 11, 1946). Mimeograph, courtesy Roger Grenier, private collection.

2   Catherine Camus, interview with the author, March 2015.

3   Jean-Paul Sartre, *Existentialism Is a Humanism*, trans. Carol Macomber (New Haven: Yale University Press, 2007).

4   Roger Grenier, *Albert Camus: Soleil et ombre* (Paris: Gallimard, 1987), 168. Grenier tracks a first print run of 22,440 in June and reprints on a nearly monthly basis, with first-year sales figures at 161,000. The Gilbert translation of *The Plague* published by Knopf in 1948 sold 3,000 copies in the first week of publication—a record number. See *Dictionary of Literary Biography* 355: *The House of Knopf 1915–1960*, ed. Lanae Isaacson (Detroit, MI: Gale/Cengage Learning, 2010), 131.

5   Camus to Michel and Janine Galllimard, quoted by Roger Grenier, *Albert Camus: Soleil et ombre*, 168.

6   As of April 1960, *The Stranger* had sold 180,951 hardcover and paper copies combined since its publication in 1946. *The Plague* had sold 50,489 copies (though there is no paperback total for *The Plague*, so these figures need to be balanced accordingly), *House of Knopf*, 152. In the late 1940s and 1950s,

La Peste far outsold L'Étranger in France; in 1973, with two mass-market paperbacks in circulation, L'Étranger (307,500) finally bypassed La Peste (301,500). See "Longsellers et bestsellers: Évolution des tirages," 1911–2011, Gallimard: un siècle d'édition, ed. Alban Cerisier and Pascal Fouché (Paris: Bibliothèque nationale de France/Gallimard, 2011), 387–91.

7   Albert Camus, "Avant-Propos," L'Étranger, ed. Germaine Brée and Carlos Lynes, Jr., (New York: Appleton-Century-Crofts, 1955), v.

8   "Lettre à propos de l'affaire Guyader," February 12, 1951, Œuvres complètes, ed. Raymond Gay-Crosier, vol. 3, 1949–1956 (Paris: Gallimard, Bibliothèque de la Pléiade, 2008), 870–87, and note 1414.

9   See Eve Morisi, Camus contre la peine de mort (Paris: Gallimard, 2011).

10   Roger Ferdinand coined the term in 1943, in a play called Les J3.

11   Panconi was sentenced to ten years in prison; his accomplice, Bernard Petit, to five years. See Macha Séry's vivid evocation of the trial and its coverage, "Joseph Kessel et les enfants perdus," Le Monde, August 7, 2014. For contemporary accounts, see Françoise Dolto, "Quand le bachelier moyen devient criminel: L'Affaire Guyader" (when the student becomes a criminal), Esprit 155.5 (Mai 1949): 678–84: "No hatred, no love, no justice, no despair—no meaning, to be honest" (my translation). Joseph Kessel, "Le procès des enfants perdus" (the trial of the lost children), in Paris-Presse, rpt. La nouvelle saison, reportages 1948–1954 (Paris: Tallandier, 2010).

12   Camus to Michel Gallimard, July 2, 1950, quoted by Olivier Todd, Albert Camus: Une vie (Paris: Gallimard, 1999), 701, my translation.

13   Inscribed copy of the first edition of The Stranger, in Albert Camus de Tipasa à Lourmarin: une exposition pour le centenaire, ed. Hervé Valentin and Eva Valentin (Orleans: Sisyphe, 2013), 40, exhibition catalogue.

14   The Stranger, trans. Mathew Ward (New York: Knopf, 1988), 71.

15   Camus, "Avant-Propos," L'Étranger, ed. Brée and Lynes, viii, my translation.

16   Emmanuel Roblès, Camus, frère de soleil (Paris: Éditions du Seuil, 1995), 73, reproducing a letter from Camus dated 1947.

17   Camus to Rolf Hadrich, German theater director, September 8, 1945, reprinted in Catherine Camus and Marcelle Mahasala, Albert Camus : Solitaire et solidaire (Paris: Lafon, 2010). Also reprinted in Bernard Pingaud, L'Étranger d'Albert Camus (Paris: Gallimard/Foliothèque, 1992) 190–93. Nicola Chiaromonte's review was one of the first to view Camus as a hero of truthtelling. See New Republic, April 26, 1946, https://newrepublic.com/article/115492/albert-camus-stranger (accessed January 9, 2016).

18   The recording is available on CD from Frémeaux et Associés.

19   The translation is from Ward, 31: "Ce qui l'ennuyait, 'c'est qu'il avait encore un sentiment pour son coït." Also among the censored lines is the cruder "Je lui ai dit que tout ce qu'elle voulait, c'était s'amuser avec sa chose." This idiomatic expression might also be translated as "All she wanted to do was play with her thing"—"chose" refers to female sexual organs. See Alice Kaplan, "The American Stranger," South Atlantic Quarterly 91.1 (1992): 87–110, for a list of expurgated sentences in the Appleton-Century-Crofts French-language edition and the way they were translated by Gilbert in 1946 and Matthew Ward in 1988.

20   "Teacher furnishes Lewd Books to Children; Is Fined and Jailed Here," Esca-

naba Daily Press, May 20, 1960, and Ray C. Olson to Knopf, Inc. (n.d.): "Is *The Stranger* so lewd and obscene that my son should lose whole future in the teaching profession?" After Olson's arrest and sentencing, the prosecutor's wife was hired by the school board to teach Olson's classes! *The Stranger* clippings file, Box 1318.5, Knopf Collection, Harry Ransom Center, University of Texas at Austin. *Time* reported his misadventure with tongue in cheek, after the case was thrown out. "Education: Stranger in Town," *Time*, September 12, 1960, http://content.time.com/time/magazine/article/0,9171,897557,00 .html (accessed July 7, 2015).

21   "Albert Camus—presentation speech by the permanent secretary of the Swedish Academy, December 10, 1957, http://www.nobelprize.org/nobel_ prizes/literature/laureates/1957/press.html (accessed September 27, 2015).

22   Knopf used the Cartier-Bresson portrait on the back of the dust jacket of his 1956 *The Fall*, published in translation in 1957. See Blanche Knopf's reminiscence in "Albert Camus in the Sun," *The Atlantic*, February 1961, 77–84.

23   *Carnets 1935–1948*, *Œuvres complètes*, ed. Jacqueline Lévi-Valensi, vol. 2, 1944–1948 (Paris: Gallimard, Bibliothèque de la Pléiade, 2006), 1075; in English, *Notebooks 1942–1951*, trans. Justin O'Brien (New York: Knopf, 1965), 147, edited.

24   It would be misleading to say the first "paperback" edition, since Gallimard first editions in the traditional "blanche" collection have soft covers. Their price and trim size differentiate them from the reprints known as "livres de poche"—pocket books.

25   See Herbert Lottman, *Albert Camus* (Corte Madera, California: Gingko Press, 1997), 601.

26   Ibid., 668.

27   Camus, from a 1958 preface to his 1937 *The Wrong Side and the Right Side*, "Préface" for *L'envers et l'endroit*, *Œuvres complètes*, ed. Jacqueline Lévi-Valensi, vol. 1, 1931–1944 (Paris: Gallimard, Bibliothèque de la Pléiade, 2006), 31–38; in English, *Lyrical and Critical Essays*, trans. Ellen Conroy Kennedy (New York, Vintage, 1970): "two opposing dangers that threaten every artist, resentment and self-satisfaction."

28   See "Mastroianni sur le tournage 'L'Étranger,'" including an interview with Visconti in the Algiers courtroom. http://www.ina.fr/video/105151993/mas troianni-sur-le-tournage-l-etranger.video.html (accessed June 23, 2015).

29   Adaptation projects had been brewing for years. Gérard Philipe, who had played the title role in *Caligula* in its first postwar production on stage, had been eager to play Meursault in a Jean Renoir project that reached the planning stages, but Gallimard and the producers couldn't agree on finances and Renoir backed out. Gérard Philipe to Albert Camus, 25 September 1950, quoted in "Quand Gérard Philipe voulait être Meursault," *La vie de la Pléiade*, http://www.la-pleiade.fr/La-vie-de-la-Pleiade/L-actualite-de-la-Pleiade /Quand-Gerard-Philipe-voulait-etre-Meursault (accessed May 1, 2016).

30   Antoine de Baecque, "L'échec de Visconti," *L'histoire* 347 (November 2009): 28, http://www.histoire.presse.fr/actualite/infos/1 -echec-de-visconti-01-11 -2009-8986 (accessed September 27, 2015).

31   Visconti asked him to play the judge, but he didn't want a speaking part. Roblès, *Camus, frère de soleil*, 116.

32   Patrick McCarthy, always a tough critic of Camus, points out that Visconti
      might have used his camera to zero in on objects, in just the way that Meur-
      sault experienced them, but chose to keep a realistic distance. See Patrick
      McCarthy, *Camus: The Stranger* (Cambridge: Cambridge University Press,
      2004), 108. Other critics suggest Visconti was tired of the negotiations, that
      he had grown indifferent to the project and wanted to finish the job. See de
      Baecque, "L'Échec de Visconti," and Roblès, "'L'Étranger' au cinema."

33   Katherine Kinnaird, "'L'Étranger meets Al-Gharib: A Deconstruction of
      Translations," unpublished seminar paper, Yale University Department of
      French, May 2105, studies two translations of *The Stranger* into Arabic: *Al-
      Gharib wa Qisas Al-Gharib Ochra (The Stranger and Other Stories)*, trans. Aida
      Matraji Idriss (Beirut: Dar al Adab, 1990); *The Stranger/Pastures of Heaven*,
      trans. Mohamed Ghattas (Cairo: Al Dar Al Masriah Al Lubaniah, 1997).

34   Jon Pareles, "Rock Group Accedes to Arab Protest," *New York Times*, January
      21, 1987, http://www.nytimes.com/1987/01/21/arts/rock-group-accedes-to
      -arab-protest.html (accessed January 10, 2016). The American Arab commit-
      tee pointed out that many people hearing the song had not read *The Stranger*
      and could not understand the connection. Smith commented in 2001, when
      "Killing an Arab" was once again subject to controversy: "One of the themes
      of the song is that everyone's existence is pretty much the same. Everyone
      lives, everyone dies, our existences are the same. It's as far from a racist song
      as you can write. It seems though that no one can get past the title and that's
      incredibly frustrating. The fact is it's based on a book that's set in France and
      deals with the problems of the Algerians, so it was only geographical reasons
      why it was an Arab and not anyone else." Chart Attack, October 29, 2001,
      http://www.chartattack.com/news/2001/10/29/oh-god-not-again-robert
      -smith-on-killing-an-arab/ (accessed August 30, 2015). It's interesting that
      Smith, who is British, uses the American title *The Stranger* in his lyrics, not
      the British *The Outsider*.

Chapter Twenty-Six

1   For Said's evolving views, see Edward Said, "Representing the Colonized:
     Anthropology's Interlocutors," *Critical Inquiry* 15.2 (Winter 1989): 223, and
     Culture and Imperialism (New York: Knopf, 1993), 185.

2   Edmund White, "What is the American for Maman: *The Stranger* by Albert
     Camus, translated by Matthew Ward," *Los Angeles Times*, May 29, 1988,
     http://articles.latimes.com/1988-05-29/books/bk-5522_1_matthew-ward
     (accessed January 10, 2016).

3   Cyril Connolly, introduction to the British edition of Stuart Gilbert's 1946
     translation, *The Outsider* (London: Hamish Hamilton, 1946), 7.

4   Pierre Nora, "Pour une autre Explication de L'Étranger," *France-Observateur*
     557, 1961, 17. See also his *Français d'Algérie* (Paris: Julliard, 1961), with its
     diagnosis of a reactionary French Algerian populism. Nora spent two years
     teaching history at the same Oran lycée where Francine Camus had taught
     math.

5   Thank you to Anita Samen whose query about Louis Vaillant led to this un-

expected discovery. On the importance of Sétif, see Mohammed Harbi's column in *Le monde diplomatique*, available in English as "Massacre in Algeria," https://mondediplo.com/2005/05/14algeria (accessed January 2, 2016). Vaillant's career is outlined in the directory of the French magistrature, available online: http://tristan.u-bourgogne.fr:8080/4DCGI/Fiche/46573 (accessed January 2, 2016). Army documents from 1945 give a list of Europeans killed, including Vaillant ("V . . . L..: retired President of the Tribunal") but only the most abstract sense of the mass killing of Muslim demonstrators: *La guerre d'Algérie par les documents*, t. 1, *L'Avertissement 1943–1946* (Vincennes: Service Historique de l'Armée de Terre, 1990), 403.

6   *L'Écho d'Alger*, the Algiers daily, devoted a single small paragraph to the story on August 4, 1942, in its North African news column, under the subtitle "Asphyxiation at Zéralda: Four Arrests." The mayor and his accomplices were indicted for negligent homicide ("homicide par imprudence").

7   On the Zéralda and Orléansville incidents, see the August 1, 1942, report of the Centre d'Informations et d'Études de l'Activité Indigène dans le Départment d'Alger (Center for Information and Study of Indigenous Activity in the the Department of Algiers), Archives Nationales d'Outre Mer, Aix-en-Provence.

8   *Meursault, contre-enquête* was first published in Algeria in 2013 by the Éditions Barzakh, quickly made its way across the Mediterranean to an enthusiastic French reception (a separate French edition was published by Actes Sud in 2014) and then on to translations into more than twenty-three different languages, including a US translation by John Cullen (New York: Other Press, 2015). In France, the book won the Prix des Cinq continents de la francophonie, the Prix François Mauriac, and the Prix Goncourt du Premier Roman. A play and a film are in the making, still more indications that *The Meursault Investigation* is a true heir to *The Stranger's* success. In Paris, people are rereading *The Stranger*, then picking up *The Meursault Investigation*. It's an unusual revival.

9   Haroun becomes Harun. Many reviewers have pointed out that Musa and Harun are Arab variants on the biblical Moses and Aron.

10 See my "Kamel Daoud, *Meursault, Contre-Enquête*" in *Contreligne* http://www.contreligne.eu/2014/06/kamel-daoud-meursault-contre-enquete/; in English, "Making The Stranger Contemporary: Kamel Daoud's *Meursault, contre-enquête*" in *Being Contemporary: French Literature, Culture, and Politics Today*, ed. Lia Brozgal and Sara Kippur (Liverpool: University of Liverpool Press, 2016), 334–36. See also Lia Brozgal's brilliant analysis of the novel's ambiguities, "The Critical Pulse of the *Contre-Enquête*: Kamel Daoud on the Maghrebi Novel in French," in *Contemporary French and Francophone Studies*, special issue, "The contemporary *Roman maghrébin*: Aesthetics, Politics, Production, 2000–2015," ed. Patrick Crowley and Megan MacDonald, 2016.

11 Daoud, *The Meursault Investigation*, 126.

12 Ibid., 11.

13 Ibid., 98, 109.

14 Ibid., 138.

Epilogue

1   Consult also "Kamel Daoud nomme l'invisible dans *Meursault, contre-enquête*," Daoud interviewed by Augustin Trappenard on "Boomerang," France-Inter, November 4, 2014. http://www.franceinter.fr/emission-boomerang-kamel-daoud-nomme-linvisible-dans-meursault-contre-enquete (accessed January 29, 2016).

2   The circumstances of Olivier Todd's research in Algeria are remarkable. He traveled to Annaba (formerly Bône, near Camus's birthplace), Oran, and Algiers in the summer of 1992, filming the site of the farm where Camus was born, visiting the writer's childhood apartment on the rue de Lyon, and interviewing leading intellectuals about Camus's Algerian legacy. He lectured under the auspices of the French Institutes. Since February 1992, the country had been living in a state of emergency, and soon the violent civil war between Islamists and the army made travel impossible. Mahfoud Boucebci, a psychiatrist and human rights activist who spoke to Todd about Camus in 1992, was stabbed to death in front of his hospital less than a year later.

3   Albert Camus, *Carnets 1935–1948*, *Œuvres complètes*, ed. Jacqueline Lévi-Valensi, vol. 2, 1944–1948 (Paris: Gallimard, Bibliothèque de la Pléiade, 2006), 899. In English, *Notebooks: 1935–1942*, trans. Philip Thody (New York: Knopf, 1963, rpt. New York: Rowman & Littlefield, 2010), 159. Chicago, in 1939, meant glamorous gangsters.

4   *L'Écho d'Oran*, July 31 and August 3, 1939.

5   Mairie d'Aix-les-Bains. Acte de décès no. 422, courtesy Djilali Touil.

6   Camus described the drive: "From the top of the coast road, the cliffs are so thick that the landscape becomes unreal through its very qualities. Man is an outlaw there, so much so that all this beauty seems to come from another world." *Carnets*, *Œuvres complètes* 2.905. *Notebooks*, trans. Thody, 167–68.

7   The Boukhatems' ancestor in the nineteenth century had been a "magsen," fighting alongside the French when they landed in Oran in 1830 to capture the town from the Turks. Caïd Boukhatem-Boukhatem Bahari, born January 10, 1879, native assistant in Aïn-el-Turck, Oran departement (adjoint indigène à Aïn-el-Turck, département d'Oran), GGA 19H 300, and Oran série C carton 4941, containing the "notice signalétique" on Boukhatem and a May 8, 1935, letter from the prefect to the state prosecutor reporting the threat. Archives Nationales d'Outre Mer, Aix-en-Provence. The caïd owned seven hectares of vineyards and rented out four of them. Next to his land was land owned by Kaddour Touil's father, a cattle and produce merchant.

8   *Carnets*, *Œuvres complètes* 2:881. *Notebooks*, trans. Thody, 134, edited.

9   He escaped the fate of the Arabs in French Algeria, who either enlisted or were drafted into the French forces as early as 1939, and were drafted again into the Allied army at the Liberation—"indigènes" who have had to fight for their pensions and their recognition in France. The film *Indigènes* called attention to their plight (dir. Rachid Bouchareb, 2006, released in English as *Days of Glory*.)

10 "Aïn-el-Turck: La mort tragique du caïd Boukatem" (Aïn-el-Turck: the Tragic Death of Caïd Boukatem), *L'Écho d'Oran*, January 24, 1942. "Funeral for the

Caïd Bahari Boukhatem, murdered the night of January 17, 1942," *L'Écho d'Alger*, March 11, 1942, reports the death of Djilali Touil in prison. (The Djilali Touil I met in 2014 was named for the brother who died.)

11 Although Cyril Connolly compares the world of *The Stranger* to the American Deep South of Faulkner and Caldwell (introduction to *The Outsider*, 1946), the strict racial segregation of the Jim Crow South did not hold sway in Algeria. The French "civilizing mission" was paternalistic and discriminatory, with consequences that ranged from the murderous rage of the official at Zéralda to the assimilation of a small elite.

Bibliography for *The Stranger*

Instead of a complete bibliography of literary studies of *The Stranger*, which would come by now to hundreds of entries and overwhelm even the most dedicated scholar, I've opted for a selected, annotated bibliography of individual articles and collections representing a variety of critical approaches.

Manuscripts, Records, and Collections

William Bradley Collection. The Henry Ransom Center, the University of Texas at Austin.

"Crise de l'homme." Typescript corrected by Camus; English translation by Lionel Abel; related correspondence. Dorothy Norman Papers. Beinecke Rare Book and Manuscript Library, Yale University.

Files on members of the Resistance. Sous-série GR16P. Service Historique de la Défense, Vincennes.

Alfred A. Knopf Collection. The Harry Ransom Center, the University of Texas at Austin.

Manuscripts of *L'Étranger*; Camus's notebooks. Centre de Documentation Albert Camus. Cité du livre. Bibliothèque Méjanes, Aix-en-Provence.

Manuscript of *Le Mythe de Sisyphe*. Beinecke Rare Book and Manuscript Library, Yale University.

Pantheon Books Records. Columbia University Rare Book and Manuscript Library Collections, New York.

Reports on the activities of natives in the Departments of Algiers and Oran, 1940–1941; Prefecture of Oran files on Associations, 1899–1957; reports on individual Caids, 1932–1949; file on the Abbé Lambert, 1936–1953; police reports on the Algiers Communist Party, 1935–1937. Archives Nationales d'Outre Mer, Aix-en-Provence.

Relations Culturelles, 1945–1959. Archives du Ministère des Affaires Étrangères et du Développement International. La Corneuve. Correspondence regarding Camus's lecture tour of the United States and Canada and reports on ongoing plans for French lecturers.

Newspapers

Alger-Républicain (Algiers). Bibliothèque nationale de France (BNF), Paris. This large paper, founded in 1938, became the smaller evening paper *Le Soir Républicain* (Algiers) in 1939, when *Alger-Républicain* was shut down. Camus worked for these papers as an editorialist, literary critic, and investigative reporter from 1938 to 1940. Both are archived at the Bibliothèque Nationale de France.

Combat. Underground issues, December 1941–April 1944. BNF, Paris. Available online at gallica.bnf.fr.

Combat. Above-ground issues, August 21, 1944–1947. BNF, Paris.

L'Écho d'Alger (Algiers). BNF, Paris. Available online at gallica.bnf.fr.

L'Écho d'Oran (Oran). At the offices of *El Djoumhouria*. Oran, Algeria.

Paris-Soir (1940–1941), éditions de province. BNF, Paris. Note that this is the *Paris-Soir* Camus worked for, which left Paris with the German invasion and set up shop in Clermont-Ferrand, then in Lyon. This is not to be confused with the version of the newspaper reproduced in the BNF Gallica collection, which is the German-controlled paper that remained in Paris.

Selected Editions and English-Language
Translations of *The Stranger*

L'Étranger. Paris: Gallimard, 1942.

L'Étranger. New York: Pantheon Books, French Pantheon Books Series 9, 1946.

The Stranger. Trans. Stuart Gilbert. New York: Knopf, 1946. Camus wondered why it had so many more quotation marks than his original.

The Outsider. Trans. Stuart Gilbert. London: Hamish Hamilton, 1946. Identical to the Knopf edition, with the addition of an introduction by Cyril Connolly, who first brought the book to Hamish Hamilton's attention.

L'Étranger. Ed. Germaine Brée and Carlos Lynes, Jr. New York: Appleton-Century-Crofts, Inc., 1955. School edition in French with introduction and vocabulary in English. Expurgated—parts considered by the publisher to be inappropriate for students were removed.

The Stranger. Trans. Kate Griffith. Washington, D.C.: University Press of America, 1982.

The Outsider. Trans. Joseph Loredo. London: Hamish Hamilton, 1982. The first attempt by the original British publisher of *L'Étranger* to improve on Gilbert's translation.

The Stranger. Trans. Matthew Ward. New York: Knopf, 1988. Now the most widely read translation in the United States, it corrects the stylistic defects of the Gilbert edition.

The Outsider. Trans. Sandra Smith. London: Viking/Penguin, 2013. Also recommended, though at the time of this writing it is unavailable in the United States.

Other Works by Camus Related to *The Stranger*

American Journals. Trans. Hugh Levick. New York: Paragon House, 1987.

A Happy Death. Trans. Richard Howard. New York: Knopf, 1972.

Cahiers Albert Camus 3: Fragments d'un combat 1938–1940, Alger-Républicain, Le Soir Républicain. Ed. Jacqueline Lévi-Valensi and André Abbou. Paris: Gallimard, 1978.

Caligula: version de 1941 suivi de La poétique du premier Caligula par A. James Arnold (the 1941 version of *Caligula*, followed by A. James Arnold), *The Poetics of the First Caligula*. In *Cahiers Albert Camus 4*. Ed. A. James Arnold. Paris: Gallimard, 1984.

Caligula and Three Other Plays. Trans. Stuart Gilbert and Justin O'Brien. New York: Knopf, 1958.

Camus à Combat: éditoriaux et articles. Ed. Jacqueline Lévi-Valensi. Paris: Gallimard/Folio, 2013. Available in English as *Camus at Combat: Writing 1944–1947*. Trans. Arthur Goldhammer. Princeton, NJ: Princeton University Press, 2006.

The First Man. Trans. David Hapgood. New York: Knopf, 1995.

Lyrical and Critical Essays. Ed. Philip Thody, trans. Ellen Conroy Kennedy. New York: Vintage, 1970. Includes "The Wrong Side and the Right Side" (1937); "Nuptials" (1939); "The Minotaur, or Stopping in Oran" (1954); "On Jean-Paul Sartre's La Nausée" (1938); "Intelligence and the Scaffold" (1943); "No, I am not an existentialist" (1945).

"Misery of Kabylia." In *Algerian Chronicles*. Ed. Alice Kaplan, trans. Arthur Goldhammer. Cambridge, MA: Harvard University Press, 2013.

The Myth of Sisyphus and Other Essays. Trans. Justin O'Brien, New York: Vintage, 1991.

Notebooks, 1935–1942. Trans. Philip Thody. New York: Knopf, 1963, rpt. New York: Rowman & Littlefield, 2010.

Notebooks, 1942–1951. Trans. Justin O'Brien. New York: Knopf, 1965

Notebooks, 1951–1959. Trans. Ryan Bloom. Chicago: Ivan Dee, 2010.

Œuvres complètes. Ed. Jacqueline Lévi-Valensi (vols. 1 and 2) and Raymond Gay-Crosier (vols. 3 and 4). Paris: Gallimard, Bibliothèque de la Pléiade, 2006–2008. The definitive scholarly edition in four volumes, known as The Pléiade, assembled by leading Camus scholars working with original manuscripts. An earlier two-volume Gallimard Pléiade edition compiled by Roger Quilliot shortly after Camus's death, *Théâtre, récits, nouvelles* (1962) and *Essais* (1965), is still valuable for its editor's notes. Whereas Quilliot's Pléiade is organized by genre, the series edited under the direction of Jacqueline Lévi-Valensi looks at the work in chronological order, and includes texts that weren't yet published in the 1960s, such as Camus's notebooks and the posthumous novels *A Happy Death* and *The First Man*.

The Plague. Trans. Stuart Gilbert. New York: Vintage, 1991.

The Plague. Trans. Robin Buss. New York: Penguin, 2013. Buss has modernized Gilbert's translation.

"Reflections on the Guillotine." In *Resistance, Rebellion, and Death*. Trans. Justin O'Brien. New York: Knopf, 1960.

Youthful Writings. Trans. Ellen Conroy Kennedy. New York: Paragon, 1990. With an introduction by Paul Viallaneix.

Correspondence

Albert Camus–Jean Grenier, Correspondance 1932–1960. Ed. Marguerite Dobrenn. Paris: Gallimard, 1981. Available in English as *Albert Camus and Jean Grenier Correspondence, 1932–1960*. Trans. Jan F. Rigaud. Lincoln: University of Nebraska Press, 2003.

Camus, Albert, and Pascal Pia. *Correspondance, 1939–1947*. Ed. Yves-Marc Ajchenbaum. Paris: Fayard/Gallimard, 2000.

Camus, Albert. Letters to André Malraux. Fonds Malraux 9 (Malraux archives). Bibliothèque Jacques Doucet, Paris.

Ducailar, Yvonne. Correspondence with Albert Camus. Raymond Gay-Crosier Albert Camus collection. Smathers Library. University of Florida at Gainesville.

de Fréminville, Claude. Correspondence with Albert Camus. Centre de Documentation Albert Camus. Cité du livre. Bibliothèque Méjanes, Aix-en-Provence. The majority of Camus's unpublished correspondence is housed at the Cité du livre and can be consulted with permission of the Camus estate.

"La publication de L'Étranger," *Camus: Cahiers de l'Herne*. Ed. Raymond Gay-Crosier and Agnès Spiquel-Courdille. Paris: Éditions de l'Herne, 2013. Excerpts from the correspondence about the manuscript and publication among Camus, Gallimard, Malraux, and Pia.

Malraux, André. Letters to Albert Camus. Centre de Documentation Albert Camus. Cité du livre. Bibliothèque Méjanes, Aix-en-Provence. A publication of the Malraux–Camus correspondence, edited by Sophie Doucet, is forthcoming from Éditions Gallimard, Paris.

Selected Biographies, Documentaries, and Memoirs

Calmettes, Joël, director. *Albert Camus, le journalisme engagé*. Paris: Chiloé Productions, 2010 (DVD). A documentary that explores Camus's work both at *Alger-Républicain* and at *Combat*.

Camus, Catherine, Alexandre Alajbegovic, and Béatric Vaillant. *Le monde en partage: Itinéraires d'Albert Camus*. Paris: Gallimard, 2013. Texts and images from Camus's many travels.

Camus, Catherine, and Marcelle Mahasela. *Albert Camus: Solitaire et Solidaire*. Paris: Lafon, 2010. In English, *Albert Camus: Solitude and Solidarity*. Ed. Catherine Camus. Zurich: Edition Olms, 2012. A rich iconography, public and private.

Garfitt, Toby. *Jean Grenier: un écrivain et un maître*. Rennes: Part Commune 2010.

Grenier, Jean. *Albert Camus: Souvenirs*. Paris: Gallimard, 1968.

Grenier, Roger. *Albert Camus: Soleil et ombre*. Paris: Gallimard, 1987. An essential introduction to Camus, organized by work, with emphasis on Camus's influences and creative process, written by Camus's friend and editor.

Hawes, Elizabeth. *Camus, a Romance*. New York: Knopf, 2009. A cultural history in the form of an American writer's memoir of reading Camus. Especially fine on Camus's health and on his travels in the United States.

Knopf, Blanche. "Albert Camus in the Sun." *Atlantic*, February 1961, 77–84.

Lottman, Herbert. *Albert Camus.* Corte Madera, California: Gingko Press, 1997. Still unsurpassed for its chronology and for its interviews with so many of Camus's close friends and colleagues, this American-style, fact-based biography was first published in 1979 by an expatriate journalist at *Publishers Weekly*.

Musso, Frédéric. *Albert Camus ou la fatalité des natures.* Paris : Gallimard NRF Essais, 2009. A poetic reckoning on Camus and nature.

Oxenhandler, Neil. *Looking for Heroes in Postwar France: Albert Camus, Max Jacob, Simone Weil.* Hanover, NH: University Press of New England, 1995. A moving reading of *The Stranger* by a World War II combat veteran and literature professor.

Radish, Iris. *Camus: Das Ideal der Einfachheit. Eine Biographie.* Berlin: Rowohlt, 2013.

Roblès, Emmanuel. *Camus, Frère de soleil.* Paris: Le Seuil, 1995. A fellow journalist and writer, born in Oran, Roblès tells the story of a lifelong friendship and intellectual complicity.

Séry, Macha. *Camus à 20 ans: premiers combats.* Lalaune: Au Diable Vauvert, 2011. A precise and gripping political and cultural mapping of Camus's young adulthood by one of France's best literary journalists.

Todd, Olivier. *Albert Camus: Une vie.* Paris: Gallimard, 1999. Especially strong on Camus's correspondence, citing letters not otherwise available, and with a deep understanding of the Parisian literary world by one of its insiders. An emphasis on the writer's romantic life. A French-style biography, writerly and interpretive. Note that the English translation by Benjamin Ivry, *Albert Camus: A Life* (New York: Knopf, 1997) is substantially abridged.

Tanase, Virgil. *Camus.* Paris: Gallimard/Folio Biographie, 2010. In this concise yet elegant biography Tanase, a Franco-Romanian writer and dramaturge, is an insightful guide to Camus's political choices and to his work in the theater.

Vircondelet, Alain. *Camus, fils d'Alger.* Paris: Fayard. Centered on Camus's ties to Algeria and written with nostalgia. Especially rich on the 1930s.

Zaretsky, Robert. *Albert Camus: Elements of a Life.* Ithaca, NY: Cornell University Press, 2010. A moving and eloquent intellectual biography.

———. *A Life Worth Living: Albert Camus and the Quest for Meaning.* Cambridge, MA: Harvard University Press, 2013. Organized according to major concepts— absurdity, silence, revolt, etc.—that inform Camus's life and work.

Selected Reviews of *The Stranger*

REVIEWS OF THE FIRST FRENCH EDITION, 1942–1943

Arland, Marcel. "Un écrivain qui vient." *Comœdia*, July 11, 1942. Paris: occupied zone.

Blanchot, Maurice. "Chronique de la vie intellectuelle: le roman de L'Étranger." *Journal des débats politiques et littéraires*, August 19, 1942. Paris: occupied zone.

Fieschi. "Chronique des romans," *Nouvelle Revue Française*, September, 1942, 364–
    70. Paris: occupied zone.
Grenier, Jean. "Une oeuvre, un homme." *Cahiers du Sud* 30 (February, 1943): 224–
    28.
Hell, Henri. *Fontaine*. July–September, 1942. Algeria: unoccupied zone.
Henriot, Émile. *Le Temps*. November 3, 1942. Lyon: unoccupied zone.
Rousseaux, André. *Le Figaro*, July 18–19, 1942, Lyon: unoccupied zone.
Sartre, Jean Paul. "Explication de l'Étranger." *Cahiers du Sud* 30 (February 1943):
    189–206. Translated as "The Stranger Explained" by Chris Turner and reprinted
    in *We Have Only This Life to Live: The Selected Essays of Jean-Paul Sartre 1939–
    1975*, ed. Ronald Aronson and Adrian Van Den Hoen. New York: New York Re-
    view Books, 2013.

REVIEWS OF THE FIRST US TRANSLATION, 1946

Arendt, Hannah. "French Existentialism." *Nation*, February 23, 1946. The article
    consulted by the FBI in its investigation of Camus.
Bentley, Eric. "Not in the Reviews: A Note on French Existentialism." *Books Abroad*
    20:3, (Summer 1946): 263–66. "You are safe too in ignoring Camus's assertion
    that he is not an existentialist. After all, Karl Marx said he was not a Marxist."
    "The French existentialists are 'the most lithe, elusive and fast moving group.'"
Brown, John L. "Albert Camus, Apostle of Post-Liberation France." *New York Times
    Sunday Book Review*, April 7, 1946.
Calas, Nicolas. "Books by Camus and Blanchot reviewed by Nicolas Calas." *View:
    Paris*, March–April, 1946.
Chiaromonte, Nicola. *New Republic*, April 26, 1946. Chiaromonte considers *The
    Stranger* as "the tragedy of integrity."
Clark, Eleanor. "Existentialist Fiction: *The Stranger*." *Kenyon Review* 84, (Autumn
    1946): 674–78. "The translation, completely inaccurate, hides both the flaws and
    the merits of the work. The novel is as weary as France—and ultimately unsuc-
    cessful."
Gannett, Lewis. "Books and Things." *New York Herald Tribune*, April 12, 1946. Exis-
    tentialism: "a pompous refuge from pompous tradition." Camus's own life in the
    Resistance contradicts the "irresponsible and defeating logic" of his philosophy.
George, Albert J. "L'Étranger" *Symposium* 1.1 (November 1, 1946): 170. A review of
    the novel in English, but quoting from the French-language edition published in
    New York by Pantheon Books in 1946.
Guérard, Albert J. "Albert Camus," *Foreground: A Creative and Critical Quarterly* 1:1
    (1946). Says Camus's early writing, taken together, constitutes a spiritual biog-
    raphy, comparable to the early Whitman. Admires the style in French, which he
    predicts will be extremely difficult to translate.
Hansen, Harry. "Apostles Arrive to Introduce Existentialist Ideas in US." *Chicago
    Daily Tribune Magazine of Books*, March 3, 1946. The existentialists "may be
    about to fill a void in US intellectual debate—people are tired of war issues and
    no longer interested in political ideologies."
Hoskins, Katherine. "A Novelist of the Absurd." *Partisan Review* 13:1 (Winter 1946):

121–23. Hoskins suggests that the novel might have been translated as "The Alien." For her, the fact that the man killed was an Arab appears to have no sociological connotation.

Jackson, Katherine Gauss. "Books in Brief." *Harper's* 192, no. 1153 (June 1, 1946): 16, 19–20.

Kirkus, (March 1, 1946): 109. Unsigned review. "A certain odd fascination though its market will be limited."

"Man in a Vacuum." *Time*, May 20, 1946. Unsigned review. "The fuzz-buzz" of existentialism.

O'Brien, Justin. "Boldest Writer in France Today: Albert Camus, Novelist, Dramatist, Philosopher of the Absurd." *New York Herald Tribune*, March 24, 1946, F2. Situates Camus as independent from the slavish followers of existentialism.

———. "Presenting a New French Writer: In His First Novel, Albert Camus Sets Forth a Parable of Man's Fate." *New York Herald Tribune Weekly Book Review*, April 14, 1946, 10. "It always takes courage to introduce a new foreign writer."

Plant, Richard. "Benign Indifference." *Saturday Review of Literature*, May 18, 1946, 10. "A master craftsman."

Poore, Charles. "Books of The Times." *New York Times*, April 11, 1946. https://www .nytimes.com/books/97/12/14/home/camus-stranger.html (Accessed January 9, 2016).

Rogers, B. W. "Ignoring Fate Won't Make It Pass You By." *Washington Post*, April 14, 1946, 56.

Sullivan, Richard. "So, Nothing Matters in Life, At All!" *Chicago Daily Tribune*, April 14, 1946, G4. "Adroitly attitudinized despair."

Wilson, Edmund. *New Yorker*, April 13, 1946. Wilson is lukewarm, calling James M. Cain's *The Postman Always Rings Twice* "somewhat more satisfactory."

PUBLISHED IN US PERIODICALS, 1946–1947

"The Crisis of Man: Inertia is the Strongest Temptation." *Vogue*, July 1, 1946.

"The Human Crisis." Lecture at Columbia University, trans. Lionel Abel. *Twice A Year* 1, no. 16–17, (1946–1947).

"The Myth of Sisyphus" (excerpted from the longer work) and "Hope and the Absurd in the Work of Franz Kafka," from *The Myth of Sisyphus, Partisan Review*, 13:2, (Winter 1946): 188–200.

"*The Stranger*: An Excerpt." *View: Paris*, vol. VI, no. 2–3 (March/April, 1946): 21–23.

REVIEWS OF THE FIRST UK TRANSLATION, 1946

Ayer, A. J. "Novelist-Philosophers XIII: Albert Camus." *Horizon* 13, vol. 75, (March 1946): 155–59. Presents Camus as a former teacher of philosophy, and puts him through his paces. The question of suicide raised in *The Myth of Sisyphus* is metaphysical, not moral; descriptions in *L'Étranger* are admirable but it is difficult to be interested in someone uninterested in himself, and the novel adds nothing to the doctrines of the absurd in "The Myth of Sisyphus."

Bowen, Elizabeth. "Elizabeth Bowen's Book Reviews." *Tattler and Bystander*, July 24, 1946. "One of the most talked about novels of this summer"; "odd, disconcerting, unamenable."

Charques, R. D. "A Victim." *Times Literary Supplement* (London), June 22, 1946, 293. "Halting and rather artificially composed."

Fane, Vernon. "The World of Books." *The Sphere*, (July 13, 1946): 60. Tongue-in-cheek: "the subject is a sort of male twilight sleep"; "too elusive for either admiration or disagreement."

Fausset, Hugh I. H. "New Novels." *Manchester Guardian*, June 28, 1946.

Hale, Lionel. "From Algiers." *Observer*, June 23, 1946, 3. African and new.

Lehmann, Rosamond. "New Novels." *Listener* 913, (July 11, 1946): 558. "Brilliant and disturbing." If we sweep away Christian morality, will we be "reaching for our revolvers?"

"New Novels." *Scotsman*, June 27, 1946. In the Gallic tradition of relentless impartiality and lucidity.

Straus, Ralph. "New Novels." *Sunday Times* (London), June 16, 1946, 3. "Exciting, uncomfortable and clearly impressive."

Books, Articles, and Critical Anthologies
on the Making of *The Stranger*

Abbou, André, Brian Fitch, René Girard, et al. *Autour de L'Étranger*. Les Lettres Modernes: Albert Camus Vol. 1. Paris: Lettres Modernes: 1968.

Bloom, Harold, ed. *Albert Camus's The Stranger*. Philadelphia: Chelsea House, 2001. Includes many of the classic articles on the novel, including René Girard's "Camus's Stranger Retried" and Germaine Brée's "Heroes of our time: the Stranger."

Bloom, Ryan. "Lost in Translation: What the First Line of *The Stranger* Should Be." *New Yorker*, May 11, 2012. http://www.newyorker.com/books/page-turner/lost-in-translation-what-the-first-line-of-the-stranger-should-be (accessed September 24, 2015).

Britton, Celia. "How Does Meursault Get Arrested?" *French Studies Bulletin* 31 (2010): 1–3.

Castex, Pierre-Georges. *Albert Camus et L'Étranger*. Paris: Corti, 1965.

Cerisier, Alban. *Brève histoire illustrée de la publication de* L'Étranger *d'Albert Camus*. Paris: Gallimard, 2013.

Fitch, Brian T. *L'Étranger d'Albert Camus: un texte, ses lecteurs, leurs lectures (étude méthodologique)*. Paris: Librairie Larousse, 1972.

Francev, Peter , ed. *Albert Camus's The Stranger: Critical Essays*. Newcastle: Cambridge Scholars Publishing, 2004.

Gay-Crosier, Raymond. *The Stranger*. Gale Study Guides to Great Literature: Literary Masterpieces Vol. 8. Detroit, MI: Gale Group, 2002. Recommended for its analysis of the novel, its history of the criticism, and a rich array of illustrations from the Camus archives.

———, ed. *L'Étranger, cinquante ans après*. Les Lettres Modernes: Albert Camus Vol. 16. Paris: Lettres Modernes: 1995.

————, ed. *Toujours autour de l'Étranger*. Les Lettres Modernes: Albert Camus Vol. 17. Paris: Lettres Modernes Minard, 1996.

Hughes, Edward J., ed. *The Cambridge Companion to Camus*. Cambridge: Cambridge University Press, 2007. Covers all of Camus, but see especially Toby Garfitt, "Situating Camus: The Formative Influences," 39–52 (on Camus and Jean Grenier); David Carroll, "Rethinking the Absurd: le Mythe de Sisyphe, 53–66; Colin Davis, "Violence and ethics in Camus," 106–17; and Peter Dunwoodie, "From Noces to L'Étranger," 147–64.

King, Adele, ed. *Camus's L'Étranger: Fifty Years On*. London: Macmillan, 1992. A useful snapshot of studies of the novel in the 1990s, as issues of race and identity came to the fore.

Lévi-Valensi, Jacqueline, ed. *Les Critiques de notre temps et Camus*. Paris: Garnier, 1970. Includes influential essays by Roland Barthes, Nathalie Sarraute, Jean-Paul Sartre.

Matsumoto, Yosei. "Le Processus d'élaboration de *L'Étranger*." *Études camusiennes: société japonaise des Études camusiennes* 12, (May 2015): 72–86.

McCarthy, Patrick. *Camus; The Stranger (Student Guide)*. Cambridge: Cambridge University Press, 1988, 2004.

Pingaud, Bernard. *L'Étranger d'Albert Camus*. Paris: Gallimard/Foliothèque, 1992. Brilliant reading and interpretation by a leading French writer and critic.

Prouteau, Anne, and Agnès Spiquel-Courdille, ed. *Lire les* Carnets *d'Albert Camus*. Lille: Presses Universitaires du Septentrion, 2012.

Rey, Jean-Louis. *L'Étranger d'Albert Camus: Profil d'une oeuvre*. Paris: Hatier, 2003. Designed for French students preparing their baccalaureate exams.

On Publishing and Literary Life during the German Occupation

Assouline, Pierre. *Gaston Gallimard: A Half-Century of French Publishing*. New York: Harcourt Brace Jovanovich, 1988.

Atack, Margaret. *Literature and the French Resistance: Cultural Politics and Narrative Forms, 1940–1950*. Manchester: Manchester University Press, 1989.

Burrin, Philippe. *France under the Germans: Collaboration and Compromise*. Trans. Janet Lloyd. New York: New Press, 1997.

Corpet, Olivier, and Claire Paulhan. *Collaboration and Resistance: French Literary Life under the Nazi Occupation*. Trans. by Jeffrey Mehlman. New York: Five Ties Publishing, 2009. Preface by Robert O. Paxton.

Fouché, Pascal. *L'Édition française sous l'occupation: 1940–1944*. 2 volumes. Paris: Bibliothèque de littérature française contemporaine de l'université de Paris VII, 1987. Reproduces primary-source documents with information on the censorship and control of editors and books by the occupiers.

Kaplan, Alice. *The Collaborator: The Trial and Execution of Robert Brasillach*. Chicago: University of Chicago Press, 2000.

Poulain, Martine. *Livres pillés, lectures surveillées: les bibliothèques françaises sous l'occupation*. Paris: Gallimard, 2008. On pillaging and censorship in libraries and bookstores by the occupiers.

Riding, Alan. *And the Show Went On: Cultural Life in Nazi-Occupied Paris*. New York: Vintage, 2010.

Sapiro, Gisèle. *La guerre des écrivains 1940–1953*. Paris: Fayard, 1999. In English, *The French Writers' War 1940–1953*. Trans. Vanessa Doriott. Durham, NC: Duke University Press, 2014. A rich analysis of publishing and literary institutions during the Occupation; see especially her chapter on the *Nouvelle Revue Française*.

Algeria in the 1930s and 1940s

Abbou, André, and Jacqueline Lévi-Valensi, eds. *Albert Camus: journalisme et politique, l'entrée dans l'Histoire 1938–1940. La Revue des Lettres Modernes: Albert Camus 5*. Paris: Éditions Lettres Modernes, 1972.

Abitbol, Michel. *Les Juifs d'Afrique du Nord sous Vichy*. Paris: Riveneuve, 2008.

Abbas, Ferhat. *Le Jeune Algérien: de la colonie versa la province; (suivi de) Rapport au maréchal Pétain: avril 1941*. Paris: Garnier Frères, 1981.

Ageron, Charles-Robert. *Histoire de l'Algérie contemporaine, T. II., 1871–1954*. Paris: PUF, 1979.

Azza-Bekat, Amina, A. Bererhi, C. Chaulet-Achour, and B. Mohammed-Tabti, eds. *Quand les Algériens Lisent Camus*. Alger: Casbah Editions, 2014. Organized as a series of dictionary entries by readers/critics of Camus, from Camus's contemporaries to the present.

Blanchard, Pascal. "La vocation fasciste de l'Algérie coloniale dans les années 30." *De l'Indochine à l'Algérie: la jeunesse en mouvements des deux côtés du miroir colonial, 1940–1962*, ed. Nicolas Bancel et al. Paris: La Decouverte, 2003.

Carroll, David. *Camus the Algerian: Colonialism, Terrorism, Justice*. New York: Columbia University Press, 2007.

Djemaï, Abdelkader. *Camus à Oran*. Paris: Éditions Michalon, 1995.

Graebner, Seth. *History's Place: Nostalgia and the City in French Algerian Literature*. Lahnam, MD: Lexington Books, 2007.

Hubbell, Amy. *Remembering French Algeria: Pieds-Noirs, Identity, and Exile*. Lincoln: University of Nebraska Press, 2016.

Kateb, Kamel. *Européens, "indigènes," et juifs en Algérie, 1830–1962*. Paris: Presses Universitaires de France, 2001.

Le Foll-Luciani, Pierre-Jean. *Les juifs algériens dans la luttle anticoloniale: Trajectoires dissidentes, 1934–1965*. Rennes: Presses universitaires de Rennes, 2015.

LeSueur, James. "The Unbearable Solitude of Being: The Question of Albert Camus." In *Uncivil War: Intellectuals and Identity Politics During the Decolonization of Algeria*. Lincoln: University of Nebraska Press, 2005.

Sebbar, Leïla, ed. *Une enfance algérienne*. Paris: Gallimard, 1997. *An Algerian Childhood: A Collection of Autobiographical Narratives*. trans. Marjolijn de Jager. (St. Paul, MN: Ruminator Books, 2001). A collection of childhood stories by writers and intellectuals of diverse origins, born in Algeria before independence.

Schreier, Joshua. *Arabs of the Jewish Faith: The Civilizing Mission in Colonial Algeria*. New Brunswick, N.J.: Rutgers University Press, 2010.

Stora, Benjamin. *Nationalistes algériens et révolutionnaires français au temps du Front Populaire*. Paris: l'Harmattan, 1987.

Viollette, Maurice. *L'Algérie vivra-t-elle? Notes d'un ancien gouverneur général*. Paris: F. Alcan, 1931.

Vrillon, Pierre. Plans d'Alger (9 plans). Alger: Éditions Pierre Vrillon, n.d. (est. 1940 or 1949). Map Room, University of Illinois at Champagne-Urbana. Vrillon began making his beautiful art deco–style maps of Algiers, neighborhood by neighborhood, in the 1930s. The University of Illinois collection has an early map that shows both Camus and Simone Hié's villa in Hydra and the winding streets around the House Above the World.

Method

Audiat, Pierre. *La biographie de l'œuvre littéraire : esquisse d'une méthode critique.* Paris: Champion, 1924.

Bly, Robert. *A Little Book on the Human Shadow.* New York: Harper & Row, 1988.

Gorra, Michael. *Portrait of a Novel: Henry James and the Making of an American Masterpiece.* New York: Liveright, 2013.

Marcus, Greil. *Like a Rolling Stone: Bob Dylan at the Crossroads.* New York: Public Affairs, 2005. On the life of a song.

Adaptations and Afterlives

Bachi, Salim. *Le Dernier été d'un jeune homme.* Paris: Flammarion, 2013. Writing in Camus's voice, Bachi evokes his life in the 1930s, including the brawl on the beach that inspired *The Stranger.*

Daoud, Kamel. *Meursault, contre-enquête.* Algiers: Éditions Barzakh, 2013; Arles: Actes Sud, 2014. In English, *The Meursault Investigation.* Trans. John Cullen. New York: Other Press, 2015.

L'Étranger. Drawings by Jacques Ferrandez. Paris: Gallimard, 2013. A comic-book version of *The Stranger*, imbued with Ferrandez's knowledge of colonial Algiers.

L'Étranger. Ink drawings by José Munoz. Stunning black-and-white ink drawings illustrating the text of *The Stranger.* See Alice Kaplan, "L'Étranger, 1942–2012, avec des dessins de José Munoz." *Contreligne*, Printemps, 2015. http://www.con treligne.eu/2012/06/l-etranger-dessins-de-jose-munoz/.

Smith, Robert. "Killing an Arab." *Standing on a Beach.* Recorded by The Cure. Elektra Records: 1986.

Index

Page numbers in italics refer to maps.